A LICENSE TO STEAL

The Untold Story of
Michael Milken
and the Conspiracy to
Bilk the Nation

BENJAMIN J. STEIN

SIMON & SCHUSTER
New York   London   Toronto   Sydney   Tokyo   Singapore

SIMON & SCHUSTER
Simon & Schuster Building
Rockefeller Center
1230 Avenue of the Americas
New York, New York 10020

SIMON & SCHUSTER and colophon are registered trademarks
of Simon & Schuster Inc.

Designed by Irving Perkins Associates
Manufactured in the United States of America

10   9   8   7   6   5   4   3   2   1

Library of Congress Cataloging-in-Publication Data
Stein, Benjamin, date
    A license to steal : the untold story of Michael Milken and the conspiracy to
bilk the nation / Benjamin J. Stein.
        p.   cm.
    Includes index.
    1. Milken, Michael.   2. Stockbrokers—United States—
Biography.   3. Junk bonds—United States.   4. Drexel Burnham Lambert
Incorporated.   5. Securities industry—United States—Corrupt
practices.   I. Title.
HG4928.5.M55S74   1992
364.1'68—dc20
[B]   92-31121
                                                                                  CIP

ISBN 0-671-74272-8

For Alex, Tommy, and Trixie

CONTENTS

	Introduction	11
ONE	LEGEND	15
TWO	THE MESSIAH	28
THREE	THE NETWORK	43
FOUR	ARCHITECTURE	66
FIVE	FRED CARR, SUPERSTAR	85
SIX	THE PROMISED LAND	97
SEVEN	ENSTAR	110
EIGHT	INFINITE JEST	119
NINE	TANGLED WEBS	127
TEN	SMILING FACES	137
ELEVEN	TRUTH FOR SALE	143
TWELVE	SED QUIS CUSTODIET IPSOS CUSTODES?	152
THIRTEEN	IN THE LAND OF NOD	157
FOURTEEN	STATISTICS	161
FIFTEEN	BUYING BACK THE BROOKLYN BRIDGE	172
SIXTEEN	RUINS	178
SEVENTEEN	PRECEPTORS	183
	Epilogue	188
	Acknowledgments	200
	Appendix: The Casualty List	205
	Index	213

Justice . . . is the main pillar that upholds the whole society. If it is removed, the great, immense fabric of human society . . . must in a moment crumble into atoms.

ADAM SMITH,
The Theory of the Moral Sentiments

Michael Milken's First Law: "The constant ME is always greater than the variable U."

HERBERT STEIN,
The New York Times

A LICENSE
TO STEAL

INTRODUCTION

O death, where is thy sting? O grave, where is thy victory?

I. CORINTHIANS

CERTAIN FLOORS OF the building at the corner of Wilshire Boulevard and Rodeo Drive in Beverly Hills were never finished. They had raw concrete floors, exposed wiring, sour-smelling heating ducts, and little balls of insulation in corners. Unsheathed steel supports stood in neat, brawny rows down the middle of huge rooms. Yet this was a building at the most prestigious corner in Beverly Hills, office space that in the late 1980s was probably the most expensive in California. Thousands of square feet of it were simply empty and unusable, as far as I could tell when I visited the building in February 1990, on the day after the investment banking firm of Drexel Burnham Lambert, its prime tenant, filed for bankruptcy. No people were there from Drexel, except for the uniformed and mufti-clad Drexel Burnham Lambert security guards who still manned posts at the front door of the building. Appropriately enough, the "front door" faced an alley behind the building and the entrance to a below-ground parking lot.

At the entrance to the parking lot there was a sign telling prospective parkers that space therein was reserved for Drexel Burnham Lambert, for Columbia Savings, for First Executive insurance, for E-II Holdings, for Rapid-American and for The Limited. The last was and is a clothing store that occupies much of the ground floor of the building. The others were companies that were key parts of the

11

Drexel empire, indispensable principalities of what had been the most powerful, feared, envied financial operation of all recorded time until just a few months before. Their own dukes and earls certainly deserved parking spaces at the emperor's headquarters.

Those spaces were empty now, and so were the offices of Drexel Burnham Lambert. The telephone had stopped being answered nearly one week before. The employees who mattered had all been told the score and given their bonuses, often amounting to millions, for their fine work in the year in which Drexel became insolvent. Even on the floors that had been finished, the desks were piled up in the corners. There were no calendars, no memo pads, no photos of wives or children at tennis camp. But on the floor where the mortgage-backed securities unit had worked, there were two large posterboards of the firm's last outing. In disarmingly homely poses, the Drexel boys and girls and their families sat at picnic tables, kicked a soccer ball, ate on blankets. One snapshot showed Michael Milken himself in picnic clothes, looking extremely fit. The captain of this Drexel Burnham Lambert team, he was posing near a soccer ball, almost like a professional soccer player, lean and confident and alert.

At the back of that room there was a copying machine, still hooked up, still humming. On top of the machine was one sheet of paper. It was a corner of a page of the February 12, 1990, *Wall Street Journal* with a story about how the collapse of the junk bond empire was putting some pension funds in jeopardy.

On another floor, in the heart of the machine, the so-called "trading" floor of Drexel, where Michael Milken and his top aides stoked the engine that made them all wealthy almost around the clock, there was no sign of power any longer.

The room was dimly lit, stripped to its essentials and converted into a litigation defense file room. From its famous artificially high floor (so that additional communication wires could be brought in to feed Milken's many phones) to its modest ceiling, it was filled with piles of boxes such as any participant in truly major litigation would recognize.

Some of the boxes read "CGR," which just might stand for "Cahill Gordon & Reindel," a reference to one of the mighty New York law firms that guarded Milken through his mighty endeavors. Other boxes read "MAD," which might stand for "Milken Area Defense" or maybe for something else. In the center of the room a huge shredder sat next to an even bigger gray-green plastic trash barrel with a clear plastic lining. On the barrel, someone had written in Magic Marker, "For Shredded Material Only."

The real estate woman who was showing me around that day explained that about one hundred thousand square feet of space in this building were for lease. In the adjoining building there was roughly comparable space available, except that the first floor had already been completely rented to a very high-end women's clothing store called Amen Wardy where dresses were said (probably apocryphally) to cost $25,000.

There was a heady feeling for me about walking around the throne room of the deposed strongman of Drexel Burnham Lambert. On the one hand, I could almost sense the exhausted exhilaration that Milken's henchmen must have felt as they looked out the windows toward the priciest parts of Beverly Hills and realized that they could, after months, not even years, afford to buy anything they saw. In the city where getting and spending were considered godly, they were divine. No matter what colleges they might have attended, no matter how worried their moms might have been that they would not make it in the real world, being on that floor, near The Man, was proof positive: They had the world by the balls.

On the other hand, especially in the empty concrete rooms, especially when the real estate broker left me alone for a few minutes, I could almost feel that even though the Emperor was gone, his spirit might still be around, lurking. The Power might still be ready to tap into the most basic parts of the human psyche and thrive and throb again, buying and selling, turning the world upside down. "Could have been the whole world, Michael Milken," and maybe it still can be.

Or, on a less lofty note, maybe the place just looked like a boiler-room phone sales operation that got busted. The metal desks and the copying machine and the tangled web of telephone wires remained, and the con men had moved on to their next game.

CHAPTER ONE

LEGEND

The world wants to be deceived.

SEBASTIAN BRANT, 1494

IF THE STORY OF Drexel Burnham Lambert and Michael R. Milken becomes a movie, as it very well may, it might begin with a symbolic scene, perhaps of an automobile graveyard where hugely expensive vehicles are crushed flat by a compacter and, worth a tiny fraction of their original cost, sold for junk. Or it might open with a panoramic view of a once verdant and prosperous land strewn with wreckage in the wake of some implacable force. But symbolism aside, if the story begins in late 1992, the following objects of reality can be discerned on the landscape.

Drexel Burnham Lambert is in reorganization as something to be called New Street Securities. It is no longer functioning as an investment bank or as anything else except a rich trove of salaries and perks for a few remaining employees as they slowly liquidate its assets. Its former leader and guru, Michael Milken, is in a prison east of San Francisco, having pleaded guilty to six felony counts.

The landscape is also littered with the ruins of a number of other financial giants such as Columbia Savings & Loan of Beverly Hills, CenTrust Federal Savings of Miami, Lincoln Savings of Irvine, California, San Jacinto Savings of Dallas, CityFed of Bedminster, New Jersey, and about fifty others. All of these institutions are in receivership or some other form of involuntary reorganization. Without exception, they were sunk primarily because of their large holdings of Drexel/Milken-issued high-interest, low-rated "junk" bonds. When these bonds had to be "written down," that is, adjusted on the books of the S&Ls to reflect their real market value because of a federal law, the institutions all slowly or rapidly sank into collapse. In fact, the real market value of their junk assets was so much below what they had paid that the value of their overall assets in relation to liabilities turned out to be below federally required levels.

The taxpayers are on the hook, through the federal deposit insurance system, for whatever it will cost to make up the difference between the real market value of the assets of these S&Ls and their obligations to their depositors. Or, to put it another way, taxpayers are on the hook for the difference between what Drexel said the junk in the S&Ls' portfolios would be worth and what it's really worth. This amount is likely to be about ten to fifteen billion dollars.

As of March 1992, Michael Milken had agreed to pay about $900 million to a set of claimants in the cases brought against the offending S&Ls, mostly to the Resolution Trust Corporation, the federal agency charged with "cleaning up" the debris of the debacle. This payment was in connection with prolonged suits alleging that Milken had systematically looted the federally insured thrifts. It has not yet actually been paid.

The largest single buyer of Drexel junk, the once fast growing First Executive insurance company (also late of Beverly Hills), is in receivership. Its two largest insurance subsidiaries, Executive Life of New York and Executive Life of California, have been seized by state insurance regulators. The seizures, again, took place because the value of the assets of First Executive, very largely junk bonds, turned out to be so much less than First Executive and Drexel had claimed that they appeared to be inadequate to meet the obligations to policyholders.

Executive Life of California and its sister, Executive Life of New York, were seized in spring of 1991. Ever since, tens of thousands of policyholders of First Executive have been on tenterhooks as to exactly how much, if anything, they would be paid on annuities and even on life insurance claims. In California, in particular, where there were uncertain provisions about what losses would be covered by the state insurance fund, policyholders were in fear. Thousands of other Executive Life "beneficiaries," who were entitled to payments from pension plans whose assets were in the form of Milken/Drexel bonds "guaranteed" by affiliates of First Executive, have been in similar danger. It is still by no means perfectly clear how much any of these people will be paid on policies that insure their very lives and ability to live.

If the state insurance funds of California or New York are tapped, that means additional charges on taxpayers who were not in any way involved with Drexel or Milken. Their taxes will go toward paying for Milken/Drexel failures in the insurance industry, just as the taxpayers are also being tapped to pay off the losses in Milken/Drexel federally insured S&Ls.

Cities and counties and special revenue districts across the country bought investment contracts made up of Drexel/Milken bonds "guaranteed" by affiliates of First Executive (and Milken). The losses on these instruments, losses directly borne by taxpayers in many cases, are in the billions.

First Capital Holdings, a Drexel-affiliated diversified financial company, owning mostly insurance companies, is also in default and receivership due to its heavy load of Drexel/Milken junk. Again, state insurance funds are at risk, and policyholders, beneficiaries, and annuitants are on edge. A "rescue" is in the works, but its exact effects are still unknown.

The Drexel financial services companies are all either going or gone. Southmark of Dallas, one of the most ethically questionable entities of all time, with a full plate of disastrous limited partnerships, catastrophic savings and loans, and defaulted subsidiaries of every stripe, is in bankruptcy. Southmark was also involved in complex, bizarre, fraudulent markup schemes with other Drexel players such as MDC Holdings and American Continental, parent of the infamous Lincoln S&L. American Continental is gone, but not before taking about $250 million from elderly, mostly not wealthy pensioners by fraudulently selling them "high yield" bonds at desks in savings and loan lobbies. Trained salesmen told them that Lincoln junk bonds were every bit as good as federally insured savings, but paid higher interest.

Integrated Resources, also a questionable diversified financial services company, is in receivership. ICH is in trouble. In fact, all of the publicly held diversified Drexel satellite financial services companies are either dead or in reorganization with the exception possibly of some obscure small ones. The proud ships of the Milken fleet, Ben Franklin, Mercury, Gibraltar, Imperial (none of them had modest names), if publicly held, are almost all now gone to a watery grave or about to be melted down for scrap.

The industrial companies for which Milken and Drexel raised money are in more diverse states. Triangle Packaging, one of the most bizarre corporate stories of all time, is now part of a huge French packaging combine, Pechiney. TWA, out of which Milken crony (and rival) Carl Icahn took hundreds of millions, is in bankruptcy. Texas Air is gone. McCrory and E-II, diversified consumer goods and retailing companies flying the Drexel banner, are in bankruptcy or default. On the other hand, Revlon is alive and well.

Enstar, in many ways the single most arresting part of the Drexel saga, is gone. In its inception, it was called Kinder-Care Learning Centers and was to have heralded a glory day of nationally standardized, high-quality child care for the middle and working classes. Under the guiding hand of Michael R. Milken, it also became owner of one of the largest S&Ls in America, at least two insurance companies, several small retail chains, and hundreds of millions of dollars worth of Drexel junk. It has sold its day-care operation to other owners as well as to its own stockholders, and now works mostly on litigation against Milken.

Junk bonds, the fuel that drove the Drexel machine, recently were defaulting at the rate of about 5 percent to 10 percent per annum, or about five to ten times the rate predicted by Milken and his friends in business schools across America. If the recent rate of default continues (and it may well have peaked in 1990 and 1991), at least half of all of the Drexel public debt issues since 1975 will default before payoff.

Drexel issued approximately $220 billion of debt. In a general way (and the calculation is very much affected by how long it took to default and how much the bond was worth—if anything—at default), the loss to American investors and taxpayers will be on the very approximate order of $40 billion to $100 billion. The high end of this range is about the same as the wages of all of the armed forces of the

United States for one year. A great deal of that money ended up in the pockets of the men who created and sold Drexel junk. Milken personally may well still have a fortune of about $6 billion, according to a lawyer familiar with Drexel. His top lieutenants in Drexel, such as Peter Ackerman and Leon Black and James Dahl, are believed to have fortunes of several hundred million dollars apiece and perhaps more.

Meanwhile, America in general fell into a widespread recession. And one major segment of the economy, real estate, and especially commercial real estate, is hurting at least in part because of wildly excessive building in the 1980s, spurred by Drexel S&Ls in various regions of America lending to their own principals. The financial services sector, especially the mergers and acquisitions area, is likewise in a major hangover, apparently at least in large part as a reaction to the spree of Drexel-financed mergers and acquisitions of the 1980s, many of which ended badly, for acquirers, acquired, and especially subordinated-debt lenders.

Hundreds of lawsuits against Milken and Drexel, mostly for fraud, are going on in courthouses around America. A few (very few indeed) Drexel players are briefly in jail, while many others of the ancien regime are accumulating new fortunes trading in Drexel junk.

This is some, but by no means all, of the devastation left in the path of Hurricane Michael. There are damages yet to be assessed, casualties yet to be counted, history yet to be written, while survivors wondered how it could have happened. Where did Milken come from, how did he acquire such force and, above all, why was there no warning?

There was one story put forward for about ten years by Drexel, its publicists, and its many friends that was supposed to organize the data about Milken. The story could be culled from books, articles, and speeches by Drexel players and apologists, all of which portrayed Milken in a dazzlingly benevolent light, transforming mere biography into the stuff of legend. It went as follows.

In the beginning there was born a little child in Encino, California. It wasn't Bethlehem, but, as far as Milken's friends were concerned, it was better than Bethlehem because, after all, Bethlehem didn't have freeways and accountants and access to higher modern mathematics. His name was Michael R. Milken, and he was a brilliant, friendly, helpful child, who was loved and revered by all who knew him. A devoted son to his accountant father, he was so good at figures that even as a ten-year-old he helped his father and was considered a prodigy of money management.

Young Michael attended a large public high school, Birmingham High School, at the corner of Victory and Balboa boulevards in Van Nuys. He played tennis. He was a cheerleader. He was Prom King. He went to college at the University of California at Berkeley and while other kids smoked dope and burned draft cards, Michael studied accounting. He was a very good boy.

While Milken was at Berkeley, he made a phenomenal and unique "discovery." A great many defaulted and lower-rated bonds were circulating in financial markets and many of them were underpriced. Further, a diversified portfolio of these bonds would pay off at a rate that made them a much superior investment to investment-grade bonds.

This "discovery" was supposedly made by Milken while he was browsing through a famous book about bonds and bond default rates, presuming that a great discovery can be made by one person reading another person's already published book. The book was and is *Corporate Bond Quality and Investor Experience,* by Walter Braddock Hickman, and it was to become the bedrock "data" upon which the revivifying work of Milken and Co. was based. Too complex for mortals, in the hands of Milken, it was the long-sought book of alchemy for bond buyers, who sought to turn base metals into pure gold.

The legend of Michael Milken went on to say that he did graduate work at the Wharton School of Business at the University of Pennsylvania, but left in a great hurry to join with other Wharton grads such as Saul Steinberg, Dennis Levine, Nelson Peltz, and Tom Spiegel, to put his "discovery" to the test. He first worked at a small shop in Philadelphia that was supposedly in pathetic shape until Milken arrived. Then he moved to a larger version of that firm in New York City. That entity became Drexel Burnham Lambert, a supposedly prestigious brokerage house but no money maker until Milken started his careful review of defaulted bonds and how much they were really and truly worth.

Thereafter, Milken gathered around him some large investors, such as Laurence Tisch, Carl Lindner, Meshulam Riklis, and Victor Posner, and taught them the gospel of careful study of junk bonds. How an obscure fledgling who reputedly wore a miner's cap to work so that he could study junk bonds in the dark could have been able to make contact right out of school with the likes of Carl Lindner, Victor Posner, and "Rik" Riklis was never explained, nor was how a mere stripling knew more about junk than its acknowledged masters.

Despite Milken's personal shyness (again according to the legend), the national media began to take note of the man who made such amazing profits in junk bond plays. A March 27, 1975, *Wall Street Journal* article about Milken noted particularly his daring mixed with his self-effacement. "Mike Milken," said the article, "vice president and manager of Drexel Burnham & Co.'s high yield corporate bond department, is undisputed king of the junk bond market."

The article went on to quote Milken as saying, "Let those big investment bankers bring their new issues to market at one hundred, and I'll buy many of them later for fifty cents on the dollar." The article then cited a number of Milken's miraculous buys in the junk bond world, especially his buys of the bonds of defunct or distressed real estate investment trusts. He had been, as one might say, "discovered." His comment about the probable fate of investment-grade bonds was mysterious, however, in that in the period of Milken's adulthood, the default rate on such instruments was always barely above zero.

Milken guided his clients into such supposedly arcane bonds as those of the then-bankrupt Penn Central Corporation. The bonds went up markedly and dramatically. The large players made money. They made so much money that they brought in other large players such as Saul Steinberg, the genuine boy genius who had made a run at buying Chase Manhattan when he was twenty-nine and far from a billionaire.

Milken continued to make money for his clients and turned his little firm, Drexel Burnham Lambert, into a barnburning money-maker in defaulted bond plays. By the mid-1970s, he had done so well for his inner circle of investors that he was asked, so the legend continued, to start forming mutual bond funds that would allow a more diversified group of buyers to enter the picture. Along with a number of persons who became close and vital members of the Milken Revolution, such as David Solomon of First Investors Fund for Income and Talton "Tally" Embry of Fiduciary Trust Company and affiliated mutual funds, Milken and Drexel set up about a dozen "high-yield" bond funds, which raised money from investors and then funneled it into Drexel bonds, either picked by Milken or under-written by him.

In 1977, however, again according to the lore of Milken, he decided he wanted to be in California, land of his birth, for a variety of reasons. First, his father, Bernard, was ill. His mother, Ferne, missed him. And Michael missed his brother, Lowell, a bright young lawyer. Plus, he wanted his children to be able to go out and play in the sunshine every day and not have to worry about rain. And he was uncomfortable with the supervision he got from the powers that were at Drexel Burnham Lambert. He wanted to fly without hovering and overly cautious corporate suits looking on.

Milken did move out to Beverly Hills in 1978, established an office in Century City at 1901 Avenue of the Stars (which was once called "Avenue of the Flakes" because it had so many offices filled with scammers), and began selling his bonds, or rather, as he was fond of saying, "trading" his bonds. His "trading" was so successful, and the people who "invested" in his defaulted bonds made so much money, that soon Milken became convinced that he had unique skills at valuing low-end debt. He was also convinced by his good friend Steve Wynn, owner of a smaller Las Vegas casino called The Golden Nugget, that he, Milken, should issue bonds to raise capital for Wynn's new venture in Atlantic City.

This issue was so successful that Milken was besieged by other medium and small businessmen who wanted to raise capital. Small oil companies, chemical companies, travel companies, and others came to Milken to issue low-rated, high-interest bonds for them, too. And because Milken had done so very well for his long-time clients, he was able to sell large amounts of his new form of debt. His innovation, low-rated high-interest debt for small and medium-sized corporate issuers who supposedly had been denied credit before the days of Milken, came as a joyous daybreak for American business.

Soon, mining companies, airline companies, movie producers, savings and loans, insurance companies, packaging companies, and more casinos joined the list of Drexel issuers. This Milken innovation was so important, again according to legend, that corporate America began to revive after having been smothered for two centuries by traditional debt issuance. Through Milken, middle and small American business could at last breathe the stimulating air of easy access to capital.

By the mid-1980s, Milken's power at raising the money that new, energetic players needed was so great that he could and did raise vastly larger sums than he had a scant few years before. He could raise money for obscure players like Boone Pickens and Carl Icahn to mount takeover raids on mammoth corporations such as Phillips Petroleum. He could bankroll takeover attempts hovering around Walt Disney. He could fund the "successful" takeover of Revlon by the relatively unknown Ronald Perelman. He could boast about having purchasing power of hundreds of billions of dollars available for his deals.

His ability to raise money so that relatively small players could attempt to seize power from far larger players was hailed by many in the halls of academe as a vital help to American business. Major names in American finance such as Michael Jensen of Harvard wrote articles praising Milken's work and the new form of corporate takeover funded by Milken's junk bonds, as a key way to make corporations more responsive to the needs of international competition. High government officials at the Council of Economic Advisers (especially Joseph Grundfest) and at the Securities and Exchange Commission (especially John Shad's associates) hailed the so-called "leveraged buyout" funded with Drexel junk as a new era in "the market for corporate control" and issued reports bearing the seal of the president of the United States that said what crucial, vital, wonderful things junk bonds were for their help in keeping American management on its toes.

United States senators and congressmen such as Al D'Amato and

Timothy Wirth (of New York and Colorado, respectively) spoke forcefully at conferences sponsored by Drexel about the brilliant helpfulness of the Milken innovations. Trusted members of the Ronald Reagan White House staff went to work for Drexel in various capacities. Ken Lerer, a publicity man for Reagan, became the publicist for Milken. He brought along with him another erstwhile Reagan publicist, Linda Robinson, daughter of Freeman Gosden of *Amos 'n' Andy,* former wife of the son of California Republican power Justin Dart, and present wife of the fascinating James Robinson, CEO of American Express.

James Lake, likewise a Reagan publicist and helper, joined Lerer and Robinson to grind out materials praising Milken, and especially his innovation, junk bonds, as a miracle cure for almost any financial or economic ill. Also on the Drexel payroll in Washington were Stuart Eizenstat, former domestic policy adviser to Jimmy Carter, now a Washington lawyer, and a fantastically successful lobbying organization called Alliance for Capital Access, headed by David Aylward, a longtime aide of Timothy Wirth.

Famous journalists such as Jude Wanniski, recently of the editorial page of *The Wall Street Journal,* and George Gilder, an iconoclastic best-selling author, spoke at the Drexel conferences and heaped laurels upon Milken. Major partners of Milken such as Ivan Boesky spoke at business school graduations (at Wharton in particular) and told grads (who hardly needed to be told) that greed was good for them and for America generally, and the grads roared back their approval.

The Drexel-funded takeover boom, along with the takeover activities of others, along with a deficit-fed consumer spending spree, along with a major fall in interest rates, generated huge fees on Wall Street. The major investment banks and securities firms expanded stupendously. Starting salaries leaped into the mid-six-figure range for aggressive, hustling investment bankers. At Drexel, the power of the innovation was so great that unknown bond "traders" reaped eight-figure salaries year after year.

Still more national media praise rained down upon the shy, self-effacing Milken. In August of 1985, *Forbes* ran a long story about Milken entitled, "One-Man Revolution." The piece gushed, "Essentially Milken has created his own universe. He isn't just a step ahead of his Wall Street peers—he's a quantum leap ahead, acting as venture capitalist, investment banker, trader, investor.'' (That this combination of roles by a bond and stock issuer might involve some ethical and legal conflicts did not merit extensive notice at the time.)

In July of 1987, when certain clouds had started to appear on the Milken horizon, *Forbes* still noted that he was a visionary in finance. "In an industrial society, capital is a scarce resource," he was quoted as saying, adding, "but in an information society such as today's, there's plenty of capital." (What this could possibly mean was not explained, nor could it ever be.)

Again, this parade of praise, according to the Drexel/Milken template, occurred because Milken had created a new financing instrument that was superior to other previously existing instruments, made for a fine investment for American savers, helped American industry to grow, made American management more effective, and made Americans generally economically better off.

The Milken creation, the original issue low-rated, high-interest bond that benefited everyone, according to the Drexel/Milken theory, was lauded in Congress, at Harvard, in boardrooms, in endless editorials in *The Wall Street Journal*. The Milken group's innovations were even explicitly endorsed by the United States government as a good investment for the savers and taxpayers of America. In a report on the suitability of Drexel junk for federally insured S&Ls, the General Accounting Office said that it was a fine buy, since its high coupon assured that interest payments would more than make up losses on default, thus helping S&Ls, their depositors, and the federal savings and loan insurance fund.

The buyers of the bonds were helped because the bonds were crafted to pay a yield so high that even after deducting for the defaults that would inevitably occur, the bond buyer would still be ahead of where he would have been if he had bought boring old Treasury bonds with their nil default rate and their lower yields.

The borrowers were better off because with the proceeds of the Drexel junk debt, they could apply their ingenuity, their talent, and their own innovations to make their businesses grow.

The American worker was better off because the companies

funded by Drexel would provide new jobs while the old, stodgy, investment-grade American companies got smaller and laid off workers.

The American consumer was better off because Drexel issuers would provide new kinds of goods and services, such as larger and better casinos and nationally franchised day-care centers.

America as a nation was better off because thanks to Mike Milken the republic was more prosperous and freer in several basic ways. Access to capital was now democratic. If any American had a good idea, he could bring it to Milken, get it funded, and try his hand at capitalism. The entrepreneur could be white, black, Hispanic, Eskimo, anything. Capital would not be provided only to rich WASPs of old family, but on the basis of the aristocracy of merit.

Or, to boil it down, the Milken legend held that:

- Michael Milken was an unselfish genius of finance and industrial organization.
- His bonds were a sound financing entity.
- Buyers of his bonds were, in general and on average, extremely secure and would be well-paid.
- America as a nation would benefit very substantially from Drexel/Milken junk bonds.

Why then did Milken and his junk bond empire come tumbling down? The tailor-made narrative of his life and works would claim that Milken was done in by a jealous, vengeful establishment. Stung by his abilities at democratizing capital, fearful of losing their vast privileges, enraged that Milken had taken them off the links for even a day or a month, the WASP establishment and a few cranks nailed Milken to a cross precisely to punish him for his "essential goodness," a phrase that actually fell from the lips of the otherwise intelligent George Gilder at a gathering of Milken forces.

For his work on behalf of clients, some of which, Milken had been compelled to admit, might have been too zealous, he was put in prison. Because of his absence from the scene, the longest peacetime expansion in American history (so-called) came to an end, industrial vitality ebbed, and America suffered. *Forbes*, which had been right there recognizing Milken's greatness for years and even decades, while oddly enough skewering some of his closest colleagues mercilessly, recognized the man's greatness by printing a laudatory interview with him in March of 1992. A staggeringly enthusiastic book on Milken, *Highly Confident*, was published in the summer of 1992 and immediately optioned by Robert DeNiro to be a major motion picture starring DeNiro as Milken.

The myth would conclude by saying that America now slumbered fitfully, awaiting the return of The Man and whatever miracles he would spin next to unleash our native power and prosperity. The only big change would be that next time, Milken would not let himself (a relatively trusting, innocent type) be taken in by such scoundrels as Ivan Boesky. Next time, Milken implicitly vowed, no more Mr. Nice Guy. Yes, he would continue to lead his people out of the desert and into the promised land of high interest and restructured balance sheets, but this time he would not be led astray by those more cunning and evil than his pure self.

To apply this legend as an explanation of the utter ruin of the Drexel-controlled S&Ls and the consequent multi-billion-dollar losses to taxpayers, the default of many Drexel-controlled insurance companies and the losses to policyholders of those companies, the bankruptcies of the Drexel financial service companies, the default rates of close to 10 percent a year in Drexel junk, the bankruptcy of dozens of large Drexel players, and the criminal convictions of a number of substantial Drexel operatives is a far fetch.

Perhaps then there is another explanation of who Michael Milken was and is. It's a rationale based upon observation, comment, hypothesis, and analysis. Whatever else, it does organize the data more efficiently than the pro-Milken myth, and bears study.

CHAPTER 2

THE MESSIAH

The first principles that are instilled take the deepest root.

ABIGAIL ADAMS, 1776

MICHAEL ROBERT MILKEN WAS BORN, ironically enough, on July 4, 1946, and grew up in the border zone between the affluent San Fernando Valley area of Encino and the more middle-class suburb of Van Nuys. The Milkens' house was just on the Encino side of the line, unfashionably north of bustling Ventura Boulevard.

His father's background was extremely painful. Bernard Milkevitz's mother died shortly after he was born, in the Wisconsin city of Kenosha. His father died in a car crash when Bernard was seven. He was passed to various relatives and spent time in an orphanage. While he was growing up, he suffered from a bout with polio, from which he recovered more or less completely, except for a limp.

Bernard was an extremely industrious man. He worked his way through the University of Wisconsin by, among other things, selling snacks at sororities. At one such, he met and became engaged to Ferne Zax, also of the upper Midwest, but from much more affluent circumstances. Bernard married Ferne, changed his name to Milken, and moved to Los Angeles. All this took place during the Second World War, when the San Fernando Valley was exploding with prosperity, was still relatively smog free, and had a reputation as a dry, hot Garden of Eden for middle-class Americans.

Bernard Milken had studied accounting and worked as an accountant. According to all reports, authorized and unauthorized, he was an extremely hard-working, meticulous man, who truly struggled to save his clients money on their taxes and to keep their affairs ordered neatly. His wife worked as a real estate broker in the Encino/Van Nuys area. She is reported by some who knew her to have been extremely interested in the sales of homes in the more expensive sections of the San Fernando Valley, such as Encino, and in particular to have been concerned by the fact that she worked at selling homes to women not anywhere near as hard-working as she was, but who nevertheless could afford far larger homes than hers.

Compounding the problem, Bernard Milken reportedly worked largely on the accounts of men and women also far more affluent than the Milkens. Thus, young Michael and his brother, Lowell, born in 1948, grew up with the strongly motivational view of a mother and father who slaved at providing comfort and wealth to those more wealthy than they.

There was yet another potent influence on young Michael, one that turned out to be critical in his life. Among Bernard Milken's many satisfied clients were a number of extremely successful men linked to Las Vegas and to labor relations law. According to a family friend, some of these men would take young Michael aside after watching him help his father with their accounts and tell him that he was a very smart lad but that they had some advice for him: he should go out and make some real money for himself, instead of using up his life seeking to make money for others. According to this same source, some of these men said that when the time came, they would be happy to help Mike make his way.

As a teenager, Michael could best be described as a model son (even as a federal judge would later find him a model prisoner). In addition to helping his father with his accounting chores, he was also a stellar student, ran track, played varsity basketball, and was head cheerleader for sports other than basketball and for basketball when he was not playing. In a comically apt precursor to his later career, he was once criticized for calling for more points when his Birmingham High School team was already ahead by forty-two points in a football game.

As far as is known, Milken did not smoke or drink and did not even consume carbonated beverages or coffee. He reportedly slept only a few hours each night (a habit he would share with his later partner, Ivan Boesky). His one imperfection was that he apparently loved to play pranks upon substitute teachers, confusing them about who was who and about what they had learned in earlier classes, and eventually driving them from their temporary positions of authority in tears.

A very revealing facet of Milken's teenage years, told in an authorized magazine biography of the man, had to do with his ability to suppress the reality principle in his life, as well as with his blindness about matters near and dear to him. According to an interview with Milken and his wife, Lori Hackel Milken, he was fifteen before he was made aware, by a high school classmate, that his father had a limp from his bout with polio or even that he walked with a brace. Further, even in middle age, Milken refused to admit or (seemingly) emotionally accept the fact that his father had lived as a child in an orphanage. He "preferred" to think of it as a "boarding school," Milken said. This startling inability to confront truth and his equally uncanny Orwellian ability to create a parallel reality out of touch with objective reality would later be called into major service in the Drexel world, where fantasy became reality.

Apart from his own family, Milken has apparently never loved anyone else in his whole life except a girl from his neighborhood whom he met in either seventh or ninth grade, depending on what one reads. She was Lori Hackel, the daughter of a salesman, and they "went together" through high school and college at the University of California at Berkeley, where she had transferred from UC, Santa Barbara. Lori was president of the Alpha Epsilon Phi sorority and Michael was president of the Sigma Alpha Mu fraternity.

The extreme energy Milken had displayed all of his life—perhaps learned from Ferne, who, according to Milken, worked sixteen hours a day and kept many projects in the air simultaneously—served him well at Berkeley. He was a good student, active in his fraternity and totally focused on his own advancement. These were the years from 1964 to 1968 at Berkeley, the precise moment when student radicalism was at its peak, at the exact spot in the universe where that rebellion was hottest and heaviest. However, for Milken there were no demonstrations in People's Park, pot smoking, laying down his body in front of cars, naked slip-and-slides, or tripping while listening to the Grateful Dead (although Lori was reported to be a devout rock music fan). Instead, there was study of accounting, the prestidigitators' quarters of economics, and actual practice within his fraternity walls at becoming an amateur magician. He would later deny that he had ever been interested in magic.

While in the fraternity house, Milken was a demon of energy and competitiveness. A later article reported that he was so incredibly competitive that when a frat brother talked about how much TV he watched, Milken said he could watch more, and stayed up for twenty-four hours watching TV, just to show he could do it. Otherwise he quietly dated Lori, studied his accounting, and all the while tried to give the impression that he got his good grades without studying, going so far as to get up in the middle of the night to study to fool his roommates.

It was at Berkeley that Milken was said to have read one volume (at least) of a multi-volume work on corporate bonds. This volume, supposedly, changed his life. The book was called (as noted) *Corporate Bond Quality and Investor Experience* and was part of a lengthy study by the prestigious National Bureau of Economic Research about how bonds had fared in the period from 1900 to 1943.

The author of the study was an economist and statistician named Walter Braddock Hickman, whose work was supervised and checked by some of the most famous names in economics, including Geoffrey Moore, long-time head of the Bureau of Labor Statistics, Arthur F. Burns, the long-time presidential adviser about economics and Federal Reserve Board chairman, and Rose Director Friedman, a famous economist in her own right, and wife of the genius monetarist and free marketeer Milton Friedman.

This study was to play a vital role in the Drexel/Milken world, and it's well worth examining what the Drexel legend said it was, and what the truth about it was. It is at this point that one of the key breaks in the legend of Michael Milken appears. It is also here that the *purpose* of the Drexel/Milken myth first starts to emerge from the mist of fabrication.

Hickman's book, thoughtful and well-written, made some points that were vaguely similar to what the Milken myth claims. He did indeed find that, by some measurements, some lower-rated bonds outperformed some higher-rated bonds overall in the period from 1900 to 1943. However, what Hickman also found and wrote was that, by most measurements, the difference between the overall yield from high-rated bonds and lower-rated bonds was usually small, that the yield on the lowest-rated bonds was less than the yield on the highest-rated bonds, and that by a number of measurements the yield on poorer-quality issues was consistently worse than that on better-quality issues.

Far, far more important, Hickman pointed out repeatedly that the time period he studied was extremely unusual in that it included the worst depression in history followed by the largest boom in history (the rearmament boom of World War II). This, as Hickman was at pains to explain, meant that bonds bought in the trough of the Depression showed fantastic gains in the wartime period, when there were essentially no defaults, there were many, many calls at above par, and some securities that had been exchanged for defaulted bonds rose spectacularly in value.

Hickman said over and over that without the phenomenally low prices for low-grade bonds in the Depression, followed by the equally phenomenal high prices for those bonds after war broke out, his results would have been completely different. He also said that one of his key findings was that bond investors can and do suffer large losses if they are lulled by prosperity into believing that low-quality issues are anything other than low-quality. He also suggested that bond buyers might be well advised to study what their probable losses will be and to take reserves against them. For any single investor or group of investors, he added, the best bet by far over any normal period was to stick with the most highly rated issues.

All this was different from what Milken's legend claimed Hickman wrote and how Milken himself would interpret it and later put it to work as part of his sales pitch for Drexel junk. In essence, he took a few portions of a large scholarly work, left out the most crucial parts of the study that discussed what it really meant, and then used those few portions as a "proof" of his Unique Selling Proposition. It was much the same as if he had read a medical study that found that fasting was good for people if they did it once a month, and then had begun a program advocating fasting six days per week. Or, more to the point, Milken's misuse of the Hickman data was analogous to using a study that recommended occasional moderate alcohol consumption for relaxation to encourage people to drink around the clock.

An invaluable and indeed brilliant document to those who troubled to read it, Hickman's book in the hands of Michael Milken became a dangerous instrument. Just how dangerous was hinted at by the frequency with which Milken cited it in dozens of interviews to support his exaggerated claims about junk bonds. In fact, it was revealed in July of 1992 by a pro-Milken hagiography that he had never read Hickman, but only a summary of it. Had he read the whole book, with its conclusions that junk over time was *not* likely to be superior to investment-grade bonds, it is conceivable that the whole Milken/Drexel catastrophe might have been averted—but only conceivable.

Also at Berkeley, Milken began a "money management" service for his friends and fraternity brothers, and even some of his father's accounting clients, promising them that he would take on all of their losses as his personal obligation if he could have half of the gains. It was an ingenious ploy and a fascinating example of the fantasy with which Milken clothed and sold himself. "Mike was supposed to be a brilliant numbers guy," said an investment banker who had recent, extremely painful experience with Milken and with Drexel junk in the form of a "collateralized bond obligation." "But look at it by the numbers. If he was so absolutely sure he could make money that he would absorb all of the losses, why not invest only his own money? By the same token, if he could afford to absorb all losses, there, too, it showed that he had enough money to put it all up himself. But nobody in his right mind makes that kind of deal—half of the gains and all of the losses. You don't even get that kind of deal with the IRS.

"What Mike was doing was either that he never did the thing at all, and he just made it up later to add to his mystique, or maybe he did something a little bit like it, only the terms were a lot different," said the investment banker. "Or maybe he made that kind of a deal when he had both sides of the deal fixed, like maybe if he had a stock or a bond and he already had the trade worked out before he got the investors into it. But if it was that kind of deal, why not, again, put only his own money into it? The whole thing as it's reported is extremely similar to the kinds of boasts that used to pour out of Drexel about the rates of return on his junk: a lot of hot air and if you looked behind it, it was just a way to sell the next guy.''

In the summer between his junior and senior years at Berkeley, Milken worked as an intern at the Los Angeles office of Touche Ross, a large accounting firm that was eventually merged with another large accounting firm to become Deloitte, Touche. He worked for Touche again in his senior year, taking off most of the last quarter at Berkeley to work as a junior member of the tax audit division of Touche. This pattern of being too impatient to get into the world of real money to stay in school was to be repeated later at Wharton. Milken also became officially engaged to Lori Hackel in his senior year in college. By all accounts, they lived a quiet life, and again, did not participate in any overt way in the "revolution" in manners and mores that was sweeping the campus.

In June of 1968, Milken graduated as a Phi Beta Kappa. His degree was in business administration, although he later told an interviewer that his major was mathematics. "That's typical of Mike," said a childhood friend who has stayed in touch with him ever since. "He was already a good student, and he was in a perfectly good field, but he wanted to make himself look more brilliant, to look as if he was both a whiz at business and also able to get into those ivory-tower, more academic areas like higher mathematics. He wanted to have it every possible way, to look good from whatever angle people were looking at him.

"That was always Michael, doing what he did, and then trying to manipulate how people saw what he did. He lived north of the Boulevard, but he always wanted people to think he lived south of the Boulevard, and then, on the other hand, he also wanted people to think he was hard-working and unpretentious and didn't have any of the snobby habits that people south of the Boulevard had. He was very eager to control what people thought about him, even if the truth was good enough.''

Upon Milken's graduation from Berkeley, Milken and Lori were married at the same sprawling but ramshackle San Fernando hotel— the Sportsman's Lodge—where Michael had had his bar mitzvah reception in 1959. They went to Hawaii for a modest but apparently happy honeymoon. Then, after another summer of work as an accountant, Milken and his bride moved to Philadelphia, where he entered the Wharton School of Business, a part of the University of Pennsylvania. There, Milken was as distinguished a student as he had been at Berkeley. He moved effortlessly through his accounting classes and supposedly discussed matters of high finance with his professors. He was especially engaged with two of his professors, James Walter and Morris Mendelson. Both of them were interested, as Milken was, in the potential rewards of investment in undervalued bonds.

In particular, Milken, Mendelson, and Walter were interested in the idea that the bond market priced bonds inefficiently—meaning that the market for bonds did not price them so that they all yielded the same amount over long periods. In an efficient market, riskless Treasury bonds with nil default rates would have yielded the same amount as the bonds of companies in distress with their much higher interest rates but also higher rates of default. But Milken, along with his teachers, believed that the market was not functioning efficiently at the low end of the credit scale.

This discovery, seemingly arcane and laughably academic, was in fact hugely important. If true, it meant that buyers of low-rated bonds could, with some insignificant investment of time and effort, consistently achieve higher yields at this lower end of the bond scale than at the higher end. The increased default rate of poor-quality bonds would not be so large as to offset their higher yield. "Junk," in fact, would be, if carefully bought, more valuable than gilt-edged Treasury bonds. The high interest rate of such bonds would, over time and with a large enough sample, make up for all risk of loss and bring the buyer out ahead of investments in high-rated, low-interest bonds.

Again, this had been discussed and rebutted in general in Braddock Hickman's book, and some trading of junk credits was already being done in New York and elsewhere on a small scale. But Milken supposedly brought to his professors the idea that this kind of trading

35

could be done on a nationwide scale, and could be done in an orderly, well-managed fashion, instead of catch as catch can.

It is not at all clear that Milken was the first man to have the idea of enlarging and "improving" the junk bond market. Hickman had shown that such a market for junk, at least in terms of issuance, had existed before the Great Depression. In some years before 1929, below-investment-grade issues were in fact about one-third of the market's issuances. And certainly it is not clear that Milken truly brought any kind of academic rigor to his so-called "discovery." That is, there is no evidence of any thoroughly documented work by Milken that would have added to Hickman's work, or of any large study by him in addition to what he might have read in Hickman and elsewhere.

Milken came to Wharton at a particularly good time for him to confound his teachers with his supposed insights and success at finance. In 1968, America was in a state of confusion on many levels. On the streets, there was anger and violence about the war in Vietnam. In the groves of academe, there was the scent of hemp and the challenging of authority. Professors who had been listened to with something like awe were, by 1968, genuinely worried about their safety going to and from class.

Something of this anarchy had even reached into business schools. Ten years before, the emphasis in business education had been on improvement of manufacturing and distribution and research. Financial management was a small part of the curriculum. By the mid-1960s, however, a nouvelle vague, spread from the Harvard Business School, held that the manufacturing, research, and distribution problems of America would take care of themselves. The real profits for American businesses would be found in making more efficient use of their cash flows, investing their liquid assets more effectively, and arranging the distribution of their capitalization in order to take advantage of tax benefits and interest rate changes—in other words, things that professors knew about, and that did not require getting one's hands dirty.

The big winners in the rest of the century, went this notion, would not be the people who made a better widget. Rather, the major rewards to companies and stockholders would come from decisions about how much debt and how much equity a company should have, how much should be in bank loans, how much in notes, how much in bonds, how much in bonds convertible into stock. Engineers of balance sheets, not of machine tools, would be the pioneers of industrial progress in the future, said the gospel, which was preached at Wharton by (among others) the distinguished Professor Walter.

Business schools carried on this trend—as iconoclastic in its way as Mark Rudd was in his—and went even further. By the late 1960s, it was considered legitimate to try to figure out how to play the stock and bond markets; that is, the focus of study had gone from making things, to raising money efficiently, to understanding the dynamics of finance, and thence to understanding how financial markets worked generally.

This was an extremely new direction for business schools. Yet economists and business teachers follwed it eagerly. It was terra incognita, as removed from usual business school subjects as Afro-American studies and the feminine mystique had been from European history and anthropology. But in the Walpurgisnacht atmosphere of the late 1960s, it made perfect sense. Traditional disciplines were being rejected and replaced, and the worship of the new and the different was the order of the day.

Within that cult, a key icon was "relevance." In the late 1960s, outmoded ideas that the study of a subject was useful for the sake of teaching studious habits or for making a better-rounded citizen were sneered at. What counted was getting information that could help a young man or woman cope with the exigencies of daily life in revolutionary Amerika. This was how one served the people, as well as serving oneself. Hence, good-bye to the History of Economic Ideas. Hello to Racism in Modern Society.

To carry that to a business school, what could possibly be more relevant than making money quickly? After all, if the Wharton student cut out all of the antiquated garbage about improving national output and efficiency, what did business school really come down to? Getting rich quick. If a student wanted something else, he should be in Divinity School. Thus, the movement in emphasis in business schools from manufacturing widgets to manufacturing money was in a perfectly obvious way a carryover of the prevailing thought fashions of the era: novelty, relevance, and self-obsession.

There was yet another current in American academic thought that

37

washed into business schools, and that both bore up Michael Milken and offered him insight. That current had to do with the *quick* part of the phrase "get rich quick." For a variety of reasons, the time horizon of Americans was shrinking, and shrinking rapidly. The late and even mid-1960s were the era of Pop Art, instant food, instant highs, instant everything. The time horizon of the patient Minnesota farmer had been replaced by the time horizon of the screaming baby who wants his toy from his Crackerjack box, which might have had something to do with the worship of youth in postwar America, or perhaps with the fear of sudden death from atomic war or from fluoride in toothpaste.

For whatever reasons, the shift of time horizons had occurred within the wider populace; within the community centered on making money there was an additional motive, which it could and did obsess upon: inflation. What Jimi Hendrix was to music, the change in the late 1960s in the Consumer Price Index was to expectations and behavior in finance and in business generally. If the instant gratification and narcosis-inducing confusion of rock music were preferable for many young Americans to the more demanding but incomparably more rewarding genius of Mozart or even of Gershwin, the rise in the rate of inflation had much the same effect on the attitude about money and just how to get rich quick.

The inflation rate through most of the 1950s and the early 1960s had hovered at about 1 percent per year, close to zero inflation, and it had led to happiness with low-yielding (in absolute terms) Treasury bonds, high-rated corporates, and sound stocks. After all, if the rate of inflation is 1 percent per annum, and your T-bond earns triple that, or two percentage points more, you, as a lender, should be perfectly satisfied. If you are earning three percentage points more than inflation, or 4 percentage points in a corporate bond, by any reasonable historical standard, you are doing fine.

But—and this is an epic but—inflation changes everything. When the deficits and money creation of the war in Vietnam and the War on Poverty stoked the price fires in the mid and late 1960s, the rate of inflation rose to 2 percent per year, then to 3 percent, to 4 percent, and then to 5 percent per year by the end of the decade. Twenty years later, 5 percent per year would seem like relative price stability.

(It isn't.) But in the late 1960s, a doubling, tripling, and quadrupling of the rate of inflation was an earthquake.

Of course, higher prices had an effect on every shopper. But to investors, the effect was far more pronounced. The nature of investments meant that inflation's effect was felt not only for the day or year of the inflation, but for years in the future. The reason for this had to do in large part with the concept of net present value.

Net present value defines and quantifies the fact that money that will be received at intervals over future time is valued as a present sum by "discounting" to present value. To perform this operation, the absolute amounts of the future payments are revised downward depending upon the interest rate, which is in turn powerfully and directly affected by the expected rate of inflation.

For example, as interest rates rise, the whole stream of future payments from a stock or a bond become worth less. (Not worthless, but *worth less*.) If interest rates rise from 3 percent to 6 percent, the value of a dollar received twelve years from today falls, not by 3 percent, but by roughly half. For payments made more than twelve years from today, the present value falls by more than half. Thus, it was inevitable that inflation and higher interest rates put fear and confusion into financial markets toward the end of the 1960s. Old standards collapsed. Old instruments seemed less valuable and a struggle began to find financial instruments that would at least in part offset the loss, fear, and uncertainty of conventional, long-term investment strategies. Again, this had to do with the *quick* part of "get rich quick." If a dollar received far in the future has smaller present value than it did ten years ago, there are two ready solutions: one, get more dollars, and two, get the dollars today or tomorrow instead of in the distant future.

As a case in point, building plants and developing better manufacturing techniques and new products takes years, sometimes decades. Changing financing techniques, altering balance sheets to take advantage of changes in interest rates or tax laws takes days, weeks, and months. An innovative way to finance a corporation can bring results to the bottom line immediately, with corresponding rewards for the managers who do it. By the time a new widget is mass-produced, the managers behind it could easily be retired or dead. And, again, those widget-making revenues will have to be discounted to present value, which could make them worth little indeed. Thus, "Money Now" came to be a far more important phrase than "Love" or "Peace," and far more suited to helping individuals grow rich.

Michael Milken came to Wharton in the midst of all of these trends and currents: the contagious iconoclasm of the age, the cult of relevance and instant gratification, and the inflation-driven (and perfectly sensible) wish to slip in the quick fix instead of the long-term solution. In other words, Milken came to a place in time and space that was ready and waiting for someone with what looked like new ideas, what looked like a convincing rationale for them, and what looked like a real track record in making money.

Milken had all three. To be sure, they were based upon salesmanship and extremely questionable use of scholarly data and perhaps fictitious experience. But the whole Milken story is about "seems" as compared with "is."

Although Milken is said to have earned straight A's at Wharton and to have been the darling of his professors, he left before finishing his required master's thesis to work at a small but prestigious "investment bank" in Philadelphia, presumably because he was so eager to enter the real world and start testing his hypotheses about bonds and default rates and yields. He did, however, turn in his master's thesis in 1973, three years after leaving Wharton. Perhaps the most fascinating and foreboding thing about the work is that Milken wrote it with James Walter, the man who had been his highly complimentary professor in his days at Wharton. That is, unlike most students, who write their theses *for* a professor who then grades it, Milken wrote his in partnership *with* his professor.

The thesis itself, entitled "Managing the Corporate Financial Structure," Wharton School of Finance Working Paper 26-73, is a bizarre document indeed. For a paper written by a financial genius and his professor of finance, it is an astonishing mishmash of basic, obvious facts such as that corporations often call bonds during periods of falling interest rates so that they can refinance at lower rates, or that adjusting for changes in interest rates, the prices of corporate bonds vary with the price of stocks of the same corporation. Mixed in with these elementary school lessons is a bewildering array of graphs and formulas to prove these propositions. The overall effect is about the same as a speech by the Kingfish in the old *Amos 'n' Andy* radio series: a lot of bluster to prove something everyone already knows.

There are also paragraphs and sections that are unrelated to the paragraphs and sections adjoining them, in different typefaces. There are sweeping generalizations about finance (which really could use a Braddock Hickman) supported in the Milken/Walter work by newspaper clippings reproduced in full and pasted into the thesis. There are spelling errors, arithmetic errors, and basic errors of financial understanding.

And there are also deeply questionable assertions about the transactional costs of altering corporate balance sheets. Overall, for the postgraduate work of one of the greatest minds in finance, it is an inexplicable disappointment. It would be easy to guess that Milken was simply too busy to pay much attention to the document, but how it went out over the name of a respected professor of finance at Wharton is a mystery.

On the other hand, the thesis is of a piece with much of what Michael Milken was before it was submitted and what he has since become. It had an elegant title, which fit in perfectly with the ethos of the age ("Managing the Corporate Financial Structure," not "Making a Better Widget"). It was necessary to make Milken an official MBA; that is, to lend him a needed credential as a financial expert. It was cowritten with a name in finance to lend him still greater credibility. It had many complex-looking graphs and tables to make him look smart and facile in mathematics. In fact, it had enough charts and enough awkward, daunting sentences to accomplish two necessary additional goals: ensure that hardly anyone would read it and guarantee that those with no special financial expertise who did read it would be impressed. Serious students of finance or economics would not read it carefully until it was too late. In the meantime, it was a credential and a selling document, much like a diploma bought through the mail from a university in England that no one in Podunk would ever have heard of.

The document also has one other important clue about who Michael Milken was and is. Many of the corporations whose bonds he was "analyzing" in 1973 were the creations of men who were to be inner members of the Milken circle, showing that as early as 1973, long before the acknowledged creation of the notorious Daisy Chain, Milken was at work on learning who his key players would be and how they and he would fit together.

The paper is largely a selling document touting the bonds and preferred stock of companies whose leaders had become his pals: Tisch's Lorillard, Riklis's McCrory and Rapid-American, Lindner's American Continental. By 1973, Milken was already in the deal stream. What he lacked in writing ability, he more than made up in his ability to plan.

In 1969, in the spring, while many of his fellow Wharton classmates were writing their senior theses, Milken went to work, at first part-time and then full-time, at a Philadelphia brokerage/investment bank/ mutual fund manager by the name of Drexel Harriman Ripley. Drexel was a small firm by then-current standards. It had a name in bond analysis, and its ancient lineage, traced back to the first half of the nineteenth century, earned it a place of respect among far larger firms. It also had a larger office in New York and excellent connections in municipal finance. Milken began work there instead of at any of the larger firms where he might have found employment in large part because his professor of finance (later his writing partner), James Walter, had a connection to the firm and thought well of it as well as of Milken.

Reports vary about what Milken's duties at the firm were when he began. Some accounts say that he was a computer specialist, which sounds far-fetched, inasmuch as business school graduates are rarely used to write programs or repair machines. Others say that his work had to do with getting securities delivered more quickly in order to save on interest costs while they were on the books of the firm. This is a possibility, but again would represent extremely trivial work for someone of Milken's caliber. Still other accounts say that Milken was assigned to help organize the recordkeeping and securities delivery systems of Drexel, collectively known as the "back office." Whatever his initial duties, Milken's real work at Drexel was the indispensable labor, for a young man on the move, of Winning Friends and Influencing People.

CHAPTER THREE

THE NETWORK

The love of money as a possession—as distinguished from the love of money as a means to the enjoyments and realities of life—will be recognized for what it is, a somewhat disgusting morbidity, one of those semi-criminal, semi-pathological propensities which one hands over with a shudder to the specialists in mental disease.

JOHN MAYNARD KEYNES, 1931

IF ONE IMAGINES a male equivalent of Ann Baxter's role in *All About Eve,* one can picture Michael Milken's rise from obscurity to super-stardom. While a humble and unworthy Eve made herself useful to an established star, a self-effacing Milken set out to make life easier for a number of the most successful—and most unorthodox—money men in America. Ingratiating himself, flattering them (which they richly deserved) on their financial acumen, he soon began to display his own star qualities until he was running the whole show. But in this drama, those who had helped him to the top did not simply retire like the world-weary Margo Channing. They stayed on to become supporting players. And what an unusual cast of characters it was.

Meshulam Riklis

The remarkable Meshulam Riklis was either the first or almost the first of the weird and wealthy men to whom Milken attached himself.

Riklis, a man of mystery, came to America in the late 1940s from Israel, but just how he got to Israel is a difficult-to-pin-down matter. By some accounts, he was a Hungarian who had, as a child, fled Hungary with his parents, and had spent the years of World War II in Turkey. By another account, he had spent the war in Turkey where his parents were serving as diplomats in the British Foreign Service. By yet another account, he had spent all of World War II in what was then Palestine, working as a secret operative for the Haganah, the secret Israeli independence army. By still another account, he had spent the war as a soldier with Montgomery's Eighth Army fighting against Rommel in North Africa.

All of these accounts put "Rik" Riklis as their primary source. Whatever the case, he certainly arrived in Minneapolis in or about 1947. And once he got there, he worked as a very aggressive broker for a local firm named Piper, Jaffray & Wood. Still remembered as a boy wonder of finance, he soon made the acquaintance of a number of wealthy families in the Twin Cities region, and in the mid-1950s he organized a group of investors to buy two automated printing companies, American Colortype and Rapid Electro-type. From this merger was born what is still Riklis's main corporate vehicle, Rapid-American.

Riklis began in the late 1950s a veritable blizzard of acquisitions of other companies. Small and medium-sized companies such as Cellu-Craft, Lerner Stores, Heller Packing, and Lakeland Packing were among his first acquisitions. Using wild, and wildly imaginative, financing stratagems (which would later connect him intimately to Milken), he was able to do deals with almost no cash. He offered various exotic kinds of shares, high-paying preferreds, high-yield bonds, convertibles—anything that did not require cash out of pocket to make his acquisitions. A favorite device for Riklis was to take over a smaller company with his own strange and appealing lures of financing and then sell off some of that company's assets to raise money to pay interest on his financings. This, too, was an eerie precursor of the work of his stupendously apt pupil.

Riklis was able to keep an almost infinite number of balls in the air. He had for many years several different acquisition vehicles going at once: Rapid-American, Glen Alden, McCrory, and some even more obscure entities owned solely by his family trusts. Through the 1960s, through one company or another, he stayed on the buying trail, taking over Lanes Stores, Inland Credit, S. Klein, Best & Co., and other smaller entities, usually paying in stock, bonds, warrants, or some combination, and almost never in cash. In fact, it is hardly an exaggeration to say that the conglomerate wave of the 1960s was started by none other than the wily desert fox, "Rik" Riklis. Certainly, his innovative use of "Chinese paper," as his bonds were called, became the template for the activities of virtually all serious conglomerateurs.

Then in 1967, Riklis started to go after one of his most visible targets: Schenley Distributors, also called Schenley Industries, a company that had an interesting history, as many liquor distributors do. It had survived allegations of Mafia influence (never proved), a contretemps among various management groups, and the end of Prohibition to become a major force in the distribution of alcoholic spirits. Among its many products was the nation's most popular Scotch Whiskey, Dewar's White Label, and for a time it also owned control of Buckingham Distributors, which sold another favorite of American Scotch drinkers, Cutty Sark. For a lengthy period Schenley had as a major distributor a certain Joseph Fusco, a colleague of the late Al Capone. Joseph Linsey, who was described as a friend and colleague of Meyer Lansky, was also a major Schenley distributor. On the other hand, the company also had a well-regarded ethical drug subsidiary and a proud record of charitable giving.

The struggle for control of Schenley took well over a year, even for a man as capable as "Rik" Riklis. It involved paying a startling premium for the shares of the controlling Rosenstiel family, in cash, while paying a much smaller amount to the other shareholders, in various kinds of sub-investment-grade financing instruments. Riklis had to fend off a competing offer by P. Lorillard, which made cigarettes and pipe tobacco and which had its own interesting history. And the purchase, which also had to survive a welter of shareholder litigation, was notable for some questionable payments to some questionable people. One of them, who was apparently not paid in the final event, was a "roommate" of the famed Linsey, the associate of Meyer Lansky. Other payees were rumored, but not proved in court, to have organized crime connections, again, dating back to Capone days.

Apparently Riklis also tipped off some of his favorite investment players about his intention to take over Schenley. The deals worked in a way that was to become typical of Milken's operations: Riklis would, according to court filings, tell his pals at certain brokerages and investment companies such as Investors Diversified Services that he was planning a bid for Schenley. They would then buy about a hundred thousand Schenley shares each, which would be counted toward the total that Riklis needed to gain control of Schenley. However, he would not disclose that he had them in his grasp. He also would not necessarily file with the SEC that he had the shares under his control.

His partners in this "parking" enterprise would get the benefit of either making money on the buyout price or getting commissions and then being indemnified for losses. Such shenanigans would reemerge in the Milken era, but Riklis was engineering these archetypical latter-day Drexel transactions for sizeable corporations when Milken himself was still at the Sammy house at Berkeley, and even earlier when Milken was still at Birmingham High School.

In March of 1971, as the conglomerate era was sinking into eternity, Riklis approached a new target. He announced that he was going to try to take over the floundering, failed mutual fund empire of the flamboyant Bernard Cornfeld, whose Investors Overseas Services has been described as one of the worst Ponzi schemes in history. (He denies it vigorously.) In this endeavor, Riklis was competing with other aggressive fish such as Fred Carr of the Enterprise Fund, which was closely linked to IOS in certain transactions, and the far more notorious Robert Vesco, who finally got the remains of IOS, looted it far more brutally than Cornfeld was ever accused of doing, and then fled to Central America.

In 1972, Riklis announced that through his personal family holding company, which also owned travel agencies, he was seeking control of a company named Continental Connector, which owned, among many other things, control of certain casinos in Nevada, in particular, the Dunes, which Riklis wanted to acquire.

Continental Connector was controlled by a number of powerful figures in Las Vegas, including lawyer and long-time Jimmy Hoffa associate Morris Shenker. Riklis's early efforts to acquire a stake in Continental Connector were canceled when some of the major owners were indicted. A federal grand jury in Reno was shocked, shocked to find that there had been skimming going on at some of the casinos these persons were involved with.

By March of 1973, however, Riklis could reveal that he had an agreement to buy the Riviera Hotel from many of the same people who had been involved with Continental Connector but who were not currently under federal indictment. A valuable source who was at the time a casino owner said that Morris Shenker was also involved in the sale of the Riviera to Riklis, and indeed, that since the Teamsters' Union was then so deeply involved with the casino industry in Nevada, it would have been impossible for Riklis to buy the "Riv" without Shenker's consent. In fact, as the source said, it would have been impossible for anyone to buy any major hotel in Las Vegas at that time without the approval, tacit or explicit, of the Teamsters. And Morris Shenker was their lawyer in Las Vegas.

In the meantime, Riklis had also been occupied with the buying of an entity called Kenton. This merchandising jewel was a collection of very prestigious retail brand names, especially Mark Cross, Cartier, and Georg Jensen. Riklis acquired control of Kenton in 1972. He put it into bankruptcy about one year later but continued to run it for some years after that until it disappeared completely, although some of the brand names persisted. The bankruptcy occurred amidst a welter of allegations of self-dealing by Riklis on his own behalf and that of his family. Kenton was only one of a number of Riklis-controlled enterprises to enter bankruptcy while Riklis simultaneously drew large amounts of money from the corporations.

Outside the world of high-flying finance, Meshulam Riklis was perhaps best known as the adoring husband of the singer, actress, and model Pia Zadora. He was, apparently, so proud of his wife that he had a life-size fully nude representation of her in his living room, as well as many nude pictures, which he shared with admirers in the pages of *Playboy*. Riklis was once quoted as saying that he believes he was put on earth to serve women, but he was far more important than any wealthy stage door Johnny. Certainly, in the early 1970s, when Milken met Riklis, he was as dramatically unorthodox, as blatantly self-serving, as ingenious a trail-blazer on the path to get-rich-quick as there was on earth. If immortality reaches to Riklis, it will almost certainly be as financial role model for the kid from Encino.

Riklis, in fact, had a certain pattern of business and financial activity that was to become second nature, although on a vastly larger scale, at Michael Milken's Drexel Burnham Lambert:

- Acquire companies, using their own cash flow and assets to pay for them.
- Use as financing instruments various kinds of bonds and stocks that do not require payment in cash for some period.
- Redeem those instruments not with cash but with new instruments (Riklis once boasted that he would never pay off a bond except with another bond).
- Use control of one entity to gain control of another and then have both controlled by his family.

The issuance of a stunning array of exotic bonds, convertibles, preferreds, and warrants, each from a different company, each with different terms and conditions, was all part of Riklis's way of doing business. But it meant that there were few if any experts in the area of low-rated Riklis debt instruments. However, that changed in 1970, when Milken went to work at Drexel Harriman Ripley. He took the time and trouble to learn about the intricacies of Riklis bonds and all the rest of his bag of tricks. He would win this particular friend by knowing all about his junk issues and he would influence this same friend the one and only way that one man can influence another man like "Rik" Riklis. He would produce a way to make still more money. (Or perhaps Riklis explained it to him.) That way had to do with offering to make a market in Riklis's junk bonds.

Milken's offer was an ingenious solution to a basic problem that issuers of junk and "Chinese paper" had when the conglomerate boom faded. The vast blizzard of low-rated paper that Riklis and his imitators had sold or traded in the 1960s was largely illiquid. The unfortunate person who held Riklis bonds or convertibles rarely could find anyone else to buy them if he wanted to sell. There were good reasons for this: The bonds had a bewildering variety of coupons, dates of maturity, provisions for maturity, and priorities of lien (generally, the right to seize hard goods if the issuer defaulted). There were even uncertainties about the legal status of the issuer. Bond experts had no clear idea of how much a Riklis McCrory bond was worth as compared with a Riklis McGregor bond or a Riklis Riviera bond. If one imagines how difficult it would be to make a market in used cars if each car were destined to stop running at a certain mileage—and that mileage was a deep secret, which no one knew—one can get an idea of how hard it was to make a market in Riklis securities. There were, in a word, almost no buyers.

This presented a deep dilemma for Riklis in the 1970s. Potential sellers of corporations that he wanted to buy knew that his securities were largely untradeable, or tradeable only at a large discount. And naturally, that inhibited their interest in selling to Riklis for securities. Moreover, when Riklis wanted to issue securities for any purpose at all, he would have to pay a higher interest rate on them than he might have wished solely to compensate potential buyers for the illiquidity of his issues.

But—and this was a big but—if Milken really could make a secondary market in Riklis junk, if he could genuinely create some liquidity for Riklis and his ilk, he would be doing them a huge favor. By making their bonds more liquid, he would greatly improve their acceptability in the market, make them more likely to be accepted as payment in corporate deals, and lower their interest rates. Milken would also be able, by creating even the *appearance* of liquidity, to confuse a bond market that had a certain well-founded reluctance even to touch a Riklis bond because of his long habit of defaulting. With the appearance of liquidity, worried owners would "know" they could sell out if there were problems.

For a genius like Riklis, this meant major dollars. He had hundreds of millions, and would soon have billions, of debt outstanding. If Milken saved him even fifty basis points, or half of a percentage point on the interest, the savings would be many millions annually. If Milken made his bonds seem to be sufficiently presentable to allow Riklis to pursue the takeover deals he badly wanted to go after, Riklis would be even more indebted to him.

But how to make it all happen? How to make a market in the random, bizarre creations of the junk world? After all, a true market cannot exist without a substantial degree of knowledge of the product by both buyers and sellers, and can hardly exist where the products sold vary case by case. There can be a world market in grain or oil,

49

because everyone knows what a bushel of winter wheat is and everyone knows what Libyan sweet crude is and how many gallons are in a barrel. But how can there be a national market in such varied and mysterious products as Riklis bonds or warrants or preferreds or convertibles?

Answer: There can't. But there can be a righteous facsimile created by a group of good fellows getting together to take in each other's laundry. There might not be the possibility of a real market, but there could be an illusion good enough to help make the sale. To create that illusion, who better than other players who want it and would profit by it?

Carl Lindner

In 1972, more or less, Milken met such another player, who, while by no means as astonishing as Meshulam Riklis, was a major hitter in his own right and a mythic figure even without having been a freedom fighter or a mideast spy. Carl Lindner, of Cincinnati, Ohio, started out in his family's dairy business and built a chain of convenience stores in and around Cincinnati after World War II. With his brother, Robert, he used the momentum of the dairy convenience stores, a lovely cash business, to buy a true empire of financial and communications companies. Through a holding company with the modest name of American Financial Corporation, by 1977 the Lindner brothers controlled Great American Insurance, a holding company that owned a string of property and casualty (and occasionally life) insurance companies that together made up the twenty-third-largest property and casualty insurer in America. The Lindners also owned, through AFC, Cincinnati's fourth-largest bank, Provident, and Cincinnati's second-largest savings and loan, Hunter.

There was more. Lindner and his brother owned or controlled at least seventy shopping centers in and around Cincinnati, along with other valuable real estate. Unlike Riklis, who showed little interest in media properties other than his wife, the Lindner brothers for a time were proprietors of Bantam Books, Grosset & Dunlap, which they had acquired in a roundabout way, and the *Cincinnati Enquirer*. Carl Lindner also owned a large homebuilding and mortgage subsidiary, both of which went by the name of American Continental (Home and Mortgage) and were operated by his former counsel, an aggressive, confident fellow named Charles Keating.

Very much unlike Riklis, Carl Lindner, with the tireless assistance of Charles Keating, was a highly visible crusader against nudity and pornography. He repeatedly used his civic muscle in Cincinnati to attempt to get what he deemed to be pornographic magazines and books off the newsstands of his city and tried mightily to keep a road show of *Oh, Calcutta* from playing in the riverfront city.

He was more successful in his business ventures. Before meeting Milken, Lindner owned a group of stocks in the portfolios of his insurance companies and banks, and these companies were generally very well regarded and conservatively run, with some exceptions. His major investments included Combined Communications, a media company to which he eventually sold the *Cincinnati Enquirer,* Government Employees Life Insurance Company, and United Brands (a fruit company once known as United Fruit, whose chairman at the time was Eli Black, father of the highly successful Drexel key player Leon Black). Lindner was also a large investor in Chubb Insurance, Circle K (a convenience chain run by the same Carl Eller who ran Combined Communications), Gulf + Western (predecessor in name of Paramount Communications and owner of Simon & Schuster), Kroger, a grocery chain, and Monarch Capital, once a carefully run insurer in Massachusetts. Furthermore, Lindner was considered a shrewd buyer of bankrupt companies, and had made large sums on his buys of the bankrupt Penn Central, of which he was eventually to become chairman.

Like Riklis, Lindner had caught the attention of the Securities and Exchange Commission for allegedly illegal securities transactions. Riklis had been accused by the SEC of self-dealing in his running of Rapid-American and his failure to disclose adequately the sums and the methods by which he was paying himself and his family out of Rapid-American's public shareholders' till. Like most SEC cases, it was settled by agreement of the two sides with promises to go and sin no more. Lindner, for his part, had been accused of illegal manipulation of the price of Warner Communications shares, supposedly in order to raise the price at which he sold a six-hundred-thousand-share block of that stock back to Warner. He had also been accused, along with his good friend and colleague Charles Keating, of illegally self-dealing by giving himself and Keating and their family members highly preferential loans and then using still other loans and sham transactions at his captive S&Ls to cover up failure to repay those loans. In a bizarre twist, Lindner, already a wealthy man, also used public shareholders' money essentially to give himself a private plane owned by the shareholders, according to charges in a 1979 SEC consent decree.

Finally, Lindner was one of the most avid issuers of new securities in America, very many of junk quality. In fact, a 1977 article about him in *Fortune* quoted a spokesman for the SEC as noting that Lindner's companies were the single largest filers with the SEC, an astonishing assertion for an entity that at that time was not even among the top fifty national financial corporations.

Thus, as an issuer of junk, and as a connoisseur of junk generally, Lindner would have had sound reasons indeed to go in with Milken and Riklis in creating a seeming market in junk. Like Riklis, he would be able to sell his bonds and preferreds at lower coupons and dividends if he could show potential buyers that there was a market for them after sale. He would also be able to use them more effectively for takeovers, and further, he would be able to sell off his own junk inventory of non-Lindner issues more quickly and at a better price if a national market for junk seemed to exist. For Lindner, the rewards from playing ball with Milken would be enormous.

Within a few years of meeting Milken, by the end of 1980, the results of this insiders' game were obvious. The conservative issues of yesteryear no longer dominated the portfolios of Lindner insurance and financial companies. Instead, as his largest holdings there appeared the names of companies controlled by other men that Milken had recruited to play the game: Saul Steinberg's Reliance Corporation (with Saul Steinberg himself as savvy a player as there could be); Laurence Tisch's Loew's Corporation, itself a sizeable issuer of junk through its P. Lorillard cigarette division; and most of all, Rapid-American, the vehicle of Riklis, which had gone private in 1979, but which was still public enough for Lindner to own a large chunk. He also owned almost half of a large company called Mission Insurance

Group, which was the first of several disastrous investments, but was not run by an outright Drexel player or insider. In other words, within a fairly short time after meeting Milken, Lindner was helping in a big way to make the "market" in junk. As a loyal team player, he was taking in the other players' junk laundry and making it look good.

Although Lindner lacked the flair of Riklis, in his modus operandi were several strategies that would later serve Milken well:

- To acquire fiduciary institutions that held large amounts of money from depositors or policyholders by the use of the tiny amount of equity needed to control such organizations. For example, in 1981, Lindner had an empire of investment companies, by then the thirty-second-largest financial entity in America, which had about $3.5 billion in assets and about equal liabilities to depositors and policyholders. But it had *no* tangible equity at that time, and only about $250 million of equity in the prior year.
- To use the equity control of the fiduciary organizations to buy assets far more beneficial to the controlling shareholder of the company than to the depositors or other trustors of the enterprise, or even harmful to their interests.
- To use the assets of a federally insured S&L (in fact, several of them) to directly benefit himself and his pal Keating. Certainly he was far from the first to do so. But he was probably the first of the major junk issuers who offered an example to Milken of how to have fun and games with institutions insured by the taxpayers.

By his own life Lindner, even more than Riklis, showed that adroit public relations and image control could obscure real-life misconduct. At the same time that Lindner was being cited by the SEC and private investors for alleged stunning abuse of his own stockholders, depositors, and the federal taxpayer, he was handing out cards that sang his love of America and the old-fashioned virtues of hard work and persistence. At the same time that he was fighting pornography, he was also fighting lawsuits by his own stockholders alleging years-long pillaging of his own investors and self-dealing as a day-by-day systematic way of doing business. At the end of the day, as usual, the lawsuits were settled for pennies and the city of Cincinnati was handing out medals and ribbons to Lindner and asking him to lead civic parades. Milken, too, would become a skillful practitioner of this PR game.

Victor Posner

A third member of Milken's inner circle was Victor Posner. Born in Baltimore, Maryland, in 1919, Posner worked his way up in his father's dry goods store, then branched into real estate when he was still a young man, possibly in his teens. He was, some later said, a slumlord in Baltimore's prodigious black ghetto. Certainly, whether a slumlord or a developer, he made an excellent return on his investments, and while in his forties he "retired" to Miami Beach.

Soon thereafter, however, Posner was moved by boredom and threats to some of his investments to start taking over corporations. His family-owned investment vehicle, Security Management Corporation, which had managed his real estate operations in Maryland, first took control of a cigar maker named DWG. He then took over what was once National Vulcanized Fabric and became NVF, even though he owned less than half of its stock. He also took over a fabricator of steel-milling equipment called Pennsylvania Engineering Corporation and through the marvels of leverage, while owning only a minority of the stock of NVF, he caused it to acquire a well-regarded manufacturer named Sharon Steel.

From these companies—hardly household names—Posner drew combined salary and perks that made him the highest-paid executive in America through a good part of the late 1960s and early 1970s. The sums were in the low seven figures, chump change by Drexel's later standards, but impressive at the time. His extraordinary wages were, moreover, an example to Milken and other Drexel players of the "rule" that public companies existed mostly to benefit their top executives, not stockholders generally.

Posner went on through the late 1960s takeover era to acquire still more corporations, usually for bizarre forms of notes and stock bought by institutional investors. By the end of 1969 he had big chunks of Southeastern Public Service, National Propane, and a clothing maker named Wilson Brothers. And he, like Lindner and

Riklis, had vast amounts of "Chinese paper" outstanding and would have desperately needed to show some liquidity for this paper in order to use it for more deals and to lower the cost of capital.

In 1969, according to the SEC, just after Posner had acquired control of Sharon Steel, he caused the trustees of the company's pension fund to sell off their blue-chip stock holdings and use the proceeds to buy—guess what?—the largely untradeable Posner securities used in the takeovers of DWG, Southeastern, National Propane, and Wilson Brothers. The SEC sued, alleging that the purpose of the buys of the Posner junk was not to benefit the employees' retirement, but to benefit Posner and his acquisition program. The suit was later settled, with Posner making some slight alterations in his behavior for a brief time, or at least promising to do so.

Posner would, by 1977, again be sued by the SEC for illegally skimming money from his public corporations and giving it to his family, thereby defrauding his stockholders. This suit also was settled. But Posner would, much later, be found by the SEC to be using a captive reinsurer in a typically imaginative Drexel fashion. He caused it to charge large premiums to Posner-controlled public corporations for its primary insurance line, then used the proceeds to prop up the price of the stocks of the companies he controlled and to make other acquisitions for his network.

Posner had a few more strings to add to Milken's guitar. Not only did he demonstrate more about the joys of leverage and about self-dealing at public companies in terms of perks and pay but he also did not hesitate to use the pension assets of his captive corporations for his own purposes, independent of whether they conferred any value upon the pensioners—or even hurt them. In this attack on the basic notions of fiduciary responsibility, Posner showed a daring that might well impress Milken and his colleagues.

Furthermore, Posner had a few personal habits of doing business that would be lamps unto Milken's feet. He was said to consider any contract that did not work to his benefit moment by moment to be worthless. He was also said to be absolutely unafraid of being sued, by stockholders, rivals, customers, suppliers, or the SEC. His attitude, as quoted in the early 1970s, was that it did not matter what his legal position was: If he had good lawyers, he would be safe from justice. In this shrewd understanding of the impotence of the legal system against those who are actually moving and shaking in the executive suites—and able to use the funds of the very people they are looting, namely the public stockholders, for their legal defense—Posner was an early and articulate seer of how the real world worked. His example would be put to staggeringly effective use by Michael Milken and his colleagues.

Posner displayed another inspirational personality trait in terms of truly world-class acquisitiveness when he took over Sharon Steel. The century-old steelmaker had, in the mid-1960s, commissioned Norman Rockwell to do a series of fourteen paintings about the steel business. The paintings, reputedly masterpieces of Rockwell's straightforward yet treacly style, vanished from Sharon Steel's Pittsburgh headquarters immediately after Posner seized control in 1969. They were reported to be in Posner's office for a number of years. And then, in 1988, when Posner's Sharon Steel went into bankruptcy and the trustee for the creditors of Sharon asked for the paintings back, they disappeared again. However, after much argument, threats in court, and some public outcry—not much—the paintings were produced by Posner as mysteriously as they had disappeared—except for one, which still remains missing. Posner was quoted as saying, regarding his business, "No matter what happens, it's not going to change the way I live."

Saul Steinberg

Riklis, Lindner, and Posner had about them something that set them apart from their pupil, Michael Milken. They were all older than he was by at least two decades. But in Saul Steinberg, Milken found a man not much older than he was, a man with interests in common who had already shown that America was still the land of opportunity for the young.

Steinberg was born in 1939 in Brooklyn, New York. His father was a maker of rubber and plastic housewares, but Steinberg himself had decided by the age of eight or nine, he later reported, that he wanted to work in finance. By the time he was in his teens, Steinberg had moved to a middle-class area called Five Towns, on Long Island, as his father's business grew in size and income. Still dreaming of a career in finance, he idolized Howard Hughes and wanted to be rich and a ladies' man, as he later told an interviewer.

In a maneuver that was truly a paradigm for Milken, Steinberg attended Wharton, although as an undergraduate. He did not go on to graduate school because he was so eager to get into the "real world" of business. However, also like Milken, Steinberg did at least some work at some time with one of his professors, which later became a senior paper about opportunities in computer leasing.

Steinberg's paper and the research for it supposedly revealed a fabulous profit opportunity. The opportunity arose because IBM, then by far the dominant firm in business computers, had only recently been forced by a Justice Department complaint to sell rather than solely lease its computers. However, IBM still leased, and when it did, it charged a rental based upon a depreciable life of only four years for its machines.

Steinberg calculated that if he assumed a depreciable life of eight years, he could rent the machines for far less than IBM. There was a gamble implicit in the assumption: The machines might actually be obsolete and relatively valueless long before the end of eight years. In that case, the lease payments and the depreciation from the lease payments would not cover the cost of the computers and other business expenses, and his business would fail.

The bet that Steinberg made was the exact equivalent of the bet a car rental company makes about what the useful life of its cars will be—with one huge additional risk: Cars are fairly standard items while computers do, in fact, change and improve radically and can become obsolete and relatively worthless over a short period. However, the computer-leasing business was an almost perfect accounting opportunity while it lasted.

Here is how it might have worked: No one really knows what the true depreciable life of a computer is. True, the IRS issues guidelines about the minimum depreciable life, but the maximum is something else again. In any case, IRS depreciation and income statement depreciation are two very different concepts. And as long as Steinberg could get a friendly bank to finance the computers on a long-term basis, he could lease them as if they had a long depreciable life.

For the first few years of the lease, no one would know whether Steinberg was right or wrong. The rentals came in, and the depreciation was calculated in such a way that they seemed to greatly exceed depreciation and other costs, and the company seemed to be making money hand over fist. Was it? No one knew. The day of reckoning would come when the computers had to be sold or re-leased, and that was down the road a piece.

In the meantime, Steinberg could push it still further down the road by leasing more computers so that he continued to have cash flow even as the first year's inventory neared the day of reckoning. That is, if the first computers were leased in 1960, the investing public would not necessarily find out in 1964 if IBM's estimate of useful life (four years) or Steinberg's (eight years, just as an example) was correct. That's because a new bunch of computers was leased out in 1961, then more in 1962 and 1963. Even as the first year's computers were turned in and could be seen to be largely white elephants, there was still money pouring in from the next couple of years' rentals. And that money meant that the leasing company could start gradually revising downward the useful life of some of the computers already returned and still have impressive income.

But the truly great part of the scheme was that for those first few years, the leasing company (which Steinberg called Leasco), if properly leveraged, could show incredible earnings on its equity. It could look as if it had discovered a major financial and technical breakthrough. With the right barrage of press agentry, which Steinberg had, it could look as if Steinberg's stock should sell for fifty times earnings, which it in fact did for a brief time in the go-go 1960s.

Then, with that hugely inflated stock and reputation, Steinberg could and did trade some of his stock and warrants and other forms of Chinese paper to stockholders of more conservatively valued companies for their assets. Then he could and did blend his greatly overvalued assets, with their potential destiny of disaster, with more solid assets, and the blend could survive.

Steinberg used this approach and Leasco for acquiring a number of small companies and then for a hostile takeover of a very large insurance company. Reliance, which had solid, conservatively valued assets in its portfolio, at first resisted Steinberg's blandishments, but then agreed to be taken over by him for—surprise—a package of junk securities.

Reliance's assets supposedly exceeded its policy liabilities by so much that Steinberg could sell some of the portfolio and take the gains as income or addition to equity capital. This maneuver would wash out losses that he might have to take by the late 1960s and early 1970s when it turned out that perhaps his estimates of the depreciable life of computers had been too long. This is at least one analysis of what happened. Steinberg undoubtedly would disagree.

In any case, by 1968, when Steinberg, not yet thirty, seized Reliance, he had so much excess liquidity that he could, as he described it, "cash out" of his overvalued computers and still be above water. Meanwhile, the Reliance shareholders who had tendered in 1968 for his Leasco stock took it on the chin. The "Chinese paper" consideration they received for their solid Reliance shares dropped greatly in value and was, of course, illiquid. Legally however, they were in the same position as if they had been taken to another planet. They could sue, and some of them did, but shareholders complaining about consideration in a merger are eligible at best for a small settlement of pennies on the dollars they have lost. As they saw their package of Steinberg junk drop dramatically below what their premerger Reliance shares had been worth, they were basically shouting for justice across an interplanetary void.

(To be fair to Steinberg, however, he was clearly on to something besides pulling a possible fast one with Leasco's accounting. His estimates of the useful life of computers, while too optimistic in fact, might not have been more optimistic than IBM's were conservative.)

In addition to what was happening at Leasco and Reliance, Steinberg was pursuing, in various ways, an old line of work with a new name and new tactics. Every aficionado of gangster movies is familiar with the basic idea of "protection." In the classic case, gangland torpedoes go into a clothing store and throw acid on the merchandise, then offer to sell the owner "protection." When he asks who they will be protecting him from, they laugh, sneer, and say, "From us."

The more up-to-date version of this racket involves a person with a reputation for questionable stewardship of a public company who takes a sizeable position in a company's stock, then makes noises about buying control. Management—usually acting to protect themselves and their jobs more than the public stockholders—offers to buy back the raider's shares at a profit large enough to make him go away.

In a career move that must have made even Milken envious, Saul Steinberg started out his "protection" efforts, now called "greenmail" and not illegal, when he was still a teenager. As a college senior, he bought 3 percent of the stock of O'Sullivan Rubber, a maker of housewares, and complained to the management that they should be doing things differently. Management bought him out for three times what he had paid for the stock. Still in school and just out of it, Steinberg also had a small business lending money to the proprietors of local newsstands in some of New York's boroughs.

With Leasco and Reliance now under his belt, Steinberg is said to have approached Chase Bank in 1969 for a large loan for one or another of his businesses. Chase apparently did not treat him with sufficient respect. He retaliated by taking a small position in Chase, announcing that it was a perfect "fit" with Leasco, and that he might buy control of it.

For a large, not particularly aggressive bank Chase fought back violently. Its chairman, David Rockefeller, enlisted the aid of his clan and his brother, Nelson, then governor of New York. Old guard banks—and there were hardly any other kind—encouraged the sale of Leasco stock, got laws passed making bank takeovers extremely difficult, and generally made Steinberg feel bad about his adventure.

Having been shown the door by the WASP banking establishment, Steinberg then announced, in terms startlingly like what would later come out of Milken, that it was time for a whole new Establishment. "That's the great thing about this country," he said in a 1969 interview with *Forbes*, "the Establishment can constantly be changed." He also noted, with some wit, "I have a feeling that there are a lot of people in this country who would rather give their deposits to Saul Steinberg than to David Rockefeller."

The computer-leasing genius also wanted the world at large to know what he saw as the truth about Saul Steinberg: "I'm no takeover artist," he told *Forbes*. "My wife and I, we're decent people.

We like tennis, art, music. We have three children. We're not really bad at all." This, too, was a harbinger of the image Milken would try to project as a self-effacing man who cared far more about spending time with his family than about sordid money matters.

Like all the other Milken players, Steinberg was often quoted as saying that he did not work to get rich, but rather to build businesses and help people. But in the later years of his life, while continuing to get ever richer, he had certain setbacks in his image building. He was sued by a private school on Long Island after promising to give it a $375,000 gift in 1972, then defaulting on most of the amount with the plea that he lacked the money to make good. The case made law when a judge held that such a promise is in fact binding and ordered Steinberg to pony up the missing $200,000. In 1978, the case was heard by the New York Court of Appeals, which confirmed that promises to charities are binding.

In 1976, Steinberg was also sued by the SEC for breaches of federal law in connection with his activities in the stock of a home builder named Pulte Home. The case was settled. Then in 1975–1976, he became embroiled in a seamy scandal about building bus shelters in New York. Bribes had been paid, and Steinberg's name came up repeatedly. He was never indicted.

A further setback in Steinberg's efforts to show what a nice, family-oriented kind of guy he was came in 1980 (long after he had met Milken), when his second wife sued for divorce. (The first one, the nice one he had told *Forbes* about, had already left the scene.) As an angry wife and large shareholder in Reliance, she sued her husband not only for divorce, but for a number of more corporate causes of action. She alleged that Steinberg had used corporate stockholders' money to renovate his Park Avenue apartment (which had once belonged to John D. Rockefeller, Jr.), had bought and used the company jet only for himself, and had used company money to pay a bribe to a city official.

Overall, the similarities between Steinberg and the older members of the early Milken fraternity were startling:

- Like Posner and Lindner, Steinberg was a major stockholder of the bankrupt Penn Central.

61

- Like Lindner, he early on saw the value of owning an insurance company so that by minimal investment of equity, he could control huge amounts of investable money.
- Like Posner, he had at least considered making a bid for a company called UV Industries.
- Like Lindner, Posner, and Riklis, he had issued large amounts of junk securities, which were largely untradeable until Milken came along.

But, once again, there was a vital difference between Steinberg and the other early Drexel investors. He was much younger than they were. Steinberg had made his name and fortune while he was still a kid. Like the baby Hercules strangling the snake, he had rattled the cage of the Establishment even as a relatively young man. This was heady stuff indeed, and must have made an impression on the young Milken, who carefully researched Steinberg's Chinese paper and secured him as an early player in the game of creating a likeness of liquidity in junk securities.

Laurence Tisch

At very much the other end of the lifestyle and ethical spectrum from Saul Steinberg was Laurence Tisch, who, in fact, along with his brother Robert, brought a definite touch of class to the fraternity of early Milken players. Laurence Tisch was born in 1923 in Bensonhurst, Brooklyn, New York. His father, Al, was in the rag trade, and was an All-American basketball player. Al Tisch also owned, along with his wife, Sayde, who was not just wife, but co-owner of their various enterprises, two summer camps in New Jersey.

Laurence Tisch showed great promise as a high school student in Brooklyn. He graduated with honors from New York University, and then, like Steinberg and Milken, graduated from Wharton. In fact, many Drexel players were Wharton alumni. There was a reason. The Drexel network was very largely made up of the children of middlingly successful men in business, and the desired business school for this group was Wharton. It was not airy and intellectual, as Harvard was reputed to be. It was out of New York, another plus. It was a place to make connections, and not terribly difficult, yet it was considered part of the Eastern college elite. It offered the reality of how business worked, making connections, along with the "prestige" of an Ivy League school—the best of both worlds: a street education and an Ivy League degree.

After graduating from Wharton, Tisch served for three years during World War II in the Office of Strategic Services, the clandestine operation under "Wild Bill" Donovan that was later to become the Central Intelligence Agency.

When the war came to an end and he was released from government service, Tisch spent one semester at Harvard Law School. In April of 1946, along with his father, mother, and brother, Tisch bought a large, well-known hotel in New Jersey called Laurel in the Pines. The Tisch family, with Sayde pitching in, did major renovations, raised rates, and soon had a profitable hotel. They then went to the Catskills, bought the Grand Hotel in the Monticello region, and upgraded that, too. Their simple tactic of buying older properties and renovating them worked well for the Tisches. The Traymore was next, followed by more Atlantic City motels, all of which were profitable before the total collapse of the seaside resort or the limited renaissance there brought about by casino gambling.

In the early and mid-1950s the Tisch family branched into Manhattan hotels, then into building Miami hotels, then into Manhattan office space, riding the postwar boom in commercial property into major wealth by the end of the decade. They then bought control of a theater chain, Loew's, which had once been a part of MGM, and knocked down many of its historic moviehouses to build more lucrative buildings on the land.

Through the 1960s, the Tisches continued to build and buy and buy and build. They made their first move outside the real property area in 1968 when they attempted to buy a commercial finance firm named Commercial Credit Corporation. The firm fled the embrace of the Tisch clan, and was bought by Control Data. However, later that year, Tisch was encouraged to buy a huge cigarette maker called P. Lorillard. This company had been a suitor for or a potential merger partner with Schenley for several months, which meant it had been dancing at the same nightclub with Riklis.

Riklis got Schenley, but within a year, Loew's, in the person of the Tisch family, got control of P. Lorillard, the maker of Kent cigarettes, which about fifteen years earlier had promised smokers a whole new level of safety with something called the "Micronite" filter. This innovation "worked" by passing hot cigarette gases through a filter made of asbestos fibers. The Tisches were successful in raising cigarette sales and reducing costs, and Lorillard, in their hands, became a money machine. However, instead of paying cash for the cigarette maker, the Tisches had offered a series of junk securities bearing the names of Lorillard or Loew's, which became largely untradeable soon after issuance, as did much of the junk paper of the conglomerate era. Into this problem stepped Michael Milken, who would provide for the Tisches, along with the other members of the junk-issuing club, liquidity, or even better, the illusion of liquidity for their junk so that it continued to be a potent acquisition tool.

In even more classic Drexel club fashion, six years after the acquisition of P. Lorillard, Tisch acquired CNA Financial, a Chicago insurance holding company. Again, the Tisches laid out some cash and a lot of securities. But with this acquisition, they were astride a huge pool of investable funds.

Brothers Laurence and Robert Tisch—still being inspired by Sayde Tisch—were not even touched by the kind of accusations of self-dealing, fraud, and personal misconduct that marked the lives of Riklis, Posner, or Steinberg. By the standards of the Drexel players of early days, the Tisches were saints and still are. Laurence Tisch (the only member of this early group of Drexel players who would speak to me) remembered Milken as a young, confident, intelligent man, armed with extraordinary knowledge of his junk and that of other junk issuers, a man who offered to help make markets where none had existed. Despite later allegations that Tisch had criticized Milken, he had nothing but praise for the junk bond czar.

In 1988, by the way, a daughter of Saul Steinberg married a son of Robert Tisch in a lavish ceremony in Manhattan, for which the flowers alone were said to have cost one million dollars, paid for by Steinberg—who a scant fifteen years before had lacked a measly two hundred or so thousand dollars to redeem his pledge to a private school near his home.

. . .

These then, were the very rich men from whom Milken learned, for whom he worked as a "market maker" in their junk securities, and from whose support he, too, became a very rich man.

CHAPTER FOUR

ARCHITECTURE

Three things are to be looked to in a building: that it stands on the right spot; that it be securely founded; and that it be successfully executed.

JOHANN WOLFGANG VON GOETHE, 1808

WITH ITS WITHDRAWAL from the war in Vietnam, the furor over Watergate, and the effects of the Yom Kippur War and the Arab oil embargo, America was wobbling in the early 1970s. But like the spider calmly and methodically weaving its web in the corner of a great palace roiled by revolution, Michael Milken continued his everyday pursuits. The ability to concentrate on one's own efforts in the midst of general confusion is a hallmark of high achievers.

Drexel Harriman Ripley was short of capital, as many firms were in the early 1970s, and found a merger partner in Firestone Tire and Rubber. Shortly thereafter, Drexel Firestone merged with Burnham & Co., a firm founded by the son of a famous physician and distiller. Meanwhile, Milken himself was taking huge strides in his image-building program and had already made important friends in his sales forays into the junk-bond market. He cast himself in the guise of an outsider, a trudging, bookish plodder who could do a deal while the white-shoe crowd played golf. He got the word around—truthfully told—that he would meet any time, any place to get the right clients and the right product to sell and buy. He would meet late at night or early in the morning, at hotels and restaurants, at resorts in Southern

California. He did not stand on ceremony, and if a player had money, it did not matter if he had been in the news for financial improprieties or had not gone to the Hill School.

Milken was the guy to get the deal done.

The bookish, nerdy part of the Milken image was an ingenious touch. In fact, he did apparently take the time to learn about various bonds that no one else paid much attention to. As a colleague of those days said, the people who Milken was dealing with, Riklis, Posner, Lindner, Tisch, Steinberg, were all tough guys. They didn't want to have to compete with another tough guy. They liked the idea that they were dealing with a scholar, the type who wears a bad toupee and funny suits and sits by himself in the corner. They liked the idea of doing business with an accountant, a bookworm, not wheeler-dealers like themselves.

Meyer Lansky had operated in much the same way with his cohorts in the world of organized crime. Lansky, said a casino operator who knew him well, was liked and trusted by very violent, tough men exactly because he was not threatening. He was an accountant type who could be trusted to keep the books straight. As bookkeeper for the bosses, he was indispensable, and so became the chairman of the board. Milken, in his role as bookkeeper for the businessman big boys in the world of junk bonds, would become equally indispensable.

The next step for Milken was crucial. Obviously, his work in arranging trades among junk issuers had value. It created the illusion of liquidity, allowed for getting cash out of illiquid and possibly valueless securities, and enabled junk issuers to realize higher prices and lower costs for their issues. It also made money, even a great deal of money, for the broker. He was creating so much value that he deserved an unusually high fee.

The problem was that there was a limit to how much of that kind of inter-frat-house trading could be done. If buyer A buys the bonds of buyer B for a price above their worth on the open market, obviously, buyer A is taking a loss on the trade, in the sense that he cannot resell those securities freely and receive a price equal to what he paid. The only way that he can be made whole at the beginning of the scheme is for buyer B to overpay for buyer A's bonds. In this way, both are adding value for the other guy while losing it themselves. But in the wash, the gains and losses were supposed to roughly tally, according to a lawyer who was close to the Milken empire for many years.

However, no rich person wants to take the chance of coming up short on his washday tally—or even to be exposed to the possibility of winding up being owed when accounts are due and payable. The sweet part of the Milken/Posner/ Lindner/Riklis/Steinberg paradigm, as it evolved, was that if A and B owned banks or savings and loans —or best of all, insurance companies—they could get together, set price supports for each other's bonds, and then use their policyholders' or depositors' money to buy them. They were not using their own money.

Further, that there had been an overpayment out of such funds for the other guy's bonds would not be known for years or maybe decades, because the securities bought usually had no public market, no established prices, and could—by accounting rules, very loosely applied—count as being worth their cost for as long as they were in the portfolio. Even if they in fact defaulted—and this was really beautiful—the issuer could replace them with a handful of new securities to which the buyer could assign any value he wished. Defaults could simply be made to disappear.

Moreover, by actuarial standards, most of the money needed to pay off depositors or policyholders would not be needed for many years. In the meantime, one might hope that the bonds would continue to pay coupons, or that gains elsewhere would offset losses on the junk, or that someone new would own the company that had issued the bonds, or that rising life expectancy and fewer mortality claims would create lower needs for assets. There had to be accounting fraud for the company to fail to take adequate reserves for default, but accountants are often flexible and present little problem.

Even so, there was a limit. Yes, regulation was lax, especially in the insurance business, but it was not nil. Regulators visiting the Steinberg or Posner or Lindner insurance companies might have wondered just why they had concentrations of junk bonds of the same few issuers over and over again—or stocks or warrants or debentures.

Also, while the arrangement might have suited the issuers in Milken's circle, it did not suit Milken. Again, there was only so much Posner, Lindner, Riklis, Tisch and Steinberg junk. Trading it back and forth was a great beginning, but a finite business. For a really larger and more successful angle, there had to be more buyers and more sellers.

In his own brief experience Milken had seen, as all of American finance had seen, that truly huge commissions were to be made selling below-investment-grade bonds. Rates of 3 to 4 percent on multi-hundred-million-dollar issues, exemplified by Lehman's bond issuances for LTV, made Wall Street mouths water. Milken saw no reason why he and his firm should not issue their own junk and collect the same commissions.

He was uniquely well set up to do so. He was an acknowledged expert in low-rated credit, was at the center of a world of low-rated credit issuers, and knew—supposedly—how to navigate the shoals and whirlpools of credit. If there were a natural limit to what his usual pals would buy, and if they wanted mostly to take in each other's bonds, for obvious reasons, Milken could go outside that club and form his own circle of issuers and buyers.

There was no shortage of those eager to issue their own junk to raise capital. Milken had made the accurate observation that major investment banks would issue (as investment grade) debt for only a few hundred corporations. All the others had to borrow from banks, which required passing certain credit muster, or meeting other fairly rigid qualifications. Thus, for the many companies that wanted to borrow for a longer term than banks liked to lend or that did not necessarily have credit ratings up to bank standards, even in the go-go years of lending, Milken could offer them something like a dream come true: long-term money, at a fixed rate, without anything like perfect or even good credit.

Yes, their bonds had to pay an unusually high rate of interest to compensate for their low credit rating. Yes, Milken charged an additional 3 percent or 4 percent off the top. Yes, his seal of approval meant that the borrower usually then had to become a lender to someone else. And yes, the borrower might become part of a world over which he had little control. But he got the money, and as any hard-pressed homeowner knows, at some point, the need for money can become so urgent that the price is almost immaterial. The desire for cash, or the apparent opportunity to make money with that cash, is so great that it simply blocks out many other concerns.

Early Milken issues in the mid and late 1970s included about $30 million for a small oil and gas concern named Texas International, about $28 million for something called Michigan General, $8 million for Emerson Radio (not to be confused with Emerson Electric, a top-grade credit), $20 million for Polychrome, $10 million for Smith's Transfer, $13 million for Tannetics, and $15 million for Comdisco, a computer leasing company. Attracting borrowers to Drexel was the easy part. But Milken had also wired the hard part. He had the buyers for this junk, buyers on an enormous scale.

His first large-scale new buyers were mutual bond funds, which already existed as places to hold different varieties of bonds, including junk. All Milken had to do was to contact the managers of these funds and persuade them to buy his bonds when they wanted high-interest, low-rated instruments. He had started with Riklis and Posner bonds to sell, but would soon have many more original issues.

By every account, Milken was a highly plausible bond salesman. He had that sense of assurance that buyers like, a complete mastery of the patter, and a startling array of statistics and references. He could go to the managers of Massachusetts Mutual's high-yield bond fund, Keystone B 4, or to Lord Abbett Bond Debenture Fund, another low-credit, high-coupon fund, and most of all to David Solomon of First Investors Fund for Income, and easily sell them on buying what he had to offer. Solomon, in particular, was a man with whom Milken could do business. He would not only buy the Drexel issues Milken recommended, but would proselytize about what a fine bond-picker Milken was.

In a way, Milken's and Drexel's work with First Investors Fund for Income (or FIFI as it was called) came to be representative of what they could and did do. In the mid-1970s, Milken and Drexel toured the country selling the First Investors Fund for Income to investors, and then stuffing it full of Milken and Drexel issues. They even arranged for interesting variants on FIFI, including selling shares in something they called "First Income" Fund, which, when they were bought, were immediately invested in FIFI.

This sort of transaction was beautifully paradigmatic for Milken and Drexel because it allowed them to collect fees at an unheard-of number of levels:

- In commission or transaction fees for selling the First Income shares.
- In commission or transaction fees on converting First Income into FIFI.
- In commission and transaction fees for selling bonds to FIFI.
- In commission and transaction fees for trading bonds within the account of FIFI.

Added to this would be, of course, the fees that Drexel and Milken could then charge to the issuers of the bonds because it controlled the buyers.

David Solomon boasted a record of such amazing success with Milken that he could and did claim that FIFI was the most successful bond fund in America in 1974. He also was rated the most successful pension fund manager for that year and other years in the decade. His prowess was such that he was selected as a pension fund manager for the International Bank for Reconstruction and Development, also known as the World Bank.

In later years it would be recognized and admitted in court that Solomon had been taking favors of various kinds from Milken and Drexel to buy their bonds. Investors in FIFI would lose hundreds of millions if not billions, and the fund itself would be the defendant in dozens of lawsuits. But in the early and mid-1970s, the fund seemed to be a miracle. Indeed, any bond fund that was involved with Drexel seemed to be a gift from the heavens, gushing money in an extremely uncertain economy.

Another excellent bond buyer for Milken in his beginning years was the national corpus of pension funds. In particular, the huge pension fund—at one time the nation's largest single union pension fund—of the Teamsters' Central States region, the part of the Teamsters said to be run by Jimmy Hoffa and others with suspect connections and reputations, became a buyer of Drexel/Milken junk.

The Central States Teamsters' Pension Fund had a colorful history. In particular, certain players long associated with control of the fund

71

had been accused of using its assets for their own purposes. Much of the casino industry in Las Vegas had been built by money from the fund, a large part of which was never repaid to the fund, although it made a number of casino entrepreneurs rich. And as one might have predicted, those same casino builders and operators were often closely connected with or perhaps even identical with the people who had control over the fund.

A goodly chunk of Central States Teamsters' Pension Fund money went into building the famous La Costa Resort in Southern California. Noted names in gangland history, such as Moe Dalitz—who later insisted he had gone straight and was a legitimate businessman when accused in a national magazine of being a criminal—were allegedly part of the plan to "invest" pension fund money in the La Costa resort. The fund did not quite make its money back on that investment, either.

Other entities controlled and run by men who were associated with La Costa, Moe Dalitz, and the Central States Teamsters' Pension Fund also became issuers of and buyers of Drexel junk at various times slightly later in Milken's career. Indeed, within a short span of years, major buyers or issuers—and issuers were usually also buyers —included the fund itself, the casinos the fund had financed, its advisers, and a host of related businesses.

Possibly, the purchases by the Central States Teamsters' Pension Fund of Drexel bonds had to do with the stewardship of that fund. One major adviser was Equitable Life Insurance, which later came into dangerous waters itself, largely due to the purchases it had made of Drexel junk. Its long-time chairman, Leo Walsh, was a business partner of Martin Wygod, a close friend and long-time business partner of Michael Milken. Walsh was also closely linked to Milken in a major real estate transaction in the mid-1980s. In that deal, a buy of thousands of co-op units at one swoop, Milken, Wygod, and Walsh were all partnered with the redoubtable Fred Carr, head of First Executive Insurance, the most key of all key Drexel players.

Milken was also setting up potential large buyers in the insurance arena. From the mid-1970s onward, Leo Walsh's Equitable was a fan of Drexel/Milken junk on a large scale. Other players such as Massachusetts Mutual and Mutual Benefit Life were also buyers, as was

Northwestern. These buyers, indebted to Milken for allocating bonds to them out of his high-coupon deck, which then made their bond or pension funds look successful, were absolutely critical in his rise to stardom. In finance, as anywhere else where selling is involved, captive buyers make a huge difference.

Here is the reason all the parts of this issuing, selling, and buying scheme were so deeply interdependent, and why it was so vital for Milken to keep them humming smoothly. As any Wall Street player —or anyone who has ever made or applied for a loan—well knows, borrowers have to pay far more to borrow if they are in shaky condition than if they are rock-solid and creditworthy. In fact, borrowers not only have to pay more interest for "hard money," they are also willing to pay the "fixer" of the loan a far larger commission. Milken wanted that business.

As for the buyers of the debt of questionable borrowers, they will take high-interest, low-rated issues as long as the buys look as if they are making money. That is, the trustees for the World Bank pensioners, presumably a group above suspicion, would buy Milken/Drexel junk, the obligations of rather suspect borrowers, but only if they consistently got returns that appeared to be at least as good as those on riskless Treasury bonds. Otherwise the supervisors of the pension fund managers would rightly ask why the fund did not stick with riskless Treasuries. Both issuers and buyers would be satisfied, and happy to pay Milken his commissions, if, but only if, his junk could be rationalized as a sound purchase, or if it could be made to look like a sound purchase with the connivance of buyers who were in on the large fees.

But here came the giant flaw in the Drexel world, which was eventually to undo it, if only temporarily. The fact was that the Drexel bonds were not even close to as good a buy as Milken said they were. To put Milken's claims more specifically, in a statement published in the official Drexel house organ, "The High Yield Newsletter," Milken claimed that his bonds had coupons far above those of investment-grade bonds (which was not in dispute). But he added, about the fear of defaults on his poorly rated bonds and the prospect that such defaults might eliminate the advantage of higher interest rates, "defaults have absorbed only about 15% of the yield advantage which

73

has been available in the high yield market. The other 85% has been 'gravy.' "

In another pronouncement published in "The High Yield Newsletter," Milken and his colleagues said, on the subject of future defaults in junk, "Future losses due to uncured defaults should be no greater than in the past. From 1977 to February 1986, we estimate this loss (from debt originally issued as high yield) at 69 BP (basis points) per year. Excluding the depressed energy industry, the loss is under 50 BP per year."

These statements, seemingly about business matters of interest only to accountants, were in fact blinding bursts of light in American finance if true. They meant that the higher interest Milken's bonds paid was not meaningfully lowered by losses upon default.

If, in truth, his bonds consistently yielded far more than investment-grade bonds, and if his defaults accounted for less than one-sixth of the difference in yield, they were manna from heaven. Any self-respecting insurance company portfolio manager would be a fool not to buy such bonds. He would almost be breaching his fiduciary duty to his policyholders if he did not do so. If, for every three percentage points of difference between the junk yield and the investment-grade yield, only about half of a percentage point (three times .15 equals .45) would be lost due to defaults, the buyer would absolutely have to own a good chunk of Milken bonds.

However, the truth was somewhat different. Even as Milken was saying that the default rate of his junk was trivial, it was in fact extremely large and meaningful, as would later be revealed. And it would make his junk definitely not a good investment if Milken had not been able to take heroic measures to make the default rates temporarily seem to be much smaller than they actually were. To put it in a nutshell, his real rates of default were easily high enough to demolish the attraction of his bonds. And even those default rates would have been much, much higher without his extraordinarily inventive measures of concealment. Milken had to obscure just how junky his junk was. If he did not, he was selling sure losers, which, of course, no one would freely buy.

Milken also had to tackle the liquidity problem, which buyers of conglomerate-era junk had faced, and did so brilliantly. One of his favorite selling points, also published in his "High Yield Newsletter," was that by buying junk bonds, insurance companies were in effect buying commercial loans (such as a loan that a bank might make to a local contractor) and getting the much higher rates on such loans than on riskless Treasuries. And, he added, what keeps you, Mr. Insurance Company, from buying the commercial loans that pay high interest is their illiquidity. You cannot add them to your portfolio because if you did, and if you suddenly needed money, you could not sell them. After all, there is no liquid market for commercial loans. Once you have made the loan, you're stuck with it.

But, Milken said, I have solved that problem by essentially securitizing the commercial loan business (that is, making commercial loans into liquid securities). Not only that, I have also been able to make an active, liquid market in them, so that you don't get stuck with them until they pay off or default. Specifically, said Milken, "High yield bonds are no more than securitized loans, often with fewer covenants." To which he added, "Buyers and issuers of high yield debt are assured of a liquid trading market—an important asset, particularly to potential debt investors."

In another Drexel-controlled publication, Milken said, "High yield [bond] investors can choose to move out of a weakening credit at any time, while traditional lenders must allow such a loan to remain outstanding until it either matures or an event of default occurs."

This was a vital inducement to the insurance company portfolio managers, pension fund managers, or any other investors whom Milken approached. Buyers of bonds don't want to get fired for having excessive, illiquid, low-credit-rated issues in their portfolios at an inopportune moment. Milken promised them that he would "take them out" of the bonds at a moment's notice. This not only made the bonds a better buy, but also made their buyers feel more secure in their jobs.

The truth was something else again. In fact, as junk buyers would soon learn, Milken bonds did not fit the conventional definitions of liquidity in markets. Milken bonds could usually (although not always) be sold, but at a price that many buyers did not like. The usual understanding of liquidity—that trades can be freely made with few costs of trading, and at a price identical to other trades of identical

75

goods at that exact moment—simply did not apply in the Milken world.

New ideologies require new definitions, and Milken's movement was so comprehensive and so tightly wound in upon itself that it too needed new meanings for words. The Milken "high-yield" bond was originally to be called the "high opportunity" bond, and this, along with other verbal acrobatics and the facts and figures of Drexel origin to support them, was largely intended to prevent meaningful research into junk bonds.

A "trade" in Milken's world did not mean what a trade usually meant, with adversary buyers and sellers bargaining at arm's length. Milken controlled both sides of the trade and as the middleman worked all trades for his own benefit, as was voluminously detailed in a congressional hearing, held by Representative John Dingell (Democrat from Michigan) in 1988. In the Milken world, "price" did not mean a figure arrived at by independent bargaining, which determined the market for goods or services. In the Milken argot "price" was a number arbitrarily assigned to goods or services, which bore no relation to what arm's length bargaining would have produced—and no relation to what the "price" of the same goods or services for another buyer would be, even at the same moment. "Compliance" also had a different meaning. In a securities firm context, it usually means compliance with law of federal government or state. In Milken's world, it meant "compliance with Milken's wishes." Likewise, "high-yield" meant "high-yield" to the underwriter (Milken and Drexel), not necessarily to the buyer.

When Milken began with his issues of virtually unknown companies' bonds, he knew that these companies were not flush, and indeed often were explicitly incapable of making their interest payments through current income. He knew that, except through him, there was no liquid market in these bonds. But he also knew a great deal about accounting, the movement of money back and forth, and the financial market's many equivalents of three-card monte.

Faced with the problems of high default rates and illiquidity, Milken realized that if he could keep funneling money into his bond scheme, he could obscure, more or less indefinitely, the facts about his bonds. The process was deceptively simple. If, for example, one issuer cannot raise the money to pay its coupon by its operations, it can sell more bonds and use the proceeds to pay off the first bond issue. If it then uses the proceeds of a third offering to pay off the coupons on the second offering, the process is well and truly rolling.

Even John Shad, the chairman of the SEC for most of Milken's raj (and a close pal of Milken's colleague, Drexel chairman Fred Joseph), would have spotted the con if there had been only one big issuer that used succeeding issues to pay off earlier issues' interest. But—and this was a huge but—if there is a whole empire of companies raising money, paying off each other's debt by financings and refinancings, and one magician in the middle directing traffic (for 4 percent off every transaction), the trail becomes much harder to follow, especially if your friend Fred Joseph is also helping to blow smoke over the operation.

This, in brief, was how the machine worked:

Overfunding

Overfunding, as its name implies, means raising more money for an issuer than he can make use of in his operations or legitimate investments, with the excess, in this case, going to buy more of Milken's bonds from other issuers.

Such an operation is similar to the classic pyramid and chain-letter scams and has been employed for centuries to propagate and prolong financial misconduct, even as long ago as the Tulip Boom of the late sixteenth century. The sad fact that overfunding was used as a standard tool should have been a tip-off that there was something awry with the Milken empire, just as surely as the home buyer who asks to borrow more than the cost of his home should be a tip-off to a savings and loan. Unfortunately, it was not.

Milken boasted that for his borrowers he liked to raise more than they originally asked for so they would have a "cushion" of cash to fall back on. He was as good as his word. For his good friend (and major George Bush fund-raiser) Larry Mizel of MDC (Mizel Development Corporation), Milken offered in the palmy 1980s to raise a mere $250 million to build homes, search for oil, and do the other things Mizel's company did. Within days or weeks at most, Milken had instead raised a whopping $506 million, at least $113 million of which was promptly invested in more Drexel junk of other issuers. Some of that junk can be traced directly or indirectly to Mizel's Silverado Savings, a federally insured S&L that later collapsed and cost taxpayers well over a billion dollars to bail out.

Integrated Resources, another Drexel captive, regularly had its bond issues dramatically raised in size by Milken. In 1985, an offering was raised from $100 million to $124 million. In 1986, another offering was raised from $100 million to $258 million. Federal government filings later reported that most of the excess had gone into buying Drexel junk.

Southmark, the vehicle for two of the most imaginative adventurers in the history of finance, Gene Phillips and Bill Friedman, had a 1986 issue more than doubled, from $200 million to $415 million, with most of the increase used to buy more Drexel junk. Even earlier, in 1983, Milken overfunded a proposed $500 million offering by a staggering $600 million, with much of the increase going to buy more Drexel junk. In the late 1970s and early 1980s, he also overfunded issues by AFC, Pantry Pride, Nortek, and Triangle, with much of the increase again used to buy the bonds of other Drexel companies. (Southmark, Integrated Resources, and Silverado are either gone or in distress.)

Just as a matter of fairly straightforward arithmetic, Milken's overfunding should have set alarm bells ringing in Washington and on Wall Street. His borrowers were financially weak, even if they were large companies. If they were financially robust, obviously they would not be issuing into the junk world at all, but would be selling investment grade bonds at a far lower coupon rate. But if they were financially shaky, how then could they afford the coupons on twice as much (or more) debt as they had originally contemplated? If the answer was that the excess would be invested in bonds that paid off even more than the cost of junk borrowing, then a whole other series of alarms should have gone off.

Who were these latter issuers who could pay such high interest that it exceeded the junk cost of borrowing for the overfunded issuers? If they had cash flow that rich, why were they junk borrowers at all? And if they were the junkiest of the junk borrowers, forced to pay the highest possible coupon rate, were they the kind of credit risks a corporate treasurer fiduciary wanted to lend to?

Finally, was it really sound practice—or even minimally acceptable practice—to bet your company on the creditworthiness of the shakiest borrowers in the Milken world? And betting the company was exactly what it was. If the bonds in the first overfunded issuer's portfolio defaulted, that would likely mean a default by the original issuer. And default of bonds meant—or could mean—the end of your company.

In that case, why do it at all ?

Why indeed, except perhaps as part of an ongoing Ponzi.

Overfunding looked dismayingly similar to the practice of trading each other's Chinese paper back and forth by the original Drexel players. It was, in outline, no more than the use of one Drexel player to prop up another, on a very definitely temporary basis. It was also, in many ways, extremely similar to what is done by one big issuer who simply issues more and more debt to pay off his earlier debt until the whole edifice eventually collapses.

Jerry-built "Banks"

As dangerous as it was to lenders, overfunding had a huge advantage for Milken in that it could convert an operating company into a financial holding company more or less at will. That is, without having to apply to become a bank or an insurance company, without having to go through any federal approval process at all, Milken could take a construction company or an oil company or an airline and make it into the equivalent of a bank.

The manner in which he simulated the operations of a bank or insurance company for his own benefit was as audacious as it was effective. In a way, it carried the concept of "lengthening" a blanket by cutting off one end and sewing it to the other to a new high of cunning and nerve.

For example, for a bank to do what Milken wanted it to do, namely buy his bonds, it would have to take in depositors' money so that it would have that money to buy Milken bonds. That might take a little time. It would also invite eventual federal scrutiny. As for an insurance company, it would have to sell policies and take in premiums to get the money to buy Milken bonds. Even with excellent salesmen and brilliant products, that might take years, and also attract the attention of insurance regulators.

Milken would eventually do such things and more with banks, insurers, and other financial companies, and he would do them on a staggering scale. But with overfunding, he could get the money to buy his bonds far more directly. He could give one small company, an MDC, Inc., for example, the wherewithal to buy hundreds of millions of his bonds overnight—just by having MDC borrow the money in the first place. He did not have to wait for MDC to come up with enough money to buy his bonds, or even to have a real need for his bonds. He could just overfund an MDC issue and use the proceeds to give the company a big fat war chest to buy still other bonds. No waiting for depositors or policyholders. No waiting for regulatory approval.

The really incredible part of the scheme was that for a decade no one bothered to ask in any depth what was going on. No one bothered to wonder where the pot of gold was that would "endlessly" allow this debt to be serviced. Where was the El Dorado whence came the final buyer of all this junk? No one ever bothered to follow the chain to its logical conclusion. Instead, the world watched in awe as Milken took any kind of company he felt was eligible and had that company hock itself to the eyeballs to buy more of his junk. No one ever thought to say, "It just can't be that easy to make a billion dollars overnight. If it were, why can't everyone on earth become a billionaire just by borrowing ten billion dollars and then using it to buy ten billion dollars' worth of bonds that pay a few percent more every year?"

Overfunding, uncritically allowed by markets and by regulators, was very largely a Ponzi in which earlier borrowers and lenders were kept afloat by later borrowers and lenders. It couldn't go on forever, but while it lasted, it was a miraculously simple way for Milken to pull buyers more or less out of thin air and thus to create a market for his junk. The scam worked so well that there were periods in the mid and late 1980s when Milken could create entities with no operating financial assets to speak of and raise hundreds of millions of dollars for them, to be used solely to buy his junk.

But overfunding and the conversion of operating companies into Milken financial sources were not enough. Even in Reagan's America, there was a limit to how much an operating company might borrow for purposes unrelated to its primary function. There was also a limit to how long bonds could simply be passed back and forth without anything but other junk borrowers propelling them. Real financial operations were necessary for the Milken world to survive —preferably large, happily cooperative financial institutions with money pouring in and a need to invest it in something that paid an excellent coupon.

Financial Services Companies out of Whole Cloth

That was where a third arrow for Milken's bow came in, closely related to the second: the conversion of operating companies to diversified financial companies. If there were a limit to how much funding he could shovel down the throat of an operating company, that limit could be dramatically raised if Milken induced the company to buy a bank or an insurer or an S&L. Such companies could then legitimately buy far more of his bonds. They would also need to issue bonds themselves to meet their capital requirements, and a lavish new area of financing and bond price supports would be opened up.

Hence, when a Larry Mizel came down the pike, smart and cooperative and energetic as he was, he could be encouraged to turn his construction company into the hub of a savings and loan company of monstrous size. When Charles H. Keating, Jr., had a good-sized construction company and Godzilla-sized patron in Carl Lindner and early Milken connections, he could turn his American Continental Homes into the real parent of Lincoln Savings. And Perry Mendel and Richard Grassgreen of Montgomery, Alabama, could be encouraged to use their innovative day-care centers, Kinder-Care, as the base for a multi-billion-dollar insurance and savings empire, which was a pristine example of Milkenism on the way up—and on the way down.

If one has a backer who can raise money, in America, it is extremely easy to buy a bank, an S&L, or an insurance company. Milken proved it over and over again. He was able even to raise money for Gene Phillips and Bill Friedman of Southmark—who really should have been under intense scrutiny as to any sort of financial transaction—to buy several insurers and at least one large S&L. Milken was able to transform Southmark from a fairly modest real estate operation into a national power in finance.

Naturally, every one of these players was deeply indebted to Milken. Every one knew that he was the Fixer, the Man Who Made It All Possible, the Magician who had transformed their modest businesses into true magnificence. And every one of the players was happy, indeed eager, to return Milken's favors. This meant a great many things, but mostly it meant buying back into Milken deals in a big, big way, and making their money available to the man in Beverly Hills, just as he had made his funds available to them.

The uninitiated might have wondered if the men who made these Faustian bargains with Milken really knew what they were doing, and if they knew, in particular, that the bonds that powered their companies into the stratosphere would also be likely to destroy them. For one thing, it is unclear how many of the members of the Milken conspiracy actually were aware of the flaw in the junk bonds that he was selling. Certainly, some of the big players knew, since they had been following the bonds long enough to know they defaulted at a rate far higher than what Milken was claiming.

But for a much larger thing, the men who made the Milken world go around were not building A City on a Hill. They were not in the conspiracy to slowly build a company that would last for generations and give employment to the community and a quality product to the world. No, these men were in it for the money, and preferably for the money quick. Some of them had long histories as adventurers. Others were stock speculators with questionable pasts. Few indeed were those who, when offered the opportunity to elevate themselves and their entities to the skies (even if temporarily and at the risk of a rapid, fiery end), put aside the crown. There were definitely some, and the name of David Geffen, billionaire entertainment mogul, comes to mind, since he was offered the chance to be a high-stakes player in the Milken circle and turned it down. But usually the chance to preside over a huge enterprise and take home—or to Switzerland —the profits that such stardom allows outweighed all dim thoughts about the future.

It's important to realize what men of this adventurous cast, men like Meshulam Riklis or Victor Posner or Charles Keating or Richard Grassgreen, did know: that even when your Drexel-fed company goes bankrupt, even when you are sued, even when you are indicted and serve a few months at a white-collar prison, at the end of the day, you are usually still rich. You still get to play pinochle with your pals, own a fabulous retirement home, and know that your great-great-grandchildren will still be rich.

A particularly interesting example of the growth of the Milken web was Chrysler Financial. This entity, associated with Chrysler Motors, had seen rocky times in the 1970s and 1980s, as well as good times. The parent knew that the auto business was a dicey thing, what with quality problems, high fixed costs, and foreign competition. But it also knew that its financing subsidiary had a lot of money coming in and going out. It was, in essence, a bank, only it existed largely to finance cars and trucks. One of Milken's most daring coups was to go to this mainstay of American industry, with its dashing chairman, Lee Iacocca, and explain, as he had explained to so many others, that the balance sheet of Chrysler Financial, all by itself, was a potential source of money in all kinds of markets.

To Chrysler, which had always had access to the whitest of white-shoe investment banks, in good times and bad, Milken explained his magic: borrow through Drexel, and I will reinvest some of your funds, while they await employment, in my high-yield paper. I can get you an arbitrage that will amount to a couple of hundred basis points and your money will be earning millions no matter what Toyota does or Nissan sells. It had a certain appeal, even to a heads-up player like Iacocca.

But even drawing in entities like Chrysler Financial was not enough. The problem was akin to a power outage that extends through an entire region, like the famous Northeast blackout of 1965. As the output of Milken bonds grew, the volume and potential of likely defaults also grew. As Milken issues rose into the billions and then the tens of billions through the 1980s, a constant ratio of defaults yielded far larger numbers in dollars in actual or potential losses. These had to be plugged up—or at least the ability had to exist to quickly plug them up, along with the ability to sell ever more debt.

As the system grew to monstrous proportions, possibilities of catastrophic short-circuits had to be ruled out.

This was not only necessary arithmetic—which eventually rules finance, sooner or later—but a key part of the image. In order to control his issuers and his lenders, Milken had to protect the gilded template of the junk bond schema. It had to appear that his junk bonds defaulted at a rate far below what would be necessary to eliminate the advantage in yield, and that he had captive borrowers who—because of that yield differential—were always ready to spring into action and buy a new issue of absolutely anything that Milken blessed. Milken had to keep the money rolling in to protect his franchise and to shield his steadily accruing debt from the gravity of finance.

For this, he needed a wonderful, heaven-sent friend.

CHAPTER 5

FRED CARR,
SUPERSTAR

A faithful friend is a strong defense; and he that hath found such an one has found a treasure.

ECCLESIASTICUS, 6:14

ALL FINANCIAL SCAMS basically work out to a simple equation: the trading of promises that are not kept for money.

Insurance is a legitimate example of the taking in of money today for the exchange of a promise to pay out money in the future. The insured pays premiums in the sure and certain expectation of getting future benefits. A forty-year-old pays money for an annuity upon retirement twenty-five years hence. A fifty-year-old pays for life insurance down the road. The insurer does not expect him to die for twenty-five years, and there is actuarial data to back up that figure. Meanwhile, the insurer has twenty-five years to play with that money before he has to pay any of it out.

In every way, this is a situation ripe for abuse. That's why there is supposedly stringent regulation of the insurance business. On a state-by-state basis, insurers are investigated, checked, and rechecked, supposedly, by state regulators. Insurers must have their assets (really the assets of the policyholders) in safe, secure investments, so that they will grow and be available to pay off the future—but still certain—claims of the policyholders. If there are to be investments in nontraditional assets, such as junk bonds, they must be investigated on a case-by-case, bond-by-bond basis to make sure they are suitable for insurance companies. If they are not deemed suitable, they must be strictly limited in amount.

Thus, again supposedly, the expectations and assets of the policyholders are protected by state regulation.

What if, however, something bad happened? What if a man who was ethically questionable got control of a big insurance company? What if he was also a smart, cagey man who knew the world well enough to know that state regulation was a paper tiger? He would also know that the state regulators might mean well, but that they were fantastically overworked, not particularly sophisticated, and very much impressed with free first-class trips to Beverly Hills. What if he then hooked up with the master salesman of questionable investments to pretend to regulators and policyholders that he was running a heads-up insurer when he was in fact running a classic scam?

Put all those "what ifs" together and, just possibly, you might have Fred Carr and First Executive Corporation. Carr has been described by Drexel insiders as the "one indispensable" Milken player. First Executive has been described as the largest insurance catastrophe in the history of the United States. To know about Fred Carr and his works is to understand the template that might explain just what happened in a key element of the Drexel world.

Fred Carr was born Seymour Fred Cohen. His father was an immigrant from Hungary who had a fruit and vegetable business in New York. The Cohen family then moved to Los Angeles, where Fred Cohen became Fred Carr. He attended Fairfax High School, which was then one of the best high schools in America. He went on to Cal State Los Angeles and helped defray his educational expenses by driving a truck, then by selling driveway repairs. By his early twenties, he was already trading stock for his own account.

Carr told an interviewer many years later that in these early trades he usually lost money, and after that dismal experience he determined that he would "leave nothing to chance" in his future investments, a foreboding comment from a man who supposedly toiled in the free, unfettered financial markets—which, of course, no individual can legitimately control.

Carr went from patching driveways to the far better occupation of brokering stock at the retail level. He did well in that field at Bache, even better at Kleiner, Bell, and then founded—with the help of others—one of the most glittery, successful mutual funds of the go-go years, the Enterprise Fund.

Within one year of its beginning in 1966, Carr had turned his Enterprise Fund into the hottest thing since sliced bread. It was frequently on top of those sheep's entrails of modern life, mutual fund performance indices. It was on the lips of press agents. It was hip, slick, and cool. In the space of two years, the assets under Carr's management rose from $20 million to $800 million, and in 1967, the value of the fund's shares supposedly rose by over 100 percent.

Fairly quickly, however, there were shadows over Fred Carr. Some had to do with his alleged practice of selling the new issues he had bought in a private offering not into the open market but to other buyers, such as pension funds, in private placements at negotiated, not necessarily free-market, prices. Another cloud had to do with Carr's purchase of unregistered "letter" stock and his subsequent resale of that stock to buyers without its having been registered in any known way. Still, he grew in power and in funds under management. By the end of 1969, the former truck driver had close to $2 billion in his Enterprise Fund, as investors flocked to get close to his fantastic rates of return.

In 1970, Carr went into a very temporary eclipse. Shortly after an interview in which he noted to a magazine that he sometimes used words differently from other asset managers (such as using *next year's anticipated earnings* and this year's prices to calculate his portfolio's price-earnings ratio), he abruptly left Enterprise and its related entities.

At about the same time, Enterprise Fund lost its magic, to put it mildly. The fund for 1969 ranked 339th out of 379 in performance. In 1970, the SEC had temporarily shut it down, barring it from selling new shares because of chaos in the back office and other problems. Later in 1970, the shares of Enterprise had fallen by two-thirds from their 1968 highs.

In one of those twists that enliven the financial market, Enterprise

Fund was allowed to reopen. It came under the stewardship of Gerry Tsai, a major gunslinger of the go-go years, who had become head of American Can (also known as Primerica). Tsai, one of many hedge fund geniuses who went on to find themselves in deals with Milken, later sold his can division to two of the world's luckiest men, Nelson Peltz and Peter May. Peltz and May were small businessmen who—under Milken's tutelage—put together the largest can company in America, Triangle Packaging, and made close to a billion dollars from it, less Michael Milken's cut. Tsai later went on the board of about half a dozen Drexel issuers.

After getting out of mutual funds, Fred Carr went into a consulting business in Century City, Los Angeles, where so many businessmen got their start. Then in about 1974, he became friendly with a group of people who had a small, struggling company called "First Executive Insurance." The head of that company, in extremis because of overdue loans, asked Carr to run the company. Carr agreed, and the company was ready for lift-off into scammers' heaven.

After a few stalled moves in which he basically tried to give control of the company to friends of his, Carr got some breathing room on his debt, pointed his bat at the far wall of the stadium, and promised to put the insurance company ball over the fence. The chosen product was something new and wonderful called Single Premium Deferred Annuities. The chosen teammate was Michael Milken. The combination of Milken, Carr, and Single Premium Deferred Annuities was the Tinker to Evers to Chance of insurance selling—a once-in-a-lifetime trio that would enter the record books.

An SPDA works as its name implies: The buyer of the annuity plunks down an agreed-upon sum of money. In return, the insurer promises to pay him a certain annual sum beginning at the end of a fixed number of years. A Michael Milken works as his name has come to imply: He offers to sell policyholders, through a Carr's First Executive, bonds that promise to yield an extraordinarily high rate of return.

The blending made for a fearsomely competitive product in the insurance marketplace. The rate of interest that can be paid on the initial premium for the SPDA completely controls the amount of the annuity. It can also control how much time must pass before the annuity is paid, and—obviously—how much of an initial payment is needed. Therefore, interest rates in SPDAs are the only meaningful consideration to the buyer, and First Executive offered higher interest than its competitors.

First Executive became a powerhouse in SPDAs. When Carr took over the company in 1974, it had only about $700 million of every kind of policy in force. Within five years, he was selling one billion dollars of SPDA insurance alone per annum and the proceeds were invested heavily in Drexel issues. These issues, with their stated extraordinarily high yields, allowed Carr's SPDAs to pay two or three percentage points more to policyholders per year. A Carr SPDA might well promise to double the policyholders' money in six years, while other insurers might require nine years or more. (By 1981, First Executive also had, as its largest stockholder, that other Drexel pioneer, Saul Steinberg.)

Fred Carr had so much magic coming off him from his SPDAs that he became a national leader in selling all kinds of insurance in which the payouts would be delayed for many years after the premium was paid. He became a major insurer of lives. He sold annuities to corporations controlled by other Drexel players to refinance their pension plans. The appeal of this to the Drexel world was nothing less than spectacular.

In the days before the era of fiduciary disintegration, the funding of pension plans was a serious matter. Real actuaries performing real calculations figured out the real future liabilities of a corporation to its pensioners. They then sought the likely rate of interest on the amount that would be invested. Usually their calculations were based upon the historic return on safe, extremely secure investments like Treasury bonds or top-rated corporates, on the sound theory that when a man's pension was at stake, funds for it should be invested as cautiously as possible. Then an amount was deposited in those safe instruments in order to yield an amount to match the carefully calculated future pension liabilities of the employer.

To the Drexel players, this looked very much like opportunity. Once a player had acquired a company, he naturally wanted to take all he could out of it in cash. After all, that's what "get rich quick" *means*. And a pension fund set up by older, more ethical management was ripe for the picking. The Drexel/Milken takeover player could and did enlist Fred Carr and various "actuaries" to note that the old pension plan was unnecessarily "overfunded." He could then say that if he put a much smaller amount of money to work with junk bonds, at their far higher rate of interest, he would still be able to comfortably meet the commitments of the company to its pensioners. It was, in every way, the exact analog of the sales pitch that Carr could make to individuals interested in buying SPDAs. By virtue of a higher assumed interest rate, the Drexel player could meet obligations with less cash. And he could then remove that extra cash and give it to himself.

This move actually required another interesting step because even in Reagan's America, there were still some strictures about what corporate pension plans could hold as assets. In accordance with federal law, as well as applicable state laws, and often by contract between workers and employers, seemingly high-rated obligations often had to make up the bulk of pension plan assets. This meant, in brief, that junk bonds per se were allowed only in fairly small amounts, sometimes less than 10 percent of the total, in pension plans.

But a pension plan could count a "guaranteed" investment contract as an investment-grade bond. A guaranteed investment contract (GIC) is nothing more than a promise by someone whom the law recognizes as a qualified guarantor to pay a certain amount on a certain date. By a stroke of fate that came to haunt the sleep of many a pensioner, most large insurance companies, including Fred Carr's First Executive, could affiliate with qualified guarantors. Many entities that existed largely as legal entries in a foreign corporations registry were likewise considered guarantors, without any real showing of ability to guarantee anything.

The GICs Carr sold were junk bonds, neither more nor less. But they magically became acceptable as pension assets because they were put into a bundle, made assets of a third party (often a largely fictitious third party) and then stamped with the "guarantee" of a largely questionable guarantor.

By 1990, Carr's First Executive reportedly had over $5 billion of GICs outstanding, consisting almost entirely of packages of Milken junk bonds. Thus, with the fig leaf of the "guarantee" put on the packages by Carr, Milken junk became acceptable for pension plans. In turn, this facilitated the removal of billions of dollars in "excess" pension fund assets as smaller, but supposedly higher-yielding pension fund assets from Carr and Milken replaced larger but lower-yielding assets.

By 1990, First Executive GIC "backed" pension plans had supplanted earlier versions at the following companies—all heavily influenced by Milken or his confederates:

- Pacific Lumber in Northern California
- Cannon Holdings (formerly Cannon Mills), mostly in the Carolinas
- Revlon, mostly in New York
- Standard Gravure in Kentucky
- McCrory Corporation
- Bulova Watch
- Walter Kidde
- Jade Corporation
- National Forge
- H. H. Robertson
- Strachan Shipping
- Peralta Hospital in Oakland

These plans—which were expressly not to be covered by federal protection under the Pension Benefit Guaranty Corporation (on the questionable pretext that they were annuities and not pension plans) —by 1990 covered about fifty thousand people. Many thousands of them would learn some lessons about insomnia from the experience.

Carr sold a similar product by the billions to municipalities and states. He encouraged them to float bond offerings—even taxable bond offerings—and then give him the proceeds. He would take the proceeds and invest them in Milken bonds, and give the cities, counties, or states his GICs in return. The process was basically identical to the way substitution of Carr's GICs worked for pension plans. It would have been barred for many states or municipalities to hold Drexel junk outright. But once the stamp of "guaranteed" had been applied, it was perfectly jake for the various government bodies to add it to their portfolios.

With Carr's First Executive up and running as a major league player in the Drexel world, the volume of Drexel bonds that could be absorbed was dramatically enlarged. Through most of the 1980s, Carr could be counted upon to take down at least a billion of new offerings each year if bidden to do so, and often far more. Even by the end of the 1980s, when the Drexel world was in tatters, First Executive was buying over $2.5 billion of Drexel junk each year, and trading (or churning) its account with Drexel furiously.

And the gig got even better than that. Once First Executive had bought a Drexel issue or part of it, it could then be resold into other portions of the fiduciary universe as a seasoned bond that an insurance company had held and that had kept current in payments while in the company's portfolio. Once again, the insurer's stamp of approval helped to ease the passage of Milken junk into a wider world.

Much, much more important, as Daniel Mogin, a lawyer who has often been involved in litigation against the Drexel empire, has pointed out, Carr was Milken's stick to beat the other insurance companies of America into buying his junk. Once the Prudentials, Mutual Lifes, Travelers, and Aetnas of the world saw how much of their annuity and life insurance business Carr was taking with his higher imputed interest rates, they became concerned. They, like Carr, wanted to sell a rapidly rising volume of annuities. Like Carr, they wanted to sell GICs to municipalities. Like Carr, they wanted to refinance corporate pension plans. So, like Carr, they had to (to use a favorite Milken phrase) "reach for yield."

Milken was reported to have stressed the vital importance of, so to speak, addicting his buyers to ever higher yield. When a bond in an insurer's portfolio defaulted, he would preach to the insurer's executives that the proper response was not to eschew Milken junk. No, far from it. In fact, Milken said, if you have a default and a loss of interest, what you must do to make it up is buy an even junkier, lower-rated, higher-yielding instrument. If they fell for his pitch, he could then sell the bonds of even more poorly regarded borrowers, who would pay him even higher commissions. To reach for yield, or at least the *promise* of a high yield, the insurers had to buy Drexel junk. After all, Milken was by far the largest source of junk, and his junk had—according to his own statistics, of course—by far the highest safety record of bonds issued at below investment grade.

Thus, feeling compelled to compete with Fred Carr's First Executive, insurers who should have known much better, such as Prudential, were sucked into buying very large amounts of Drexel junk—to reach for yield. In fact, by the late 1980s Prudential came to be the largest single private buyer of Drexel junk. But Prudential is such a large insurer that its losses in the junk world have not caused the havoc that the losses at First Executive wrought. That is, while junk was most of First Executive's asset portfolio, it was only a small part of Prudential's far larger, incomparably safer asset base.

There were other major insurance companies in the Milken world, which is to say, under control of Milken either by his owning large blocks of stock in them or by other forms of influence. Equitable Life Insurance, headed by Milken's close friend Leo Walsh, became a large and devout Drexel junk buyer. Several smaller companies headed by Robert Weingarten (who stood far above the usual Drexel standard as a fiduciary) and later largely owned by American Express, grouped under the heading of First Capital Holdings, became loyal Drexel players (although not until the mid-1980s). Zenith National of Los Angeles, run by Milken's cousin Stanley Zax, Ferne's nephew, also became a loyal Drexel player. Pioneer-Western, Northwestern, Transmark, Mutual Benefit, and some others were more or less in the Milken orbit, as were Clarendon, Reliance (Steinberg's company), Lutheran Brotherhood Life, Monarch Life, and several Lindner companies.

But for sheer devotion to the cause, astonishing even within the Drexel world, Fred Carr was at the top of the class. "As bad as we might have been," said a CEO of a Drexel insurer recently, "as much junk as we might have bought, we at least looked at the issue. We at least read the financials and did some due diligence on the company that was issuing the bonds. Fred just had a guy there at Drexel, right near Roy Johnson (the 'trader' who handled the First Executive account), who just signed for everything and then authorized the wire transfers to Drexel. Carr didn't even look at what he was buying. He just bought what Mike said to buy."

Through Carr and his First Executive, Milken was able to add insurance policyholders, pensioners, and many more corporate stockholders to his list of involuntary junk buyers, basically turned over by their fiduciaries. Moreover, First Executive threw off still more possibilities for the sale of Milken's bonds. Insurance companies sometimes need reinsurance companies, which insure for any abnormal losses. The prime example would be an insurer that covers a huge oil field. If a natural gas explosion demolished the field, the insurer could be wiped out. To avoid that it buys reinsurance to distribute the risk of a catastrophic event. Typically, this is done far more in property and casualty lines than in life and annuity lines, but Fred Carr and Milken decided that Carr needed reinsurers.

The result was that Milken, his brother, and other Drexel hucksters joined with Carr to start small and large reinsurers, the best-known of which was First Stratford, which was owned jointly by the Milken team and First Executive. It was to reinsure First Executive—and perhaps other firms as well—against extraordinary losses. But what to buy with the premiums First Executive paid for reinsurance? Drexel junk, of course.

There was a certain weird beauty to this part of the scheme. One element of the need for reinsurance is the possibility of a disastrous claim. But another is the possibility of a disastrous failure of assets. This would not normally be a problem with investment-grade assets. But with assets such as Drexel junk, a catastrophic failure is a very real possibility indeed—thus the need to reinsure risky assets as well as risky policies. But to reinsure risky assets with the same kind of risky assets is the sort of "in your face" slap at tradition, good sense, and fiduciary standards that made Milken and Carr true artists of modern finance.

With First Executive one of the fastest growing large insurers in America through most of the 1980s, and with its reinsurers growing at least as fast, Milken had a friend indeed in Fred Carr, a complaisant friend with billions of dollars of Other People's Money. The entire network of junk buyers was important: the overfunded issuers, the nonfinancial financial companies, the true financial companies, the pension fund advisers, the insurers, the reinsurers—all of them assured Milken of buyers. But Fred Carr provided unquestioning, multi-billion-dollar buying per year.

Michael Milken and his wife, Lori, riding bicycles on their Encino estate in 1987, before he was indicted and dethroned from his position as Junk Bond King.
AP/Wide World Photos

The three faces of Milken at a Congressional hearing in April 1988 as his empire was beginning to crumble.
Terry Ashe/SYGMA

Meshulam 'Rik' Riklis, who went from a muddled past, possibly as an operative in the mideast, to fortune as a conglomerateur, casino owner, husband of performer Pia Zadora, and likely mentor to Michael Milken in the uses and abuses of junk debt.
AP/Wide World Photos

Saul Steinberg, who started corporate raiding when he was still a teenager and tried to take over the Chase Manhattan Bank when he was twenty-nine years old. In his energy and audacity, he was another inspiration to Michael Milken, as well as one of his early business consorts.
AP/Wide World Photos

Charles Keating, a major campaigner against pornography and a staunch Republican, was a good friend and reliable customer of Michael Milken's junk bond department. Shown here in a prison van, he is likely to spend the rest of his life behind bars for fraud against his depositors at Lincoln Savings & Loan—one of the Milken captive S&Ls.
Los Angeles Times photo

ABOVE, Fred Carr, Chairman of First Executive, "the one indispensable Milken player," was Michael Milken's best customer, buying billions of dollars worth of Drexel junk year by year through the 1980s. He sometimes allowed Milken to sell junk bonds to his insurance company without even requiring a prospectus. The failure of First Executive after its losses on Milken's bonds was the largest insurance failure in American history.
Los Angeles Times photo

LEFT, Tom Spiegel, CEO of Columbia Savings, was one of Milken's most devout customers. In mid-1992 he was indicted on more than 50 criminal counts relating to the failure of Columbia Savings—a failure that cost the taxpayers more than one billion dollars.
Los Angeles Times photo

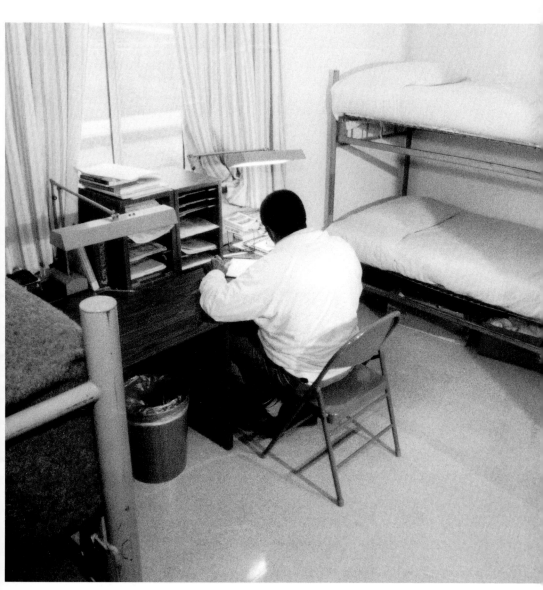

An interior view of the living quarters for inmates of the Federal Prison Work Camp at Pleasanton, California, east of San Francisco. Milken was originally sentenced to ten years for his crimes. His sentence was later reduced to twenty-four months largely because the Justice Department, at Milken's request, claimed that Milken had helped its prosecution of other financial criminals—even though the SEC filed a brief questioning the value of Milken's "cooperation." Milken's jail time will approximate that of homeowners caught passing bad checks.
AP/Wide World Photos

Meshulam Riklis might have been the number-one mentor of the Milken cathedral. But Carr was the rock on which it was built in its latter years. It was Carr, buying without asking, and by the hundreds of millions at a shot, who gave Milken instant, huge captive buying and selling power. It was Carr who helped Milken perform the miracle of raising money for anything at all overnight. Carr, the jovial former driveway repairman, was the one who allowed Milken to mesmerize borrowers and to demand fees beyond what any mere mortal in finance could have asked for. Fred Carr was Michael Milken's good fairy. "Rik" Riklis, the first number on Milken's Speed-Dial, could hardly lay claim to having done as much. He taught Milken how to play the junk bond game, but Carr actually got the ball rolling with immense sums of cash, without having to account to anyone for years if not decades. He was a good, good friend.

Again, the entire point of the exercise was control of the huge cash infusions necessary to keep things working smoothly. If Fred Carr could deliver the premiums of the policyholders of First Executive, reliably, predictably, then the Milken machine could be assured of a large amount of new cash day by day, week by week, year by year, all to be fed into the junk maw, to buy new issues, service the interest on old issues, make the junk look good, validate Milken's promises, and keep the parallel universe of Milkenism going strong.

In Milken's access to the pool of insurance premiums as a source of junk consumption, he was mining a rich lode indeed. In 1980, life insurance companies had eighty billion new dollars per year to invest, and the sum was growing rapidly. Obviously, if Milken could use only a small part of that on a consistent basis to prop up his bonds, it would represent a monumental contribution to his world. Also by 1980, total life insurance policies in force were $3.5 trillion. Even if the total of invested funds for that liability was less than a fourth of the policy amount, it represented a pool of over $800 billion of potential sales for Milken.

Just how avidly Milken pursued that market (along with other bond sellers, to be sure) is revealed by other statistics. In 1980, annual purchases by life insurers of corporate bonds were about $22 billion. By 1988, they were $180 billion, representing by far the largest percentage increase in any class of nongovernment asset. Luckily indeed for the policyholders of America, purchases of government debt rose even faster than those of corporate bonds.

Property and casualty insurers also represented a vast pool for Milken. By 1980, annual premiums for property and casualty insurance were $95 billion, and were (like life insurance premiums) rising rapidly. These vast sums, plus the inputs of buying power from bond mutual funds, corporate pension plans, and over funded corporate treasuries generally were mighty rivers into which Milken was busily tapping the best way he knew how.

However, even they were not enough. Milken, as a lad in Encino, may have heard the tale of Alexander the Great, who, after defeating the Persians, wept because he had no more worlds to conquer. Not wanting to be in that situation for long, he may have followed the adage of Louis "Lepkele" Buchalter, one of the founders of Murder, Incorporated, who said, when asked why he was so rapacious, "You have arms, you take."

And there was so much, much, much more to be taken, from a class of people even more diffuse, more easily accessed, and with far less protection than insurance policyholders.

CHAPTER SIX

THE PROMISED LAND

The public be damned.

CORNELIUS VANDERBILT, 1882

IF THE INSURANCE INDUSTRY was a dream come true to the purveyors of greatly overpriced junk bonds, the savings and loan industry was the realization of their wildest fantasies of bare-breasted maidens handing out money just for the taking.

For about forty years, ever since the Great Depression, savings and loan institutions existed primarily to make loans to homeowners. They took in deposits, on which they paid interest, and which were insured by the federal government, then lent those funds to home buyers, who also paid interest. All well and good as long as interest rates remained stable. But S&Ls began to have chronic problems from the mid-1960s onward because of the fluctuation of interest rates. In the now familiar phrase, they had to lend long and borrow short.

That is, the typical S&L had to lend to homeowners long-term mortgages at the current fixed rate of interest. But the deposits from which these mortgage loans were made paid interest generally at the current short-term rate, which fluctuated over time, especially from

97

the mid-1970s, when the famous Regulation Q was terminated. Regulation Q, the best friend banks and S&Ls ever had, even though they didn't know it, barred paying interest on deposits above a certain very low level. Thus, many of certain S&Ls could make long-term mortgage commitments at a slightly higher rate of interest and come out ahead. But Regulation Q and its clones were probably doomed by the explosive growth of money market funds, especially those tied to brokerage accounts. They paid so much more interest than bank or S&L accounts that they caused a significant hemorrhaging of deposits from these accounts.

As interest rates in general began to rise dramatically in the 1970s, the S&Ls faced a dilemma. If the bank lent at (let us say) 5 percent for thirty years, and then within a few years had to pay 7 percent on many or most of its deposits, it was playing a losing game. In fact, this was precisely the shape that the S&L industry found itself in by the end of the 1970s. It was reported in a confidential federal document by 1980 that on any realistic basis of accounting, the S&Ls as a national industry were insolvent. However, it takes some very considerable searching to find *any* S&L that actually became insolvent and had to be seized by the Federal Savings and Loan Insurance Corporation in the pre-Milken era solely because it made too many unprofitable loans to ordinary middle-class home buyers.

Still, the S&Ls were staggering, and into this bad situation stepped a number of congressmen and senators who were determined to "help" the industry. Help had already been offered in the form of variable-rate mortgages, which allowed the S&Ls to raise their receipts as interest rates rose, and in the form of a huge government-aided after-market in mortgage loans, which enabled S&Ls to liquidate low-paying loans and reinvest the proceeds at current rates. Of course, such loans could be liquidated only at a discount, which somewhat diminished the profitability of the concept.

Even so, the S&Ls, through their powerful lobby in Washington, the Savings and Loan League, wanted more relief. Under laws dating from the Great Depression, the federal government mandated that if an S&L wanted to be part of the Federal Home Loan Bank Board, which gave it such extraordinary advantages as eligibility for deposit insurance and advances from the discount window of the Federal

Home Loan Bank Board (a form of somewhat subsidized loans), it had to make loans primarily for homeownership.

The S&Ls wanted out of that restriction. Their advocates in Washington said that if they were ever to become profitable, the federal government would have to permit them access basically to all of the loan activities that a commercial bank had. They wanted to be able to make business loans, make loans for commercial property, and even buy corporate bonds, preferably without restraint upon the quality rating of the bond.

While this might have seemed risky to the hidebound, the S&L lobbyists said that in the long run it would actually save the taxpayers money. If the S&Ls expanded their range of permissible activities, they would make such excellent profits that they could take themselves out of the red. In turn, this would eliminate any liability the taxpayers might have to face down the road if some substantial number of S&Ls went bankrupt. After all, only by allowing the federally insured S&Ls freedom of maneuver, said the Savings and Loan League, could resourceful managements save their banks and at the same time save the hides of the taxpayers—savings that could reach well into the billions of dollars.

In fact, the S&L spokespersons had a large amount of merit on their side. Banks were making home loans. Even brokerages were making home loans. Others were poaching on the S&Ls' land, while the hands of the S&Ls were tied. At the time it seemed as if the returns on bonds, although they had been catastrophic during times of rising inflation, would be better if a Republican president brought down inflation. Perhaps, indeed, the S&Ls might work themselves out of their mess without having to draw in the taxpayers to bail them out. Perhaps a "level playing field," which allowed the S&Ls the same freedom of investment as federally insured banks, was the ticket.

In addition, the S&Ls deserved to have, to paraphrase *Richard II*, because they knew "the strongest and the surest way to get." It was said that every district in the South and Southwest had at least one oil man who contributed in cash to his congressman. But every congressman and senator had many S&L owners and executives in his district, and they could be generous as well. When campaign time came around, the oil men might be broke or in another part of the country, but S&L pals, and their pals at the League, were always in evidence.

Finally, the Savings & Loan League had the powerful ideology of deregulation on its side. The etiology and intellectual history of the deregulation movement originated in a few cubbyholes at the University of Chicago and was borne through decades of silent perseverance by economics powers such as Milton Friedman, Aaron Director, George Stigler, and Gottfried Haberler. It was merely a curiosity for most of the 1940s, 1950s, and 1960s. But as liberalism faltered (at least in the public mind), as new solutions were sought for national problems, as government grew into an ever larger and more cumbersome target, deregulation came to be perceived as a national panacea.

President Richard Nixon tested the waters of deregulation with his notions of unrestricted (or barely restricted) block grants to states and localities as replacements for federal grants to be used in specific ways. Jimmy Carter actually moved toward deregulation of air travel, and barely fought at all against deregulation of telecommunications. Ronald Reagan campaigned for deregulation of everything he could think of. Ever since leaving the fold of Hollywood Democrats, he had been an enthusiast of deregulation. His intellectual baggage came marked with the stamps of various hostelries in Chicago, Stanford, Washington, D.C., and Claremont, which served up deregulation as part of the daily fitness regimen. He was completely in sympathy with the idea of deregulating the federally insured Federal Home Loan Bank Board member S&Ls. As far as he was concerned, they could and would work their way out of the hole regulation had gotten them into if the government would only take off the manacles of serfdom and let the S&Ls "do business."

The confluence of a real need, a likely theory, a genuinely apparent unfairness in law, powerful lobbying, and a completely sympathetic Republican administration was more than enough to do the trick. In 1982, the Garn–St. Germain Act became the law of the land for federally insured S&Ls. It had many provisions, helpfully crafted by lawyers and friends of the League, and had been inserted into the congressional hopper by Senator Jake Garn of Utah, a devout Republican, and his colleague from the other side of the aisle, Ferdinand St. Germain, a Democrat of Rhode Island.

The act did basically what the deregulators wanted done. It allowed S&Ls to hold as assets a wide range of investables that they had been barred from holding in any meaningful amounts before. From 1982 onward, S&Ls could hold corporate bonds, stock, real property, commercial loans, and almost any other investment that a commercial bank could own. The amounts that could be held varied greatly from state to state inasmuch as federally insured S&Ls could have either federal or state charters, and there were wide variances in what each state allowed to be held. The federal statute, however, provided the minimum amount of flexibility an S&L could work within. The state statutes could not limit that amount, but they could enlarge it. In some states, particularly California under the Nolan Act of the California State Legislature, there were virtually no limits at all imposed upon what a state chartered, federally insured S&L could own.

In many ways, deregulation was the coming of nirvana for the Milken circle. With the turn of a key, a vast new market for securities from the Milken junkyard had been opened. It was even sweeter than the insurance racket, because it could go from a standing start to full-speed-ahead virtually overnight.

With an insurance company such as First Executive or one of the First Capital entities, there had to be patient, time-consuming work selling insurance policies before enough money came in to buy junk in any amounts. Salesmen had to go door to door. Prospects had to be pitched. Even when municipalities were sold GICs, there had to be presentations and contracts and detailed legal documents and actuarial calculations. It takes real work to build a major or even minor insurer.

But with an S&L, it was all so easy that it must have seemed like a dream. First, find a little S&L, preferably in California. Buy its equity with the proceeds of a Drexel offering to already captive buyers. Install Milken-friendly management or assure that the management was Milken-friendly through the usual means of argument, exhortation, and active self-interest. Next, go to the major brokers of large certificates of deposit, namely Merrill Lynch (whose continuing cooperation with Milken was as indispensable to the swindle as that of any firm besides First Executive). Pay a small fee to Merrill Lynch to draw a vast flow of deposits into the maw of the Drexel S&L. Then get rid of whatever assets the S&L already had by selling them into secondary markets. And finally, use the assets of the Drexel S&L to buy Milken junk and lots of it.

Within months of the enactment and effective date of Garn–St. Germain, the Milken circle was taking over S&Ls with dazzling speed. A Drexel equity player, Saul Steinberg, took over effective control of Imperial in San Diego. Another Drexel player, David Paul, took over CenTrust in Miami. In Beverly Hills, Gibraltar was commandeered. In New Jersey, CityFed was swallowed up. In Texas, Ben Franklin and a whole army of others joined the ranks. It would take almost three years for Charles Keating to get Drexel money to take over Lincoln Savings, but after that he earnestly made up for lost time. In Beverly Hills, father and son team Abe and Tom Spiegel took Columbia Savings to new heights of power and asset size that only they and Milken could have dreamed of.

None of this happened by accident. Drexel actively urged its players to buy S&Ls. A memo from James Dahl, a major Drexel insider in the high-yield department, to Ivan Boesky specifically urged him to buy a federally insured S&L. "We are inviting our most valued friends to look into buying federally insured savings and loans," said the memo. "The leverage is impressive, and the federal government assumes all losses" (or words to that effect). In fact, Dahl recommended that good Drexel players buy two federally insured S&Ls each, on the theory that if one went bust, that was the taxpayers' problem, and the other might make money.

This memo, from 1982, set out yet another group of appealing S&L features for the Drexel world. Leverage was one of them. Although there were variations around the margin, a federally insured S&L could generally be had for about 3 percent of its liabilities. That is, an S&L that had $100 million of deposits needed only about $3 million of stockholder equity. If an S&L had a billion dollars of deposits, it needed only $30 million of stockholders' equity.

Consider this from Milken's perspective. If he arranged for a friend to pay (let us say) $30 million for an S&L, the friend paid Milken 4 percent (including various fees) for the financing on that part of the deal. The friend now owned the assets of the S&L and could then buy at least $500 million of Drexel junk, allowing Milken commissions of another $20 million at a minimum. In turn, this buying of new

Drexel junk provided income to Drexel issuers who needed it to pay their interest. New financings paying off old financings provided not only money, but longer life for the Ponzi by allowing the bonds that would otherwise have failed to continue to pay interest. The potential for Milken was staggering. In the 1980s, the S&L hoard was heading for a trillion dollars. If even 10 percent of it went into Drexel junk, that hundred billion would keep the pot boiling for many years of interest payments.

And, as James Dahl's letter to Boesky and others in Milken's circle pointed out, there was, for the Drexel players, literally no downside. If the S&L failed due to the failure of the Milken bonds, that was the problem of the federal deposit insurance fund, which would pay off the depositors so there would never be angry mobs marching on Rodeo Drive with pikes and poleaxes. The S&L layer of the Milken world did something stupendous: through S&Ls and the Federal Savings and Loan Insurance Corporation, Milken could sell his junk indirectly to the taxpayers—by far the largest group of buyers in America.

If the S&L failed, yes, the equity would be lost, but the loss to the insiders would have been long since offset by their Milken group earnings. Moreover, how much of the equity would be in the hands of the Milken circle by that time? Most of it would long ago have passed into the hands of anonymous shareholders.

How the scheme worked in a specific case was laid out clearly and punishingly in a 1991 complaint in federal court in Los Angeles against Columbia Savings. In its own way, the story was an authentic human tragedy as well as a financial and legal catastrophe.

Abe Spiegel, a Hungarian immigrant who had been an inmate of a Nazi concentration camp, came to California in the late 1940s. He built, mostly by his energy and determination, a successful construction business. In the 1960s, he bought stock in, then bought control of, a small firm called Columbia Savings & Loan. As far as is known, he ran it very much on the up and up. Then, in 1977, he turned over the reins of power to his son, Tom, who had been in finance and wanted his family bank to rise to a far more aggressive position in the S&L world. Like many another S&L player, Tom thought he saw the easy route to riches lying through the middle of Michael Milken's junk bond room. He told Milken that he was willing to take down as much Drexel junk as he could, and Milken was happy to oblige.

To make it all work, and to keep everything in the family, Milken raised several hundred million dollars' worth of equity and debt for Columbia, which allowed it to have vastly larger assets. To make very sure that control would not be lost to outsiders less friendly to Milken, as well as to produce endless fees for Drexel, huge blocks of Columbia stock were floated and then bought by Milken personally, with his brother, or with various family members. By 1982, Otter Creek, a major Milken partnership, controlled by Milken family members, lawyers, and colleagues, owned more than a million shares of Columbia's common stock. By 1984, Drexel owned still more stock, a total of slightly more than 10 percent (not counting the Otter Creek stock). By 1985, three huge Milken colleagues and customers, Ivan Boesky, the Drexel financial captive Integrated Resources, and the Drexel/Milken pal money manager Martin Sosnoff, each owned or controlled roughly 10 percent of the stock.

By virtue of the Drexel offerings of capital for Columbia ($140 million in 1984 alone, $100 million in 1986 alone), Milken's ownership of Columbia stock, his pals' ownership of Columbia stock, and other inducements, Columbia had by 1989 bought over $10 billion worth of Drexel/Milken issues, throwing off fees of various kinds of hundreds of millions of dollars for the Drexel/Milken high-yield department. Columbia, in fact, was such a loyal, devoted customer that Milken could count on it to perform his usual stable of tricks: buying doggy issues to give the impression that he was dealing with a hot issue and thus drive up the price on resale; assuring quick arrangements of financing to give Milken the appearance—and reality—of unique financial power; pledging money for takeovers and greenmail; and parking stock to conceal Milken group ownership and thus to help Milken players take over target companies.

For this help to Drexel, Spiegel was paid lavishly. In 1985, he took home direct compensation of over $9 million, far more than the chairman of General Motors. For the year 1987, he was paid $5.6 million, which included the personal use of two company-owned airplanes (one a Gulfstream II), several condominiums (at least one in Jackson Hole, Wyoming), many, many automobiles, a vast collection of firearms (some of which he taped to his leg while jogging), and legal and accounting fees paid by Columbia.

This was just the tip of the iceberg, however. As with his most loyal inside players in other places, Milken allowed and encouraged Spiegel to buy into various Milken deals. These deals usually followed a fairly repetitive pattern: The Milken player, such as Spiegel's Columbia Savings, would buy some bonds, particularly of the more dicey varieties. In return, Milken would give equity kickers in certain transactions to the buyer. But, again, the buyer would never put up his own money. He put up the money of his depositors or policyholders while he, the Milken protégé, would personally take the equity kickers. These equity kickers were non–publicly traded stocks in various Drexel-controlled companies. It was well within Milken's power to reorganize the company in question so that its equity yielded enormous profits, no matter how well or badly the company was doing in the marketplace. It looked a lot like bribery of fiduciaries to buy Milken bonds.

For example, when the Milken group arranged for the purchase of Storer Broadcasting in mid-1985, there were some especially questionable bonds and preferred stock that Milken had to sell to make the transaction fly. Because Tom Spiegel caused Columbia to buy several million dollars' worth of these securities, Milken gave to Farnham Partners, a partnership controlled by the Spiegel family, secretly, an option to buy, for about $132,000, private equity in the Storer deal. This equity had been explicitly created and passed around by the buyers of Storer, Kohlberg Kravis Roberts, to induce buyers of the bonds and preferred stock to go forward with the purchases. In fact, the passing around was controlled by Milken, who made sure that it was mostly passed to him and his family. A few percentage points of the stock warrants were also passed to loyal buyers, such as Spiegel.

On their $132,000 investment, the Spiegel family made a profit of about $7 million within about one year. Obviously, the private equity on which these huge gains were realized was made available as a gratuity by KKR for the financing of its buyout of Storer. Just as obviously, all of the risk for the failure of the securities in question, the millions of high-risk takeover debt, fell on the stockholders and

depositors and taxpayers/insurers of Columbia. And just as obviously, all of the gain without any significant risk went to Spiegel
and his family. Further, as the complaint stated succinctly, "The
shareholders of Columbia were injured because without their SCI
equity, Columbia would have paid a materially lower price (for the
SCI securities)." (SCI became the new, postbuyout name for Storer
Broadcasting.)

Another way that Milken and his colleagues kept the Spiegels in
line was to allow them to have a piece of another Milken partnership,
AFP Investors. This partnership had stakes in a number of Milken/
Drexel deals, which could be "wired" to guarantee profits. In particular, it had a piece of a company known as American Family Products. As usual, the partners, including Spiegel, put in several hundred
thousand dollars and made a profit of 300 percent within five months.

In return for his unswerving dedication to Milken and his bonds,
Spiegel was allowed to know about a planned takeover of venerable
Safeway Stores in advance of the market generally. In his trading on
that inside information, he made a profit in excess of $10 million,
according, once again, to the lawyers who filed the complaint in the
civil action against him. Spiegel was also allowed to know about a
planned takeover of Container Corporation of America by a Drexel
player. Although someone else eventually stepped up to the plate and
bought CCA, Spiegel reportedly made a profit of about $50 million on
a $1 million investment in options on the company stock.

In 1988, in connection with the sale of a former part of Beatrice
known as Playtex Holdings, which was being sold off after a series of
transactions largely financed by Columbia, Liberty Service Corporation, a subsidiary of Columbia, was given the chance to buy about
two hundred thousand shares of private equity in the company for
$5.20 per share. Before the shares were even delivered, that order
was canceled and the shares were instead bought by Tom Spiegel,
Abe Spiegel, various Spiegel relatives and family trusts, and a friend.
Within one year, the Spiegels had sold their Playtex for $10.60 per
share for a profit of over a million dollars.

Just how close the relationship between Milken and Spiegel was
can be gathered by knowing that, at Milken's request, Spiegel actually installed a branch of Columbia Savings in the Drexel office

building at Wilshire and Rodeo in Beverly Hills. Drexel operatives could deposit checks from out-of-state banks at this branch, then write checks upon those deposits for immediate use. They often did this when they bought Drexel issues and then immediately resold them for large profits—to Columbia.

Thus, it was a standard part of Columbia's operations, eventually subsidized heavily by the American taxpayer, to make no-interest loans to Drexel players so they could then make guaranteed profits by selling bonds bought with those loans to the entity that made the loans. The most beautiful part of this operation was that the bonds in question had no market, and the price at which they were bought by Columbia—which was never less than what the Drexel players had paid for them—was simply made up by Drexel, and probably by Milken in particular.

Some of the bonds Columbia bought after they had originally been withheld by Milken (so that a profit was built in and the issues looked "hot") were Cannon Group (now defunct), Allied Supermarkets, Ambrit, Bally's (in distress), Coastal Corporation, Compact Video (recently in distress), Coopervision, Banner, Colt (in default), Southmark (in default), Pantry Pride, Golden Nugget of Las Vegas, General Host, Occidental Petroleum, Texas Air (in default), Texstyrene (ditto), Wickes (recently in default), Ingersoll (in default), and Magnetek (recently in distress).

In short, Spiegel was another very, very good friend to Milken. Through his agency, and that of his father, he plowed over $10 billion into keeping the scam going, adding money for financings, allowing little and big bits of chiseling within Drexel's junk bond department, permitting the Drexel raiders to flex their muscles, and pumping up Milken with OPM (Other People's Money) steroids. And Columbia was the flagship—but only one ship—of the potent Milken fleet of S&Ls.

To get an idea of the might that the federally insured S&L system added to Milken's armada and the power that Milken and his colleagues had over the nation's S&Ls, look first at the Milken/Drexel control over some of the largest S&Ls in America. In 1983, Drexel player Fred Carr financed the acquisition of control over Imperial of San Diego by Drexel friend Victor Goulet. Goulet bought control from Drexel friend Saul Steinberg, and then made Imperial into a major purchaser of Drexel junk. Imperial was seized in 1990. In 1983, Milken financed Charles Keating's acquisition of Lincoln S&L; Lincoln was seized in 1989. In 1983, a Drexel colleague, Richard Frary, plus another Drexel entity, bought about 11 percent of the stock of Security Savings, also seized in 1989. In 1985, Drexel bought 733,000 shares of stock in CenTrust, run by good pal David Paul until it, too, was seized in 1990. In 1985, Drexel bought about 7 percent of the stock of USAT S&L, and by 1987 had about 10 percent of it; it went under in 1988. Through the mid and late 1980s, Drexel did a series of underwritings for Southmark, the parent of San Jacinto Savings, aggregating hundreds of millions of dollars; it was seized in 1991. Through the mid and late 1980s, and beginning as far back as 1978, Drexel also did a series of underwritings for Kinder-Care, the corporate parent of American Savings, aggregating hundreds of millions of dollars; American Savings went into distress in 1990.

These provide only a hint of the financial transactions that allowed Drexel such leverage with the nation's S&Ls. The consequences were disastrous. With hindsight it seemed as if Drexel were running one huge S&L under different names, with deposits and purchasing power of at least $100 billion. Indeed, the whole captive Drexel apparatus often looked much like one large combined bank/S&L/insurance company/bond fund/pension fund/corporate treasury monster finance machine run out of Beverly Hills, at an office on the corner of Rodeo and Wilshire, with fiduciaries being "taken care of" to buy Milken's bonds.

It is clear from both civil and criminal court complaints that Milken bribes in one form or another were familiar procedure for dealing with trustees of other people's money. Within just a few months in 1992, juries found that consideration had been paid to trustees of Fidelity Funds and First Investors Fund for Income to buy Drexel junk. A grand jury returned an indictment against Tom Spiegel for his alleged acceptance of favors to use depositors' and taxpayers' money to buy Drexel bonds.

In barely disguised maneuvers in broad daylight, the Drexel machine sucked the blood of its captive S&Ls like a vampire, draining the assets of their depositors dry. Plasma available through the federal deposit insurance blood bank could not even begin to replace their losses and huge transfusions would ultimately have to be drawn from taxpayers. For the Drexel Draculas, it was a feast. For their victims, S&L depositors and American taxpayers, it was an experience from which they would not soon recover.

CHAPTER SEVEN

ENSTAR

There it was, word for word,
The poem that took the place of a mountain.

WALLACE STEVENS, 1952

To MOST AMERICANS, Montgomery, Alabama, is recalled in history as the first capital of the Confederate States of America; or as the former segregationist bastion of George C. Wallace, one-time governor of the state; or as the sleepy Southern city where Rosa Parks refused to give up her seat in the front of a bus and sparked a revolution.

However, Montgomery is also home to a federal district court, where a drama involving a genuinely astounding saga of greed, lawlessness, and contempt for stockholders has just recently been played out. The drama had to do with a company that used to be called Kinder-Care, and was once featured in an advertisement about what great financing work Drexel Burnham Lambert did for small companies. Kinder-Care was founded in Montgomery and was a source of great pride to the community, as well as an employer of thousands of men and women. It changed its name to Enstar when it became a huge financial services, retail trade, and oil company in addition to owning a chain of day-care centers.

Enstar went bankrupt. It employs exactly five people, one of whom works part-time. And now it's a source of rage, frustration, and loss for the people of Montgomery. They were taken, and taken badly. How it happened, with the final acts in the drama played out in the same courthouse where momentous decrees about racial integration used to resound, is a perfect illustration of the Drexel conspiracy, how it worked, why it achieved the power it had, and just what amazing callousness it showed toward every goal except feeding Michael Milken's bottomless maw.

In 1969, a local Montgomery developer named Perry Mendel had an idea. He would use some of his real estate and his building abilities to start a chain of day-care centers. These facilities would provide well-supervised, nationally standardized child care for working mothers and fathers. The idea was well executed and an instant hit. First hundreds and then thousands of Kinder-Care centers with their trademark red school bell came to dot the national landscape. They were occasionally criticized for being run on too much of a bare-bones format, but they were generally well-liked. They were considered, as stated in *The New York Times* and elsewhere, models of how the private sector could respond to social change.

The stock of Kinder-Care was a success story as well, gladdening the Montgomerians who bought it early and watched it go from the original twelve cents to its high in mid-1987 of almost twenty dollars per share. At its peak, an apparent phenomenon of success and probity, Kinder-Care ran 12,000 centers, employed more than 17,000 persons full-time, and had gross revenues of $900 million, with operating profits in its best year, 1987, of $75 million (although eerily enough, even then, its net profits were only about $6 million).

In 1970, a scant year after founding Kinder-Care, Perry Mendel brought on board as a director and corporate officer another Montgomery businessman. Richard Grassgreen soon rose to a position of high trust and confidence within Kinder-Care and by the mid-1970s was essentially running the company. By 1985, he would be the official president and chief operating officer.

In 1978, Mendel and Grassgreen sought out Michael Milken for a small infusion of capital through junk financing. Milken persuaded them, as he had so many others, that he had an alchemical way to help them get rich quick. The way was for Grassgreen and Mendel to hire Milken and his pals to raise money for them through his Beverly

111

Hills junk bond machine. The money, as he told them, could be used to expand Kinder-Care's powerful franchise. They would, of course, have to pay a rather high interest on the issue, but if they raised more money than they really needed, that extra money could also be used —in an even surer and faster way to get rich—to buy the higher-yielding junk of other Drexel issuers, thus putting the child-care chain into the interest arbitrage business.

Soon, starting with a paltry $10 million issue in 1978, Drexel was grinding out public and private financing for Kinder-Care, by the hundreds of millions of dollars. Certainly some of this money went to expand Kinder-Care. The company built new day-care centers and expanded by acquisitions as well. In 1985, for example, Kinder-Care bought Sylvan Learning Centers, one of its competitors, and instantly added dozens of facilities. But the bulk of the funds Drexel raised went into two enterprises far more responsive to the needs of Milken and his world than to the needs of the stockholders of Kinder-Care.

The first of these was to convert Kinder-Care into a diversified financial services company capable of buying still more Drexel junk. In 1985, Kinder-Care, at Milken's behest, bought an insurance company headquartered in the charming Florida town of Largo. Pioneer-Western, along with several subsidiaries and affiliates, was purchased for about $70 million and was soon buying Drexel junk by the tens of millions and more.

Within a few months, in 1986, Kinder-Care, again at Milken's behest, bought for about $37 million the stock of a St. Petersburg, Florida, S&L called CenterBanc. The two entities, one an S&L and the other an insurer, were put under a common umbrella within Kinder-Care. CenterBanc, too, was a major buyer of Drexel junk.

In July of 1987, acting with the promise of Drexel-raised money, Kinder-Care bought Miami's troubled American Savings and Loan. (It had been implicated in the illegal dealings of Marvin Warner and ESM, and had suffered major losses in those trades.) Soon, American S&L also was a huge buyer of Drexel junk.

Thus, in the space of about one and a half years, with the help of Drexel and Milken, Kinder-Care had been converted into a substantial-sized banking and insurance company with about $3 billion in assets. It had been Milkenized. And both the child-care part of

Kinder-Care and the financial services part of Kinder-Care were into Drexel deals in a major way. That is, money from the corporate treasury of the child-care centers, as well as from the assets of the depositors, policyholders, and stockholders of insurance and S&L subsidiaries, went to buy Drexel junk. At its peak, the sprawling entity, which had begun life as a small child-care center with a trademark red bell, owned about $650 million of Drexel junk.

Curiously enough, the company also began a retailing subsidiary, which bought in February of 1988 a chain called Shoe City, and soon thereafter also bought a series of bargain clothing stores—Max 10, Simply Six, and others throughout the southeast. At about that time, the corporate parent was renamed Enstar. By all appearances, the little child-care center had become a major conglomerate. The problem was that in many ways, the entire structure was hollow and was destined to collapse under the weight of the scheme perpetrated by Grassgreen, Mendel, and Milken.

All through the 1980s, Kinder-Care (now Enstar) was a player in Drexel deals, a faithful buyer of Milken junk floated to finance a number of takeover attempts involving, among others, Safeway, Storer, Coastal, Revlon, Unocal and Gillette. Obviously, some of these attempts went forward and others did not. The threatened takeover of Unocal by Boone Pickens never happened, and neither did the attempt to take over Gillette by Ronald Perelman. But the takeovers of Storer and Revlon did happen, conducted by Kohlberg Kravis Roberts (KKR) and Ronald Perelman respectively, with major backing from Drexel players. Still, when any takeover was begun, it was vital for the Milken team to have the financial muscle in place and evident. That was where trusty sources like Enstar, Mendel, and Grassgreen came in, along with other Drexel faithful, such as Carr at First Executive and Spiegel at Columbia S&L.

There was a reward for that kind of loyalty. For some deals that went through and some that did not, Milken paid commitment fees to his financing sources. The fees were on the order of slightly less than one percent of the amounts pledged, although they varied greatly. But while the stockholders, policyholders, and depositors of Enstar, certainly not Mendel and Grassgreen, put up the money for Drexel's deals and bonds and bore the losses, at least much of the commitment fees were paid to Grassgreen and Mendel personally. In particular, they often went into an Alabama partnership with the clever name of Megra Partners, (MEndel and GRAssgreen).

Just as some examples, and not at all a full inventory, Grassgreen and Mendel got commitment fees in the hundreds of thousands of dollars for offering to put up Enstar stockholders' money in the following deals:

- Ronald Perelman's takeover of Pantry Pride.
- Charles Hurwitz's catastrophic takeover of Pacific Lumber, which resulted in some of the worst environmental atrocities of all time against first-growth redwood trees.
- The failed takeover attempt of Unocal.
- And, of course, that most beautiful of all Drexel deals, the KKR takeover of Storer Broadcasting.

In Storer, a 1985 deal, the pickings were especially lush. In a convoluted series of events that involved a Drexel captive financial company called Atlantic Capital, the Milken/Drexel MacPherson partners, and, of course, Megra Partners, Grassgreen and Mendel, for buying into a supposedly risky part of the financing package, got actual warrants to buy private equity in the Storer deal.

When Milken issued these warrants to Grassgreen for his generous disposition of Enstar stockholders' money, Grassgreen later testified that he asked Milken, over the phone, if the warrants were for the Enstar stockholders. According to Grassgreen, Milken said, "No, they're for you and Perry." For Grassgreen and Mendel, the profits from this transaction alone, as the private equity skyrocketed in value, were roughly $900,000. In other words, Grassgreen and Mendel took money that obviously belonged by law and economics to their stockholders. (Milken and his lawyers later insisted that they had never intended that Mendel and Grassgreen keep these transactions from their stockholders. That was an amazing assertion, since the transactions would have invited civil and/or criminal legal action on a silver platter if they had been publicized in any detail.)

Even worse than that for a public company, by virtue of his control over Grassgreen and Mendel, Milken was able to compel them to buy vast quantities of his toxic junk. And because he had split the total consideration for the junk, with some going to Megra for no fee to speak of, he had made it by definition overpriced to Enstar, which did pay for it. That is, he had taken a large chunk of the income that might be expected from his junk issue and simply given it to Grassgreen and Mendel up front. The remainder, which went to Enstar, was clearly inadequate to compensate for the high risks of the Drexel junk. It was much the same as if a trustee for a pension fund bought 7 percent Treasuries and kept two hundred basis points for himself. His trustors would have been shortchanged and would have drastically overpaid for what was somewhat less than a real 7 percent bond.

In the Kinder-Care/Enstar world, the total consideration for the Milken bonds that the child-care conglomerate bought was the interest plus the warrants. If Grassgreen and Mendel took the warrants, they were simply taking a part of the consideration that made the bonds a halfway fair deal and leaving the stockholders and bondholders of Kinder-Care/Enstar with a very much overpriced bond.

But the high-jinks of Grassgreen and Mendel had really only begun with their buys of Drexel junk and their juicy commitment fees. Once Drexel had paid Megra their commitment fees, it then took further care of the two men by helping them make still more money by Milken-assisted trading. For example, through Milken, Grassgreen and Mendel bought into a Drexel account that had a position in Hill's Department Stores long before a stock split and other activities that Drexel was aware of drove the stock up and soon made a profit of about $790,000 for Megra.

But deals involving a company called TPR and its various affiliates were in some ways the most outré variants of the financial misconduct of Grassgreen and Mendel, this time committed with the help of Milken mentor Meshulam Riklis and his daughter, Marcia. TPR, sometimes called Trans Pacific Resources, was a company owned primarily by a partnership also called TPR. The partners in TPR, the Riklises, Grassgreen, Mendel, and a man named Ari Genger, who moved in and out of high financial and government circles in the United States and Israel with astounding fluidity, accomplished several transactions that merited note in the annals of contempt for law and stockholders.

In one of these transactions, in or around January of 1986, Grassgreen and Mendel led Enstar into lending about $10 million to TPR and investing roughly another $3 million in TPR equity. This money, lent and invested through a Kinder-Care/Enstar subsidiary, Care Investors, enabled TPR to put together a large potash company, to acquire control of an Israeli potash company called Haifa Chemical, to restructure this agglomeration of potash companies, and to make approximately $20 million of profit *each,* and possibly more, for Mendel and Grassgreen. It is not known whether Enstar ever saw its money back from the Riklis deal.

(In an ironic twist later on in the TPR story, after Grassgreen and Mendel had both been convicted of federal fraud charges in 1991, TPR partners sued Mendel. The erstwhile partners alleged that had they known that Mendel was taking profits from TPR for money he had caused his stockholders to put up, they would never have dreamed of letting him into their partnership. They were shocked— shocked—to find that there was gambling going on at Rik's place.)

In another transaction involving TPR, in 1987 Grassgreen and Mendel brought to the board of Enstar a plan to buy Shoe City, a large discount shoe chain. They thought of it as a possibly decent acquisition, but not one they would insist upon as a great opportunity. The board demurred, and Shoe City was then immediately bought by TPR or by the partners in TPR, including Grassgreen and Mendel, under a related name. Part of the financing came from Enstar, directly or indirectly.

On February 5, 1988, Mendel and Grassgreen went to the board again and now insisted that Enstar buy their Shoe City. The board agreed to do so, giving Mendel and Grassgreen and the Riklises an almost tenfold profit on their investment in Shoe City equity within one year. Grassgreen's personal profit on the deal was about $4.5 million. Mendel's was about $2.8 million.

In a final, almost unbelievable twist late in 1989, as Enstar was sinking into oblivion, Grassgreen, Mendel, and Riklis bought 10 percent of Enstar's common. The idea was to show their faith and confidence in the corporation and in Grassgreen's management, or so they said. What they did not say was that they had bought the stock in question through TPR, the same entity that was largely financed with Enstar money. The "confidence" that Grassgreen, Mendel, and Riklis were showing in Grassgreen's management was paid for with the stockholders' money. As usual, only the stockholders' money was at risk, and only Mendel, Grassgreen, and Riklis would have benefited unusually if gravity had been defied and Enstar had survived.

Money tends to corrupt, and Milken money, cut off as it was from the whole stream of logic and ethics, tended to corrupt absolutely. Some of the behavior of Mendel and Grassgreen as their reign wore on became almost unbelievable in its illogic and defiance of good sense. To cite one extraordinary situation, Mendel had taken up tennis as a middle-aged man. His coach and fellow player on the courts was Jackie Bushman, who, like many another Alabaman, liked to hunt deer. He also coveted a magazine about deer hunting. Like an Arabian potentate, Perry Mendel, with money from the stockholders of Enstar, bought his tennis-playing buddy *Buckmaster* magazine to run. It, like CenterBanc, American Savings & Loan, Pioneer Insurance, Western Reserve Insurance, Sylvan Learning Centers, Haifa Chemical, and Care Investors, became part of the empire that started with one little day-care center, built with Milken money into a giant house of cards.

In a similar situation, Grassgreen had a friend from college days who wanted to run a brokerage. Again, like a Middle Eastern prince, Grassgreen bought him a firm named Kauffmann Alsberg. The firm had been profitable since 1932, but by the middle 1980s, as part of the empire of Enstar, it began to lose money. It is no longer operating, at least under that name.

There were other, larger, more well-publicized miscues and misadventures by Mendel and Grassgreen. As was usual within the Drexel empire, a variety of heroic measures were attempted to raise money and somehow keep the financial services portion of Enstar operating so that it could continue taking down Drexel junk, even as the defaults on that junk began to drag Enstar into oblivion.

In a complex series of maneuvers, Enstar sold off the Kinder-Care portion of the company to its stockholders and to an investment group called Lodestar. The sell-off was distinguished by an amazingly crude trick. Originally, in 1988 and early 1989, the child-care centers

117

were to be simply spun off to the Kinder-Care stockholders without charge. But management then said that the IRS objected and that therefore a price of about $4.75 per share had to be charged for each new share of the Kinder-Care entity that the old Kinder-Care share-holders wanted to buy. Not only was this making the stockholders pay for something they already owned, but also, as it happened, there had never been an IRS ruling barring the spinoff. Management had just made that up to fool the shareholders into ponying up.

In Kinder-Care/Enstar, there was an almost pristine paradigm of the way that Milken operated: Take a small company, pump it up with debt capital by issuing junk bonds, and make it into a larger company able to buy huge amounts of other people's junk.

A genius of finance and stock picking, Warren Buffett of Berkshire Hathaway, likes to say that there is always a sucker in every deal, and if you are in the deal and don't know who the sucker is, it's probably you. Kinder-Care was a company with a bright future in-deed until its top officers were sold on the idea that they could make themselves truly rich without effort. Lured into the Drexel web, they issued their own junky bonds and used the proceeds to buy still junkier bonds. In that way, Kinder-Care became hopelessly entan-gled by its own high-yield debt costs, its exposure to the default of even more highly leveraged issuers, and the fragility of the entire Milken edifice. Milken and Drexel made money on every part of their deals with Mendel and Grassgreen. Guess who the suckers were.

As of summer 1992, Perry Mendel was in a federal prison and Richard Grassgreen was in a federal corrections halfway house. There are enormous court judgments against them both, issuing from that Montgomery courthouse. The stockholders they defrauded are free, but distinctly poorer. There may be different kinds of suckers in every deal, but some might better be called innocent victims.

CHAPTER EIGHT

INFINITE JEST

*A feast is made for laughter, and wine maketh merry:
but money answereth all things.*

ECCLESIASTES, 10:19

PUBLIC ATTENTION AND the media have for good reason focused on the massive, routine insider trading that went on among "investment bankers" during the 1980s. The media and legal focus on Michael R. Milken has also attached to this aspect of his career, particularly in connivance with Ivan Boesky. And, indeed, insider trading was a lucrative area for the Milken enterprise, the junk bond conclave within Drexel and without, and their hangers-on. Obviously, buying stock or options on stock when one knows that it is virtually certain to go up sharply is a fine way to "get rich quick." The Drexel machine, however, had incomparably better ways to make incomparably more money. Insider trading, with its romantic cloak-and-dagger quality, was really no more than a lucrative sideshow for the Drexel team. But it was not the blank check, the license to steal, that a few other Drexel practices were.

Junk issuance itself was the first and prime engine of Drexel/Milkenism. Over the ten years from 1978 to about 1988, Drexel issued about $200 billion worth of bonds, including private placements, which were of junk credit rating levels. This is the approximate amount broadcast by the Drexel publicists before their silence relating to bankruptcy in 1990. It also roughly corresponds to the amounts calculated by independent experts such as Securities Data, Inc.

Drexel got paid about 3 percent as a minimum fee for this kind of work. It also got paid in warrants and equity kickers, which raised the rate to as much as 30 percent of the total equity capitalization of the bond-issuing corporation. The amounts yielded to Drexel/Milken by such practices remain unknown, except in a few spectacular cases such as the takeovers of Beatrice and Storer. But even assuming that the total commission on all Drexel junk offerings under Milken was raised by only one percentage point, the total commission of 4 percent for the junk department at Rodeo and Wilshire would have approximated $8 billion.

In the real world of debt issuance, an investment-grade bond pays a commission to its underwriter of (at most) 0.5 percent. On $1.5 *trillion* of investment-grade bonds, or about the total face value of *all* of the bonds listed on the New York Stock Exchange as of 1988, the commission would have been close to the amount that the small group of thirty or so Milken players in Beverly Hills made on their junk in one decade. That is, the Milken group collected in underwriting fees in one decade an amount roughly equal, in current dollars, to what the commissions would have been on all of the bonds listed on the New York Stock Exchange and still traded as of 1988 (had they all been investment-grade bonds).

This sum was nominally the property of Drexel, but was really made in Beverly Hills and very largely owned and distributed or retained by one man, Michael R. Milken.

Then there was churning.

Every investor is familiar with horror stories about churning a discretionary account. Churning occurs when a broker trades a client's account unreasonably, usually to increase commissions. Obviously, that is a clear breach of fiduciary duty and a rip-off of the client. It does, however, produce income for the broker and the brokerage.

Milken did the same thing on a spectacularly greater scale. In many ways, he had discretionary accounts at all of his major captive S&Ls and insurers, and with some of his corporate players. He had control of about $15 billion worth of bonds held by institutions just within a short walk from his office—primarily at Columbia S&L, First Executive, First Capital Holdings (although the discretion there was incomplete, with CEO Bob Weingarten vastly more responsible than the usual Drexelite), Gibraltar, and for a time, part of Zenith National, plus Far West, Atlantic Financial, Coast, and others. Throughout the country, there were even more billions to be traded—at CenTrust, Ben Franklin, Santa Barbara Savings, San Jacinto, Lincoln, Mutual Benefit, Guarantee, and other captives in Milken's junk world. Had he controlled the trading of this amount of money in stocks listed on the New York Stock Exchange, that, by itself, would have conferred an awesome ability to collect commissions—whether or not he earned a profit on the trades. But Milken's money-making power was incalculably, unimaginably greater than that.

The conventional broker trading GM or Xerox earns only the standard commission allowed by Merrill Lynch or Prudential-Bache or wherever he works. This might be a fraction of a percent of the total sale, which obviously limits his ability to make money. This same broker also has to trade at current market prices dictated by the laws of supply and demand, which means he may show a profit or a loss on the trade. But Milken could not only trade tens of billions at will, he could also fix both ends of the trade to give himself any level of commission or profit he wished.

It has now been amply shown by the research of Congressman John Dingell, by lawyers in the S&L cases, and in other lawsuits that Milken could and did sell the same security at the same time to different people at different prices. He could and did do the same thing on the buy side as well. He could take one million dollars of Hypothetical Milken Issuer bonds, for example, and "buy" them out of an account at First Investors Fund for Income, a junk bond fund he controlled, for 97. He would put them in something like LorSan Partners II, just as an example, named for Lori and Sandy Milken, wife of Lowell Milken, and then, at the same moment, resell them to, for example, Columbia S&L for 102. He had discretionary power so absolute over these entities that he did not even have to consult the buyers or sellers except to make bookkeeping entries that showed the deals had been done. By jotting down a few notes, he had made a profit of $50,000.

But Milken was trading in the tens of billions each year, churning the portfolios at his captives by 100 percent each year and sometimes by far more. He was taking a few percent out of each trade, more or less, on an amount of at least $30 billion over which he had sole discretion, making for vast "trading" profits, which approximated one billion dollars annually just on this captive sum. And this assumes, conservatively for Milken, that he turned over the accounts "only" at the rate of 100 percent per year.

Then there was another $170 billion that he could trade occasionally, if not as completely arbitrarily as the captive funds. And, again, he had complete and absolute power over the prices, so that he always could fix his own profit. Even if these funds turned over at only 50 percent annually, the "trading" profit on a three-percentage-point spread on this "float" would approximate $3 billion annually.

For the men and the few women in the Drexel trading room, the money was just raining down from heaven. They could, with Milken's permission, simply write checks to Milken and to Drexel and to themselves by making "trades" all day and all night. For the ordinary citizen, it would be as if he could buy stock at any price he felt like and then, at any time, resell it at any price he felt like. The only obligation of Milken (and his fellow "traders") was to keep records and to keep the prices sufficiently within the margin of sanity that the trustees they had coopted would not be caught, tarred, and feathered, at least not right away.

Small wonder that the people in the Drexel office at Rodeo and Wilshire worked such long hours.

Then there was greenmail, which is, in many ways, one of the most psychologically and sociologically interesting "get rich quick" areas in modern industry and finance. In greenmail, a potential buyer threatens to acquire enough of a corporation's stock, at a price in excess of its current market value, to mount a takeover attempt. The officers of the target corporation respond by frantically trying to keep their jobs. They can do this by suing the potential acquirer, by performing heroic and often suicidal refinancings, or by other means. One of the most popular "other means" is to pay off the potential acquirer by buying back his stock at a price greater, sometimes very much greater, than the acquirer paid for it. The acquirer, who may

studies simply overwhelmed rumors of the truth and helped keep the Drexel junk business going through its three biggest years, 1987, 1988, and 1989. Altman's seemingly "scientific" data were the pivot on which the sale of $50 billion of Drexel junk swung. Were it not for Altman's studies and the heavy reliance the GAO placed upon them, Milken's captive S&Ls might not have been allowed to continue buying Milken junk after 1987 and 1988.

The GAO study itself would be a worthwhile object of examination for archeologists of the age of decline of fiduciary and other governmental responsibility. The GAO, asked to study whether junk was a suitable investment for taxpayers to support through the FSLIC, a question on which billions of tax dollars rested, performed almost unbelievably poorly. It brought no negative viewpoints at all to its hearing on junk. It relied almost exclusively, if not exclusively, on the anecdotal experience of S&L officers known to be affiliated with Drexel for comment on how its junk was working out at their firms. It performed no independent research to validate the data supplied by Drexel players. It cited profit and loss data from known Drexel captives without any examination of whether the data were real or in accord with standard accounting practices.

The GAO relied, in fact, on the faked superlative experience of the eleven largest junk-holding S&Ls for its primary conclusions endorsing junk. Within one year of the issue of the report, ten of the eleven were insolvent. Even so, the supervisor of the report at the GAO insisted that he would have done nothing different in his report even if he had prepared it after these failures. In a well-worn line from the Drexel playbook, he blamed excessively zealous government regulators, and not junk bonds, for the failure of the largest junk-holding S&Ls.

To be fair to Altman, however, he was joined in his pro-Milken, projunk view by two professors from Milken's alma mater, Wharton. Marshall Blume and Donald Keim produced a number of papers that were at least as intellectually and factually questionable as Altman's, and as resoundingly pro-junk. But for some reason, their work did not achieve the following that Altman's work did.

In 1988, Altman wrote that by using another method of analysis, junk had much higher levels of default than his studies had shown.

135

not have had any real intention of taking over the company, then picks up his profits and goes away. Sometimes various forms of expenses, spurious and real, are also paid by the target company to the potential acquirer.

The fascinating part of this form of financial behavior is that the real misconduct is not so much by the potential acquirer as by the management of the target corporation. To fend off a takeover, it spends the stockholders' money, weakens the company, sometimes drastically, by assuming a burdensome debt, and deprives the stockholders of the potential of making a profit on their shares.

To make greenmail work, however, the potential acquirer must be taken seriously. He must above all have credible means of financing an acquisition; that is, enough money to buy the stock necessary to gain control of the company. It does not, however, have to be cash on the barrelhead, merely a source of that kind of cash to tap if necessary. That was where the Milken group stepped in to provide the financial clout for men like Saul Steinberg, Sir James Goldsmith, Carl Icahn, and some smaller fry like Ivan Boesky to mount real or threatened takeover attempts. With the Milken junk world able to produce financing power on command, these so-called corporate raiders could and did make hostile takeover feints for such companies as Green Tree Acceptance, Goodyear Tire and Rubber, Walt Disney, Phillips Petroleum, Avco, and other entities and then walk away with greenmail.

To the watching world, the real winners of such games were the corporate raiders who waltzed away with large profits, sometimes in the hundreds of millions, not the corporate officers, even though they still had their jobs. But Milken did not provide the chips to play these games for free. He had a piece of the action. The piece, according to insiders, was about 40 percent of the upside of any deal that went right; that is, where the greenmail was paid or where the stock moved up.

In a bitter added feature to the takeover game, whatever its outcome, the taxpayers were putting up a large part of the financing muscle through federal insurance of the assets of the Milken-controlled S&Ls. Without that guarantee, the S&Ls could never have played the game, could never have had available the kind of money

Milken needed, could never have been on call twenty-four hours a day to finance hostile takeovers. In fact, none of the power tactics of the Milken group would have been possible without the implicit support of the U.S. taxpayer. It was Milken's ability to tap the collective taxpayers' almost infinite wealth that gave him real muscle.

The compulsory, nonrational restructuring of corporate debt was also a piece of Milken alchemy, made possible by his control over sources of funds, and a lucrative source of income for him. In a nonrational recapitalization, something like this happens. A Milken-friendly buyer, say KKR, buys a corporation, say Storer Broadcasting. The price is almost but not quite irrelevant. And in return for the financing work, the Milken inside group gets warrants for equity in the new, often privately held corporation that takes over the assets of the acquired corporation, as noted above.

However, these warrants will only be profitable if the new corporation is then bought by someone else. In the ordinary course of business, such a possibility is only that—a possibility. If the new entity is well-managed, in a good business, in a good economic climate, and the initial price paid was not excessive, maybe there will be a new buyer who will make the warrants worth something. In the Milken world, of course, it was all very different.

In the Milken world, the new owners could be complete incompetents. The fundamentals of the business could be terrible. The initial price paid could have been a joke of bad judgment. None of that mattered. Because of Milken's unquestioned control over financing sources, they could sell out at a large profit because Milken could always arrange financing for the new buyer at a higher price. With funds provided by other Milken players' stockholders and bondholders, by insurance policyholders, by S&L depositors and the American taxpayer through the federal deposit insurance system, the Milken group could buy out the equity at a price that guaranteed truly fabulous profits to the warrant holders—usually Milken and his pals. It did not signify if the new price was also a joke, and if the bonds issued to finance the new buyout were sure to fail. That was a problem for another day, to be handled on that day, as the stockholders and bondholders of Gillett Holdings (not to be confused with Gillette, the toiletries manufacturer), and others would discover.

The "genius" of a leveraged buyout firm, Kohlberg Kravis Roberts or another, may well have been genuine. But KKR's genius may also partly have been due in part to the ride KKR got on the back of the Milken financing machine. To make certain that his warrants in Storer, or Beatrice, or any number of other entities would be substantial, Milken could make any kind of new buyout fly. It might not fly for long, but if it flew at all, Milken had his stupendous profits out, and that was the bottom line—for him and his friends.

Cutting through the various levels of partnerships, redemptions of preferred, and other occult transfers, the transactions worked roughly like the buying of a piece of real estate for a tiny sliver of equity. For example, if one buys an apartment house for one million dollars with $10,000 down and the rest in debt, that's a risky investment. But if your brother-in-law owns an S&L and your cousin is a builder, the risk disappears. Your brother-in-law buys the building along with your cousin for $2 million, all of it borrowed from the S&L's service corporation subsidiary. The profit is not 100 percent for you, the equity holder. No, it's one hundred times your initial $10,000 down payment (or equity). If the building turns out to be worthless, your gain is still locked in. The federal deposit insurance fund might lose, but you have won, big-time. You might even buy a box of steaks and a freezer for your brother-in-law and your cousin.

This was exactly the way that nonrational recapitalizations for such entities as Storer worked out: Milken and his colleagues raised debt for the purchase of the company. The debt then was put under a very thin slice of equity, which was passed out to Milken, Tom Spiegel, Grassgreen and Mendel, and others. The company would be run for a while, then it would be sold as a whole or in pieces, at least in part, with more funding raised by Milken. The price might be "only," say, 50 percent more than in the original transaction. But if the equity in the first takeover was only 1 percent of capitalization, then the profit on the second, nonrational round would be fifty times the original investment. Hundreds of thousands would quickly become tens of millions. It was nice work.

Then Milken and his colleagues at Drexel could lay claim to smaller items of income—advisory fees, finders' fees, and such trivia. All in all, taking the insider trading profits, the underwriting fees, the "trad-

ing" profits, the "trading" commissions (which were often the same thing), the greenmail payoff participation, the equity profits on LBOs and secondary LBOs, the streams of Milken income became a mighty river, and then an ocean.

By rough calculations, the take from this admittedly very hard work during Milken's twelve or more very, very fat years, would have been as follows:

- About $8 billion from underwriting of new bonds and preferred stock.
- Roughly $12 billion from "trading" a pool of about $200 billion of junk bonds and stock, computed as follows: an average of about $50 billion outstanding each year, allowing for a slow start at the beginning of the term, times a minimum average "trading" profit of about 2 percent, or $1 billion per year times twelve.
- Very approximately, $4 billion in gains on insider trades, pieces of equity, or warrants in deals such as Storer, Beatrice, Triangle, and Wometco, and shares of greenmail profits.

It is just possible that just his take, or that of his department, again, a small staff indeed, would have been something like $24 billion over his dozen big years. This amount was about equal to the profits of every bank, S&L, financial institution of every other kind, securities company, and insurance company in the entire United States for the boom year of 1985.

Milken long ago might have been hired as the go-between, the fixer for heavy hitters like Posner and Lindner and his mentor Riklis. But by the time his financing engine was rolling, by the time the yield-addicted American financial community was moving around Other People's Money by the billions, Milken was the master manipulator. The boy from Encino was not Prom King. He was the king.

CHAPTER NINE

TANGLED WEBS

"Reeling and Writhing, of course, to begin with," the Mock Turtle replied, "and the different branches of Arithmetic—Ambition, Distraction, Uglification, and Derision."

LEWIS CARROLL, 1865

EVEN KINGS HAVE PROBLEMS and Michael Milken's problem was a killer. The entire Milken money machine, the nuclear fusion of finance in the 1980s, was fueled by an outright lie about the correct rate of default of the Milken-issued bonds. On covering up that lie and maintaining the belief in it rested every single iota of power that Milken had.

If the rate of default on his bonds was truly 1 percent per year (or close to it) as his adherents claimed, Milken had indeed repealed gravity. He had truly made a huge breakthrough in finance, enlarging vastly the postwar market for lower-rated bonds and generating healthy new economic growth. But if it was 3 percent or 4 percent or more, the Milken machine would soon run out of fuel and eventually blow up in a huge cloud of smoke. Milken bonds, adjusted for default, except in very circumscribed circumstances, would not be a better investment than Treasury bonds. If his buyers held the proper reserves for default, they would show consistently worse returns than if they had bought investment-grade bonds or Treasuries. Thus, there would be no legitimate reason at all to buy high-risk, low-rated instruments from Beverly Hills as a matter of economics.

While gifts of a box of steaks, private equity in deals, commitment fees, and free trips to Beverly Hills were still very much a part of dealing with Milken, no matter what the true rate of return on his bonds might be, even in the age of Reagan deregulation, no public company or trustee could publicly rationalize buying bonds it had to know were losers. It could not say, "Management has received certain financial and noncash considerations for buying these inferior investments." On the contrary, those in the Milken circle had to pretend that their bond buys were economically sound.

Further, the true rate of default on Milken junk had to be concealed for as long as possible. An analogy would be a drug company that sold a very expensive medicine that, it said, would prolong life for any twenty-year-old who bought it. The medicine was just sugar water with a hint of arsenic and, obviously, data about its true effectiveness would be hard to come by for a number of years. But if information then began to surface showing that the drug's buyers, in fact, had *shorter* lifespans than others, the medicine would no longer sell and the manufacturers would go to jail. To counter that threat, doctors would have to be found to offer studies that "proved" the drug worked. For the company to continue to sell the drug, deaths would have to be covered up, explained away, called something other than death.

In the Milken world, professors of finance would serve the same role.

The truth about the default rate of Milken bonds could have been observed in a variety of ways. Questioners could be referred to the Braddock Hickman book, which was clearly not in agreement with Milken, but rare indeed was the hardy soul who would read it all the way through. Other questioners could be referred to Milken's "research experts," a likely group who produced yield and default data literally at Milken's command, when, as, and how ordered. Others could talk to earlier buyers, who would give anecdotal evidence about how happy they were to have joined the world of the Milken-pods. And, in addition, in the early years of the Milken raj, the rates of default were not large. After all, if a bond issuer is overfunded, if there are still issuers and investors waiting in the wings to put in more money, the early issuers can keep going for quite some time.

But all too soon, the default rates of Milken bonds started to become worrisome, even within the Milken universe. By 1983, defaults were climbing into the hundreds of millions of dollars, and by the mid-1980s they were in the billions.

True, many of the defaults were obscured and concealed by calling them "exchanges." In these transactions, the holders of interest-earning instruments were given non-interest-bearing "stock" or "convertible zero-coupon bonds" or "payment-in-kind" bonds, which, in fact, did not yield cash payments. And to the buyers interested in bonds for their cash yield—such as insurance companies, savings and loans, or pension plans—these exchanges might as well have been defaults. After all, if insurers needed cash payments every quarter or every half-year to meet policyholder liabilities, what good did non-interest-bearing stock or payment-in-kind bonds do them?

With these defaults and default equivalents piling up, the Milken gravy train could have been derailed as early as 1985, by which time it was evident that his junk was a distinctly questionable investment. But at exactly this point, by lucky coincidence, to the rescue came Edward Altman of New York University's Business School, now called the Stern School of Management. Altman, born in 1941, had studied at the City College of New York, and then at the Business School at the University of California at Los Angeles, before he joined the faculty of NYU. There he was considered knowledgeable in the field of bankruptcies and distressed bond issuers.

In about 1984, Altman was hired by Morgan Stanley to do some research on the default rates of junk bonds. The reason, presumably, was to help Morgan Stanley get into the field of issuance of below-investment-grade bonds. Morgan Stanley, like many another investment banker, had looked on with hungry heart as Drexel had one gigantic year after another in the field of junk issuance. Morgan Stanley wanted its piece of the pie.

Apparently, the people at Morgan Stanley had not studied the field sufficiently to realize that Drexel had acquired its gray-chip clientele much the same way that they had acquired their blue-chip clientele—through ancient ties of shared interests. By doing research in junk yields and defaults, Morgan Stanley presumably thought it could show that it had expertise in the field and start selling lots of original-

issue junk, little realizing, once again, that the Milken franchise was hardly based upon research, but upon years of mutual backscratching in the back alleys of finance.

Edward Altman performed Morgan Stanley's research. Like many another academic, he had, over time, been a consultant and had written reports on many subjects for such employers as Equitable Life Assurance, that Milken crony of long standing, and Chemical Bank.

Altman dutifully performed his research on the junk bond species and then conducted seminars over a period of three years for Morgan Stanley and its clients about the "real" rates of default and yield on original-issue and other junk. He came, as Martin Luther King, Jr., might have said, as a joyous daybreak for the Drexel world.

Altman's research work was filled with tables and charts and formulas, and had a plausible quality about it that was impressive not just to the layman, but to the investment professional. He claimed his research proved that junk bonds were a good investment for fiduciaries. In fact, however, his research was spectacularly misleading.

Altman used a variety of techniques to give the impression that junk was not junk. But three, in particular, were extremely simple and seductive. His first and most questionable method was to compare defaults in any one year with the entire existing universe of junk bonds. At times he even used a comparison of junk defaults with the universe of *all* bonds of every kind. That is, Altman took the number and face value of junk bonds that had defaulted in a given year, say 1986. He then used that as the numerator while the denominator was the total amount of junk in existence as of 1986. That technique gave him extremely low rates of default, ranging around 1 percent to 1.5 percent in most years, with very rare spikes up to about 3.4 percent.

Using this method, Altman "found" that the "average default rate" on junk from 1978 to 1986 was slightly less than 1.5 percent per year, well within the limits needed to sell Milken's junk. Essentially, however, he was comparing one number with an irrelevant other number. The junk universe had been growing so rapidly, thanks to Milken and his circle, in the period from 1978 to 1986 (from about $9 billion in 1978 to about $95 billion in 1986) that any comparison of it with defaults in any one year was meaningless.

That is, if one assumes that junk almost never defaults immediately because it takes a while before overfunding and its other props are used up, and that therefore it tends (in general) to default only after several years of life, the defaults of a year in which there were only a few issues in amount (and in face value) cannot be usefully compared with the whole junk universe when that universe is vastly larger than it was when the defaulting junk was issued. The buyer of the junk that defaulted would have bought it in the earlier year, and for him the meaningful default rate could only be found in a comparison to the numbers of issues in that year, which Altman generally ignored.

For example, if one bought all of the junk issued in 1978 and then held it until, say, 1986, and if 100 percent of all the junk one bought in 1978 defaulted, that might seem to the investor like a catastrophic loss and a good lesson about junk investments. The default rate would rightly be counted as 100 percent for such an investor. But in 1978, there was only a total of about $1.4 billion of original-issue nonconvertible straight junk debt. By 1986, the total universe of junk outstanding was about $92 billion. The default of 100 percent of that $1.4 billion of 1978 issuance would mean a default rate (by Altman's method) of barely more than 1.5 percent in 1986.

In a sense, the method Altman used would be like attempting to find the mortality rate of a group of Americans born in 1900 by comparing their death rates in 1992 with the total American population in 1992. Obviously, even if all of the people born in 1900 still living at the beginning of 1992 died by December 31 of that year, their mortality rate would not even come close to 1 percent of the total population of the United States. Thus by Altman's methods, a ninety-two-year-old American would have only a less than 1 percent risk of "default" in the year 1992.

A second misleading aspect of Altman's calculations was that they did not include exchanges of interest-bearing bonds for new, often non-interest-bearing securities as defaults, or as anything at all. Such exchanges were simply counted as continuing issues or, at least, not taken into account as defaults. But an investor who thought he had a bond paying 14 percent and then got a letter from Drexel saying that instead of his bond he now had a new stock paying zero might take a view different from Altman's. Certainly, an S&L or an insurer who

thought it had an interest-bearing instrument that would defray the costs of deposits or the liabilities to policyholders could not legitimately count that exchange as anything other than a default, against which a reserve from other sources had to be taken. If one added in such exchanges—even if there were no defaults of the newly made security—the average default rate of junk bonds would be raised considerably.

The third major defect in the Altman studies was the method he used to account for the residual value of a junk bond upon default. It is true, as Altman said it was, that a bond rarely goes to zero upon default. It usually has some value as a claim against assets or in some other way. But just what is the residual value of a junk bond upon default? That arcane question has a heavy weight in the investment world. If a buyer of Drexel junk can expect that a portion of it will go into default but will still be worth forty cents on the dollar, that means something. If the bond will be worth only ten cents on the dollar in default, that is something else.

Data existed from Braddock Hickman on the residual value of "fallen angels," bonds that were originally investment grade and that then defaulted. These data showed that fallen angels averaged very roughly forty cents on the dollar in residual value upon default, or did so in the period of the Hickman study. Some further study of bond defaults in the period from 1945 to 1986 showed that more recent default residual values for all grades of bonds studied were about thirty-five cents on the dollar.

However, there was no published study at all, literally none, about the default residual value of original-issue Milken-era junk. Despite that gigantic lacuna, Altman simply assumed for his calculations that this residual value was the same as that of a mixture of fallen angels and other original-issue junk. That was quite a leap.

It was possible that the residual upon default of a Milken junk bond was the same as that, say, of a New Haven Railroad bond, just as it is possible that there is still an underwater city of Atlantis. But common sense would seem to indicate that the bonds of an investment-grade issuer, often secured with assets of considerable value, are worth more upon default than the defaulted bonds of a Milken-era borrower, often secured with little more than a promise.

In a smaller yet equally misleading device, Altman took only a sampling of junk bonds and extrapolated from them to all other junk bonds. That is, in a number of studies, he cited what he described as price and yield data from a "large" quantum of sub-investment-grade debt. The standard bond buyer might well have assumed that these data were an indication of junk bond performance generally. And he might think that for a good reason. Investment-grade and Treasury bonds tend to move in sequence, and data about them are comparable to data about a commodity like wheat or oil. If you know how fifty (or even ten) investment-grade bonds are doing you can divine the precise movement of the market and its performance. In turn this movement is almost always a function of interest rates.

But junk bonds are called junk for a reason. Whether their prices are fixed or unfixed, they tend to move erratically, and not necessarily in sync with other junk bonds. They are much more like a class of particularly unruly students than a military marching band: Some may be secret geniuses and stars and some may be drop outs. Data about even a fairly large sample are helpful, but not necessarily predictive of the results from any one or a dozen issues. Thus, the reader of Altman studies, unless he was already well-versed in the lore of junk, would have no clear guidance about any purchases he might make from such small samples. As a further problem, obviously, if the prices of Drexel junk were fixed, as they in fact were, the movement of one group of bonds would show absolutely nothing about the real value of either the bonds in the group "studied" or any other bonds.

In a closely related issue, Altman's sample was, in most instances, composed of both Drexel-era original-issue junk and "fallen angels." He lumped their performance together, but it was not clear that the two groups performed similarly, or if similarly, how wide the variations were between the two groups in general.

Another unsettling aspect of Altman's study, however, which underlay all other problems with his work, was that it relied largely on Drexel data for prices and yields. But the bonds were traded only, or almost exclusively, at Drexel. There were no publicly known prices. There were hypothetical or "matrix" prices, but these too were fancily described fictitious prices. Or rather, the prices might be real or

they might not be. No one but Milken knew, and there was no incentive at all for him to be truthful.

That is, Altman was basically making a comparison between high-grade corporates, for which there were internationally known prices, and junk bonds with fictitious prices. Obviously, to prove anything meaningful about a security for which you do not know the exact real price, yield, or default rates is impossible. And comparing such "prices" with the prices of real investment goods is even more questionable, to put it mildly.

In any event, the Altman studies came out in drops and then in streams and then in mighty rivers, eventually to become the primary "scientific" props under the Milken world. In the space of six years, Altman's amazing seventeen research papers and four books touting junk bonds were invaluable tools for the Milken strategy. With Altman's studies (and those of an active colleague, Glenn Yago of the State University of New York at Stonybrook) at hand, Milken could bamboozle many suspicious bond buyers or regulators. And Altman himself, with his highly plausible net of facts and figures, charts, complex-seeming formulas, with his seemingly impeccable credentials, including an endowed chair, honors from financial analysts' societies in Japan, France, Italy, and the United States, and with his diffident, folksy demeanor was the perfect Milken tool, unwitting or not.

The Alliance for Capital Access, the organization vigorously lobbying to allow S&Ls to acquire Milken junk, used the Altman studies brilliantly. In fact, the Altman studies were relied upon so heavily by the federal government that when the General Accounting Office, once considered the "watchdog agency of Congress," lately a sad, craven lapdog of lobbyists, issued its notorious 1988 study recommending ever more junk for America's S&Ls, it cited Altman's work over and over again.

Two years earlier, in 1986, an internal memo within Drexel had noted that the rates of default on Milken-issued junk were getting to be dangerously high. Some whispers about this problem reached the outside world, despite an explicit warning to readers of the memo to keep it highly secret within Drexel and even within the junk department. It is entirely possible, therefore, that the torrent of Altman

He noted, however, that even so, by his calculations, junk was a superior investment. But this later study was little noticed or publicized, except for its conclusions, by the Drexel army or by Altman himself.

Much academic attention was focused on studies about how the hostile takeover or the leveraged buyout affected American industry. There were also studies of how junk itself affected American industry. Many purported to show how helpful Drexel junk-funded takeovers were for America, and these studies, too, proved valuable as selling tools in the Milken world and contained an astounding amount of nonsense in many cases on the pro-LBO side.

But the most important question of the Drexel/Milken age, whether junk issues were really a decent investment, was hardly studied at all, except by Altman and by Blume and Keim. They were the physicians, very possibly sincere, who said that there was no danger from the narcotic of finance, Milken-Drexel junk, and no one bothered to look past their words and their charts to the truth. Had their studies been accurate and meticulously researched, had they pointed out the real story of junk defaults and why that made junk a poor investment indeed, especially without huge reserves, the Milken world just might have crumbled years before it did.

CHAPTER TEN

SMILING FACES

Print is the sharpest and strongest weapon of our party.

JOSEF STALIN, 1923

"SUCCESS," said John F. Kennedy, paraphrasing many another sage, "has a thousand fathers. Failure is an orphan." By the same token, making big money, tens of billions, overnight, with very little effort, has a multitude of friends. And Michael Milken in his heyday had an army of friends and admirers to protect him and keep him functioning.

There were, first and foremost, his pals from childhood who had been rescued from obscurity by Milken's stellar scam. His best friend in the whole world, Harry Horowitz, who had been made rich by Milken, toiled at the Beverly Hills office and handled Milken's donations to charity. Lorraine Spurge, a tough-talking former telephone operator whom Milken also enriched, would in all probability have laid down her life for him. Richard Sandler, a friend from boyhood who became Milken's lawyer, was ferociously loyal and tireless in the Milken cause.

Everyone in Drexel's junk bond department loved Milken at some level. True, there was grumbling at the long hours and strict discipline. True, there was envy and competitiveness. But every man and woman at the southwest corner of Rodeo and Wilshire knew that he or she was making more money than they had ever dreamed possible.

137

They all knew that, often with much less in the way of academic qualifications and actual experience, they were making much more than their counterparts at other firms. They loved Milken for it.

After all, they were not esthetes or intellectuals or spiritual beings. The men and women who worked at Milken's shop had long ago turned wholeheartedly to the Golden Calf. Small wonder that these worshipers of Mammon would consider Milken the One True Savior. Very small wonder that few would even consider turning against him, or spilling the beans about how his shop operated. They believed in him and in what he stood for almost as a matter of religious practice and he rewarded their faith. There was never a Judas within the "high-yield" department because any potential whistle-blower knew that Milken would come up with hundreds, thousands, millions of pieces of silver to top any paltry twenty-nine pieces from a prosecutor or journalist.

Then there were the Milken raiders and business moguls whom he had raised from penny-ante operators to the ranks of the richest men in the world. Former small-time salesmen who had achieved some success and then were catapulted into money superstardom by Milken, these also were his friends. His mentors and teachers and early pals, Riklis and Posner and Lindner and Steinberg, who had gotten even richer because of Milken's energy and effort, were also his devoted fans, some more so than others.

The legions of lawyers and accountants to whom he gave employment also rallied to Milken's cause. Just filing the SEC documents for his junk issues kept thousands of lawyers and accountants and their staffs busy around the clock. Vast law firms such as Cahill Gordon, Skadden, Arps, and Latham & Watkins were booming on a scale hitherto undreamed of, papering his deals, preparing merger and acquisition documents, answering shareholder lawsuits, forming the legal phalanx within which the genius could toil unhindered.

The accountants of America might well have erected great pyramids and obelisks to Milken. Every junk offering, every preferred stock, every exchange, every hostile takeover, every management LBO needed accountants as well as lawyers. At Touche Ross, at Arthur Andersen, at every Big Eight, then Big Six accounting firm, there was work to be done. Profit and loss statements, flows of funds, balance sheets, pro formas, appraisals, valuations of future prospects —all had to be produced, usually in a hurry. Often there was so much money riding on a Milken deal that hardly anyone even bothered to look at the accounting bill. For some accountants, those plastic surgeons of finance whose duplicitous job is often not to save the patient but to make him look good, the Milken boom in financings, mergers, and acquisitions was heaven-sent.

But even beyond the serried ranks of those whom Milken enriched or gave employment or both, there were other friends. "Intellectuals," who got only a $15,000 speaking fee here or a $10,000 consultancy there, nevertheless rallied to the Milken camp. Former friends of the self-educated economist class picked up the scent of money coming off Milken and made tracks to be at his disposal.

The editorial page of *The Wall Street Journal,* fresh from its triumphs in helping America endure supply-side economics, jumped into Milken's waiting arms. No slight to Milken was too trivial, no cause of his too questionable for the *Journal*'s editorial page not to take up the cudgels in his defense. Milken's publicists, first the likable Steve Anreder at Drexel, later the aggressive firm of Robinson, Lake, Lerer & Montgomery, had smooth, unfettered access to any editorial-page editor at any time. Editorial writers and columnists at the *Journal* were frequent, welcome guests at the tables of the Milken team. No question about Milken's scam could ever be raised, and no query about how the whole process made any economic sense could ever be mentioned by the staff of the editorial page of the premier financial newspaper in America.

At *The New York Times,* Milken also had friends, in part nurtured by the tireless Robinson, Lake, Lerer & Montgomery. Kurt Eichenwald, the primary reporter on financial subjects, was a frequent source of pro-Milken, pro-junk articles, especially after Milken started to get into legal trouble. At the *Los Angeles Times,* which always looked for the good in everything about Los Angeles anyway, there was rarely a critical word about Milken or his works.

The means by which the Milken/Lerer axis asserted its power was fascinatingly simple and revealing. According to a financial reporter from the *Los Angeles Times,* the Lerer people were always available with juicy comments and "inside" quotes. They were generous with praise and good cheer for a pro-Milken story, but they were on the phone with severe criticism when any story appeared that made Milken look bad, no matter how factual. Such tactics eventually took their toll, since there was no Milken critic on the other side.

Likewise, the Milken team would provide data and would ask in return to be allowed to at least comment on the copy before it appeared—a request frequently granted by reporters even for major newspapers. This process eventually produced an unwholesome relationship, to put it mildly, without money ever changing hands.

Then there were still more business school professors, more economists in small and large foundations, more people with their hands out, ready to enter the lists for Milken and his junk, to preach it round or preach it flat. Many of these people, like the staffers on *The Wall Street Journal* editorial page, were perhaps genuinely convinced that Milken was right, and that he had in fact created a breakthrough financing vehicle. But they, like everyone else, followed fads and/or fees. Papers poured out of the Milken academic machine to "prove" that the economic renaissance of the 1980s (as it was then thought to be) was created mainly by Drexel junk. Statistics were used to show how Drexel had created hundreds of thousands, then millions of jobs. The figures were completely made up, as a Drexel spokesman later said, but America is the West, and the truth rarely catches up with a lie in the West.

Still more papers and more advertisements talked about Drexel's invaluable help to individual states, especially California. Other studies claimed that Drexel was responsible for an increase in worker productivity through the 1980s. The statistics from California were comically insubstantial. The productivity increases never happened at all (except as parts of normal economic cycles within much longer-term, extremely depressing productivity trends that could not be blamed on Milken).

Academic and charitable honors rained down on Milken. He was cheered at Harvard Business School, where until 1988 no voice from the corporate finance department ever inquired about real rates of default or how one man from Encino might have disproved the entire theory and experience of financial markets. Senators and representatives came to his conferences and praised his name. Powerful universities like UCLA were at his doorstep asking for money for buildings and schools that were to be named in his honor. Amazingly, even after Milken was indicted *and had pleaded guilty,* he was still being sought out by charitable foundations and departments within UCLA for funds, and still being offered his name on large buildings at the Westwood campus. This phenomenon—get the money and everything else is just a detail, especially law and ethics—was at the heart of the Milken mystique.

Then there were Milken's foundations—incredibly trivial in size compared with his wealth—which gave out contributions and attempted to make him look like a large-scale philanthropist, even though the actual gifts were comically small until he was indicted. At a point approximating his sentencing, the Milken public relations machine issued releases claiming that he had made charitable donations of more than $300 million. According to the data from the state of California, that was a spectacular exaggeration. Milken's gifts, in fact, would more likely have been in the range of $50 million.

That was by no means a small amount. Still, when compared with his wealth, which could not have been much less than in the billions, even after all of his fines and settlements, it equaled only a few percent or less—hardly lavish charity. Further, because Milken also used at least one of his foundations, which he called The Capital Foundation, to park stock and avoid the payment of tax, some measure of making up for that abuse might have encouraged him to go over the few percent mark in his contributions.

All of this—the journalists, the academics, the legislators, the publicists, the advertising campaigns, the honors, the image as philanthropist—was in the service of sustaining the myth of Drexel/ Milkenism. Everything, every lie and puff and phony statistic was to preserve for as long as possible the basic untruths of the junk bond scam:

- That junk bonds were a superior investment, compared with other investments.
- That this was so because of the high interest and relatively low default rates of Milken bonds.

- That Drexel/Milken junk was a good investment for fiduciary organs such as S&Ls, insurance companies, and pension funds.
- That Milken had defeated market theory and found a way for lenders to get something for nothing.
- That only Milken could perform that miracle, or at least that he could do it best.

Nor did this apparatus exist only to provide sanction and blessing for Milken and his works. It also existed to smite those who dared even to question the Milken mystique.

When Connie Bruck wrote her book, *The Predators' Ball,* in 1986, 1987, and 1988, and published it in 1988, the Milken apparatus struck back. Although Bruck had done meticulously detailed and insightful work, and although her conclusions about Milken were extremely restrained, attempts were made to have the book stopped, delayed, or bought out from under her. When neither she nor her publisher yielded, malicious, false rumors were spread about her personal life. In 1991, when James Stewart of *The Wall Street Journal*'s page-one staff published his attack on Milken and other criminals of Wall Street, the Milken goons again struck back. Their attack was not on his work or its accuracy, except in tiny measure. It was a fanciful attack on Stewart's fictitious personal attitudes and prejudices. In both cases, little attempt was made to answer the questions that had been raised or to discuss the basic ethical issues under investigation.

The point was that no criticism of any kind was to be allowed. If it had been, if there had been serious querying of just what a Milken junk bond was, what the real track record of such bonds was, what their underlying economic and financial rationale was, and what kind of people Milken's peers and mentors were, the whole ethos of the junk bond would have begun to unravel. And, amazingly, even after it had unraveled and Milken was in jail, there was still a phalanx of the faithful standing guard over their fallen hero. Say this for the Milken praetorian guard: They are not defeatists.

CHAPTER ELEVEN

TRUTH FOR SALE

Better mendacities than the classics in paraphrase.

EZRA POUND, 1920

ONE OF THE MOST unexpected allies of Drexel/Milkenism came under the general category of a guard who had become extremely confused about what his job was, or whom he was supposed to guard against.

The bond-rating house of Duff & Phelps was founded at the nadir of the Great Depression in 1932. Its purpose then, as for many decades thereafter, was to value the debt issues of utility companies. One of the many abuses of investors in the 1920s and before had been the creation of vast utility holding companies. When new federal legislation required that they be broken up, it became clear that some of the surviving companies were sound and others were shells. Duff & Phelps sought to use its expertise to cut through the layers of confusion and corporate secrecy to show investors what was valuable and what was not, or what was real and what was not.

Operating at a size far below Moody's or Standard & Poor's, but still well regarded in its niche, Duff & Phelps grew steadily. By the early 1980s, it had begun to acquire various money-management and research entities in the Midwest and to enlarge its scope of operations. It was so well regarded that a large California bank, Security Pacific, sought to buy the company in 1984, largely for its highly prized team of credit analysts.

Security Pacific, however, was a member of the Federal Reserve System and needed Fed approval for the transaction. Moreover, Duff & Phelps had been recognized by the Securities and Exchange Commission as one of a tiny band of credit raters whose word it would take in assessing the value of stocks and bonds in broker-dealer inventories, a not-trivial honor. Others in the select fraternity were Standard & Poor's, Moody's, Fitch, and more recently, McCarthy, Crisanti & Maffei.

The Fed therefore paid some attention to the deal and said that it could not go through as planned. The Fed asserted that it would be extremely "unwise" to allow the precedent of a major lender, with a clear interest in the credit ratings of its borrowers, to control a company that rated the creditworthiness of such borrowers. There was an inescapable conflict of interest, said the Fed.

After that deal soured, Duff & Phelps was bought by its own employee stock ownership plan. The company continued to flourish, adding various advisory services as it went along. Its investment-research division, it noted in an SEC filing, was particularly prized because "Duff & Phelps Investment Research provides 'pure independent research' in that it is not engaged in the business of selling the securities of the companies its research covers." Its investment-management division was strong because its "fixed-income investment philosophy concentrates on identification of fundamental value and avoidance of credit risk." Duff & Phelps noted that it also, as of the late 1980s, started to work in the field of "fairness opinions" in connection with mergers and acquisitions, which it described as its area of greatest growth.

In 1988, with the good help of Morgan Stanley, the management of Duff & Phelps looked for new suitors. No suitable third parties were found, so management itself shouldered the task of buying the company away from its own ESOP. To help with this chore, Merrill Lynch put management together with the energetic leveraged buyout firm of Freeman, Spogli in Los Angeles, formerly known as Riordan, Freeman, Spogli. Richard Riordan was a noted lawyer and an apologist for Michael Milken. Ronald Spogli and Brad Freeman were former investment bankers. There was obvious enticement in the deal for everyone.

The year before, in 1987, Duff & Phelps and a border state regional brokerage firm had hit upon the idea of putting out a closed-end mutual fund in utilities, using Duff & Phelps's prized name as the come-on. The fund, Duff & Phelps Selected Utilities, was nothing less than a smashing success. Merrill Lynch, the underwriter, sold about $1.2 billion of common shares, and soon thereafter another $500 million or so of a large-denomination preferred. The public leaped at the chance to buy a utilities fund run by that master of pure, unbiased research into utilities, Duff & Phelps.

The investment-advisory income of Duff & Phelps shot skyward as it took in the fees for managing Selected Utilities. The prospects for more such funds also existed in other areas in which Duff & Phelps had expertise and the respect of investors. What had been a small credit-rating firm showed every prospect of becoming a heavy-duty fee generator.

Freeman, Spogli, flush with profits from a number of LBOs in the grocery and electronics areas, often arranged and financed and co-owned with Drexel Burnham Lambert, saw another winner.

Funding for the LBO of Duff & Phelps by its own management would hardly be a problem. Merrill Lynch and the other underwriters of Duff & Phelps Selected Utilities had taken in close to $85 million in fees on that mutual fund. They liked Duff & Phelps, wanted to see it do more such deals, and probably wanted it to have a hungry, post-LBO frame of mind.

Considering that Duff & Phelps had earned $997,000 in 1988, by far its best year in recent memory, and that managers would be paying off over $116 million of debt in the deal with Freeman, Spogli, it was obvious that junk bonds would have to finance the LBO. At the time, Duff & Phelps was heavily engaged in covering the junk market, was familiar with it, and knew the dangers as well as the rewards of the junk life. But, as distinct from Moody's or S&P, the company had often taken a fairly sanguine approach to junk. Duff & Phelps liked to tell potential clients that it had, in fact, gotten its start in utility junk, and that, in evaluating a company's junk bonds, it looked more at a company's prospects than its earnings. This approach, so refreshingly similar to the presentations Michael Milken was making, apparently impressed Duff & Phelps executives with their own prospects

145

for paying off a debt that would approximately quintuple their yearly debt-service costs.

The deal, then, was set by November of 1988. Roughly 70 percent of the equity in the transaction, around $30 million, would be contributed by a Freeman, Spogli LBO partnership and the balance by executives of Duff & Phelps. These gentlemen would be able to borrow half of their contributions. Some of the rest might have to come from the seven-figure bonuses and payments they were giving themselves to buy the firm away from its lower-ranking employees and turn it over to its higher-ranking ones.

The debt would be raised from banks (about $51 million) and from a true piece of art of the late 1980s, a $65 million issue of senior subordinated notes payable in kind—that is, in other notes—for three years, and then payable in cash if not called or bought back in disguised call. The debt was to be sold partly into the open market and partly to certain regular buyers of junk. The deal was done, and a new Duff & Phelps was born.

The employees of the reborn company worked very hard and started to pay down its bank lines and to increase cash flow. The company got more vigorously into junk bond research and aggressively advertised its services in what it described as "this highly visible market." In fact, Duff & Phelps apparently believed so strongly in the future of junk that in late February 1990, moments before Drexel, under that name, became history, Duff & Phelps brought to market an instrument, known as a collateralized bond obligation, backed by about $300 million of mostly Drexel junk. The most secure tranches (*tranche* is French for trench or gutter) were taken by institutional players, while the equity was taken by Duff & Phelps itself along with certain partners. The investment was a disaster, with Duff & Phelps losing all its equity in the deal within months.

There were, however, a few other major problems with the new, lively Duff & Phelps, the swinging bond-rating house. For one thing, the company was majority owned by Freeman Spogli Equity Partners II. This was disclosed in many different documents. What was not disclosed was that some of the partners in the FS Equity Partners II fund were the very utility companies, and their pension funds and their ESOPs that Duff & Phelps had been rating for almost fifty years.

Still other major participants were industrial companies and their pension funds and ESOPs that had been rated by Duff & Phelps for decades.

In every meaningful sense, Duff & Phelps, the pure, unbiased rater of bonds, was largely owned by the very corporations whose credit it rated. By the same token, it was also owned, in a meaningful way, by the firms whose securities it endorsed by buying them for its management clients, including the owners of shares in Duff & Phelps Selected Utilities.

Other credit-rating companies and their parents, such as McGraw-Hill, have stock outstanding. Surely some of McGraw-Hill's stock is owned by corporate pension funds or corporations. The difference was that the utilities and industrial companies rated by Duff & Phelps hadn't bought their Duff & Phelps stock anonymously in the open market. They were part of a tiny group of Freeman, Spogli investors who were shopped the deal, and who through Freeman, Spogli were specifically picked for it. The credit raters themselves solicited as investors the people they rated.

In 1984, the Fed had said that ownership of a major credit-rating company by a firm in the business of lending would be an unallowable conflict of interest. That was why it had nixed the deal between Duff & Phelps and Security Pacific. But if that was a conflict of interest, what about Duff & Phelps's being owned by the firms it rated?

In particular, there was a Drexel-related conflict of interest that was about the size of a continent. Not only were the very companies rated by Duff & Phelps part of a small group of partners who owned the company, but also among the owners through FS Equity Partners II was James Dahl. Dahl was a $40-million-a-year right-hand man of Michael Milken at the Beverly Hills office of Drexel. That is, a principal player at Drexel was (and still is) personally an owner of the Duff & Phelps bond-rating house—which was (and still is) actively rating Drexel issues.

Another owner was Imperial Corporation of America, the parent of the defunct Imperial S&L of San Diego. Imperial, another Drexel player, was run into the ground largely by its ownership of Drexel bonds and saved for a while by the machinations of other Drexel players. But by far the most interesting owner of Duff &

147

Phelps through FS Equity Partners II was something called Liberty Service Corporation, a wholly owned subsidiary of none other than Columbia Savings & Loan. And Liberty Service was used mostly to buy assets that the parent was forbidden to own for a variety of reasons, usually having to do with credit quality.

Thus, Duff & Phelps, the old-line bond house, forged in the fire of the Great Depression, proud boaster of its unique expertise in valuing junk credits, tireless booster of junk as an asset class, turned out to be owned in large part by kingpins of the Drexel empire. It was as if the judge in a murder case was in secret a blood cousin of the defendant.

The Columbia S&L tie was particularly astonishing because in early 1990, as Columbia was desperately clinging to life, violently thrashing to avoid seizure by federal regulators, it hit upon a stratagem. Its management, including Tom Spiegel, put together a collateralized bond obligation, basically a bundle of bonds with a face value exceeding the stated value of the bonds in the portfolio. This CBO was then examined by—guess who—Duff & Phelps, which gave it an investment-grade rating. In a complex series of transactions, that CBO was then sold to Far Eastern buyers with only 10 percent down, and the note that Columbia took back was also given an investment-grade rating by Duff & Phelps.

In the busy world of S&Ls and federal regulation, that investment-grade rating was life-or-death stuff. It meant that Columbia had an investment-grade asset against which far smaller reserves and capital had to be held than if it was straight junk. To Columbia, desperately short on capital, it was a chance to stay alive a little longer, take in more deposits, buy more junk—and put the taxpayers on the hook for ever more money when it eventually failed.

To reduce the rating transaction to its essence, Duff & Phelps was —at all times without disclosing the conflict—giving a high rating to an extremely dicey class of security, which was owned by one of its owners. It was akin to the son who appraises the value of his dad's vacant land before selling it to a third party who doesn't know much about land. The third party in this case was the federal taxpayer. When the transaction was written about in *Barron's*, it fell apart and Columbia was seized days later. But this was not the end of the question marks surrounding Duff & Phelps.

Apart from the Duff & Phelps buyout, Freeman, Spogli had done a number of other successful LBOs and their partner in several of these deals was Michael Milken personally. In Tops Markets, done about mid-March 1988, P&C Foods, done in 1985, and Webcraft, done in 1986, Milken took substantial equity in the deals through his colorfully named partnerships.

Usually there was no more than a handful of equity partners in Freeman, Spogli deals. That meant that they were intimately connected in ownership. Indeed, Drexel employees sat as directors of many Freeman, Spogli LBO companies, which was, in fact, disclosed in the prospectuses for junk and other securities sales for those individual companies. What was not disclosed was that Michael Milken in particular was the main Drexel employee who was in partnership with Freeman, Spogli. Far more disturbing, in no filed document related to the bond-rating firm of Duff & Phelps was it disclosed or even hinted that Freeman, Spogli, the primary owner of the bond-rating house, was a major partner in many deals with Michael Milken, effective head of Drexel Burnham Lambert.

Stripped to the essentials, Duff & Phelps was owned largely by the people it rated and by players in a gigantic junk bond organization, owned largely by persons in a partnership with a master fraudulent-bond magician. That would have been of no consequence if Duff & Phelps were rating lawnmowers. But it was in the bond-rating business, holding itself out as an unbiased observer.

Perhaps the top figures at Freeman, Spogli and the high officers of Duff & Phelps did not set out to deliver to Drexel a captive bond-rating firm. But something like that happened. Duff & Phelps, self-described as high on junk bonds, was touting them as an investment class, especially in desperate cases such as Columbia's, while being secretly owned in large part by Drexel players and partners of Milken himself. The power of Drexel to pull off something like that was impressive. The complaisance of the executives of Duff & Phelps was equally depressing.

The timing of Duff & Phelps's climb aboard the junk bond bandwagon was noteworthy as well. The Justice Department announced that Drexel was to be indicted in February of 1988. The financing of the Duff & Phelps LBO, with James Dahl, Columbia, and Imperial participating, did not take place until one year later. The Duff &

Phelps collateralized bond obligation deal, done explicitly with and for Drexel, with Drexel an equity partner, was done after Drexel had pleaded guilty, after Milken had been indicted on ninety-eight felony counts, days before he pleaded guilty. And the CBO deal, by the way, featured Duff & Phelps explicitly calling up the very firms it was rating and asking them to invest with Duff & Phelps in the deal.

It would be easy to say that while Duff & Phelps's behavior was questionable, at least investors could have relied on the two main rating houses, Moody's and Standard & Poor's, considered the stolid watchdogs of finance, the incorruptible raters of bonds. It would be easy but it would be wrong.

To be sure, Moody's and S&P had carefully and soundly evaluated bonds all through the 1980s and before. As far as is known, they did not make a practice of treating junk bonds, with their lower ratios of income to debt payments ability and other lower credit indicia, as if they were other than low-rated bonds, at least directly. But in an indirect way, Moody's and Standard & Poor's simply missed an obvious truth about the junk world and in so doing allowed Drexel and Milken to keep operating when they should have been restrained.

Starting in the late 1980s, Moody's and Standard & Poor's began to issue ratings of claims-paying ability of insurance companies. This field had been the more-or-less-private preserve of a small, private company known as A. M. Best. It was seen to be a lucrative business, and Moody's and S&P believed that they had a profit opportunity in entering the same field.

Duff & Phelps had also long rated insurers and had and continues to have a fine record in the field. But A. M. Best completely missed the truth about the financial condition of a number of large insurers that defaulted due to the proliferation in their portfolios of Milken junk, especially First Executive's subsidiaries, Mutual Benefit, and to a lesser extent, First Capital. But far more disturbing was that S&P also missed the boat, as Moody's stood on the dock right beside it. After all, S&P and Moody's had the nation's most complete files on bond defaults and exchanges. If any entities in the world besides Drexel should have known just what the record was for junk bonds, it should have been S&P and Moody's.

They also knew—or should have known—which of those bonds

was in each insurer's portfolio and in exactly what amounts. This data was not secret, but is kept in reports to state regulators. Moody's and S&P were in a position to know just what the real rates of loss on the bonds in the Drexel insurers' portfolios were, and just how severely that would affect their claims-paying ability. Before anyone else outside the Drexel world, the two rating giants should have been able to warn policyholders, annuitants, buyers of GICs, and everyone doing business with the Drexel world that the real rates of default and loss of interest on exchange were far higher than what Drexel claimed. They should have been able to warn that those losses were also far, far higher than would have been provided for by loss reserves or capital at the insurers in question.

Despite that knowledge, or what would have been easy for the rating houses to extract as knowledge, the public never learned until the very last moment—when they were warned about it in *Barron's* —just how shaky First Executive and the other Drexel insurers were. To the end of its days, until literally the last moments of its life, First Executive boasted that it was sound. The watchdogs of S&P and Moody's should have smelled a fake. They didn't.

CHAPTER TWELVE

SED QUIS CUSTODIET IPSOS CUSTODES?

Government is a trust, and the officers of government are trustees; and both the trustees and the government are created for the benefit of the people.

HENRY CLAY, 1829

MUCH OF WHAT WENT WRONG in the Milken raj might be attributed to the answer to a question asked by Juvenal the Satirist: *Sed quis custodiet ipsos custodes?* It translates roughly as, "But who will guard the guards themselves?"

Throughout the Milken regime, the Securities and Exchange Commission, charged with keeping the securities markets open, honest, and above all, free of fraud, utterly failed to do its job. It was a flat failure with no equivocation. Although a damning mountain of research about Drexel was accumulated by SEC staff attorney John Hewitt as early as the beginning of the 1980s, and said mountain showed convincingly that Milken was engaged in stupendous price fixing and bond-price rigging within his empire, the SEC took no action against him. Despite the additional fact that there was clear-cut—or at least impressive—evidence at the New York Stock Exchange that a Milken partnership, Otter Creek, was trading illegally on inside information, and that Milken had once controlled a Chicago partnership also actively trading on inside information, the SEC took no action at all.

How could this have happened? How could the largest securities fraud of all time have been committed without the SEC getting involved at an early stage?

The answer was part ideology. The Reagan-era SEC was programmed to let the financial markets function without "interference." The wicked slogan of the Reagan campaign was "government is the enemy," which, as Michael Thomas sagely pointed out, many in the business world soon interpreted to mean "law is the enemy." The Reagan appointees at the SEC were convinced that some kind of magical purifying waters would heal whatever was wrong at the nation's marketplaces of finance if they only stood back.

Alas, that conviction showed a stunning misunderstanding of capitalism and business. There is no one more ignorant of the real workings of business than a probusiness academic or a bureaucrat. And as anyone who has ever earned a living in business would have known, when the cops stay home and watch TV, the criminals go wild. Even men who were not originally tempted to be criminals become criminals. Adam Smith knew it when he said that, left alone, businessmen will always conspire against the public good by fixing prices. Joseph P. Kennedy knew it when he was the first head of the SEC. John Kennedy knew it when he talked about how all businessmen were SOBs, but steel men were the biggest SOBs.

For that matter, Ronald Reagan, with a life's experience dealing with motion picture studios, must surely have known what business is if left absolutely unregulated. However, his appointees at the SEC thought that, in some way, the laws of human nature had been repealed, and that supervision of financial markets was no longer required, except perhaps at the level of individual brokers and penny stock promoters. It was amazing how similar the sales tactics of Milken and of the penny stock kings were: fraudulent promises, boiler room sales, and a quick move on to the next deal when the game was up. (Milken and Meyer Blinder, the penny stock Napoleon, became two of UCLA's largest donors. Both are now in exile from the securities business.)

Reagan's appointees to the SEC also had close ties with the boys at Broad Street and at the corner of Wilshire and Rodeo. His long-time chairman, John Shad, had been Drexel chairman Fred Joseph's first boss at E. F. Hutton, and they had maintained a long and cordial relationship. Inside the commission, Shad's chief economist, Texas economics professor Charles Cox, was an avid fan of anything Shad said in favor of free markets and was happy to weigh in with his scholarship about how regulation would hurt American business.

Indeed, the Shad-Cox axis at the SEC was at the heart of the entire problem, according to Vise and Coll's *Eagle on the Street*. Blinded by ideology and by family ties, the SEC simply could not bring itself to act on the totality of the Milken scam. To this day, it still has not acted. Milken was convicted of insider trading and stock parking—frauds and felonies, to be sure. But they were a small part of what was going on, which has been addressed only in civil cases against him and Drexel. However, some indication that the SEC had at least a clue that Milken was engaged in a truly staggering conspiracy came from the enormity of his fine. For six relatively trivial fraud counts, it was in the hundreds of millions of dollars, with many hundreds of millions more supposedly to be paid in connection with the failure of Drexel S&Ls.

The Milken regime was also protected, surely unintentionally, by the bureaucrats of the National Association of Insurance Commissioners. The NAIC, as it is known, has been in a pivotal position relative to junk bond sales for more than a decade. It has been responsible for telling insurance commissioners of the states and the insurance companies domiciled in those states whether certain bonds can be considered eligible to be bought by insurance companies.

Although the rules for eligibility were, and still are, complex, they are also subjective at the margin. Further, they are applied to facts and figures stated by the issuers and underwriters of the bonds. Obviously, if those data are positive and are trusted by the regulators, it has a major effect upon whether the bonds can be considered acceptable for an insurer's portfolio.

The analysts of the NAIC were called upon hundreds and then

thousands of times to rate Milken junk. Upon their answers largely depended whether the Drexel captive insurers would be allowed to hold Drexel/Milken junk. Even the most captive insurers could hold only a small quantity of bonds rated "No" by the association.

Milken junk was, more often than not, rated "Yes." But the independence of judgment of the NAIC was put into doubt by a number of events. State insurance and NAIC regulators were often flown first class, at Drexel expense, to lush watering holes such as the Beverly Hills Hotel, to be feted and wined and dined and shown how great Drexel junk was. All this, of course, was on the Drexel tab.*

In addition, former insurance regulators were known to have the favor of the Drexel world if they had been friendly to Drexel when they were in office. Not only did E. Benjamin Nelson, former insurance commissioner of Nebraska and high honcho of the NAIC, get on the gravy train by becoming an employee of First Executive and its affiliate, Regency Equities, but he later became a director of First Executive and governor of Nebraska.

Then there was Roxani Gillespi, who was insurance commissioner of the state of California for most of the 1980s. (Her conduct in office was so criticized that the post became elective after her reign.) Gillespi appeared at a California state legislative hearing in 1990 to make assurances that First Executive was in fine shape, even after it had clearly gone into insolvency or very near it. She said that management could be trusted and that she as commissioner had everything under control. In fact, the insurance giant was seized only months later, at a staggering loss to its investors and policyholders.

For her pains, Gillespi was first named a state court judge by outgoing governor George Deukmejian (a major recipient of Drexel gifts, mostly via Charles Keating). When there was an outcry, she became a partner at a Los Angeles law firm instead.

An honest, aggressively skeptical NAIC would have crippled Milken's entire effort. It did not happen in the Reagan era, which might be described as the time of the government that refused to govern.

---

* As a former low-level regulator myself, for the Federal Trade Commission, I find it incredible that bureaucrats could be expected to be impartial or negative to Drexel when Drexel was paying for lavish entertainment and travel for them. It's amazing that it was even allowed.

On a continuing course, the American government has steadily declined to enforce laws, whether on the streets or in the boardrooms. That was an astoundingly lucky coincidence for Milken. Even he was not powerful enough to create an intellectual climate averse to law enforcement. Even he cannot claim authorship of a doctrine that holds that no government action is better than any. That dubious honor belongs to various intellectuals in various universities and think tanks. But Milken benefited lavishly from that line of thought. Indeed, he could never have flourished in an era of strict law enforcement.

The confluence of a demobilized SEC and regulatory apparatus that was drugged by Reagan laissez-faire narcotics (and the example of the Federal Home Loan Bank Board's repeated refusal to step in against Drexel-controlled entities has become a legend of government incompetence) and a national mentality that believed "greed is good" —these were all the gifts that the 1980s bestowed upon Michael R. Milken. He knew well how to use them.

CHAPTER THIRTEEN

IN THE LAND OF NOD

*This year in peace, ye critics, dwell
Ye harlots sleep at ease!*

ALEXANDER POPE, 1715

A PRIMARY ALLY of Milken in his efforts to obscure the facts about his junk was greater than greed, lax law enforcement, intellectual bewilderment, or willful obscurantism. It was sloth, perhaps mixed with a certain lack of motivation.

At any given time, the number of accountants, business school professors, statisticians, lawyers, economists, and journalists on the Milken pad was a small fraction of the total. Why didn't any of them bother to look closely at the financial phenomenon of the age, the Milken bond? The answer in part is hinted at by this fact: When the GAO performed a study of junk bonds to see if they were suitable for S&Ls, it did not, as noted, call one negative witness, in part because at that time there were *no* well-known critics of junk bonds. There were critics of hostile takeovers, of the "two tiered . . . bust-up take-over," as Martin Lipton, a New York lawyer, called it, of the baleful effects of mergers and acquisitions on corporate and metropolitan life. But there simply were no known figures who said that junk *itself* was questionable and might not live up to its promises.

157

But again, why not? Perhaps it was because of a basic flaw: the way financial research is organized—and paid for. Or, in other words, because there was almost no one passing out grants to research junk critically, and without such grants, there was no incentive for qualified persons to make such studies. Possibly, also, there did not seem to be any money in such a field of study because no investment banks stood ready to give a highly paid job to the MBA who had done such a thesis—although they would have been wise to do so. Or possibly Milken was throwing such a great party that hardly anyone in his right mind wanted anything except to be invited.

Journalism was also at fault in America's not knowing that the Milken pyramid was in large measure a Ponzi. We have come to look to the journalists in many forums to probe and analyze and dig into aspects of our society that are far too complicated for the ordinary citizen to understand, or even to discover, without their diligence and reportorial expertise. But journalists are particularly ill-suited to dig into a modern-day financial fraud as clever and well-protected as the Milken paradigm.

For one thing, such frauds usually involve fancy statistical footwork, which requires some training in statistics or at least accounting to see through. There are few full-time or even frequently contributing journalists who have had that kind of training. People who do go to the trouble of studying accounting usually seek more orderly, and especially better-paid jobs than are offered by print journalism.

Also, just as a fact of life, few journalists indeed would have had the time to study a scheme as complex as Milken's. It might have taken months or even years to grasp the outlines of a conspiracy so immense. It would also have taken a fair amount of reading of prospectuses and fictitious name forms for partnerships, not to mention a mountain of other documents. Not every journalist has that kind of inclination, and even if he did, not many employers would have given him the time and financial support necessary to pursue such a story. Newspapers in modern life are run lean and mean. Those few that are adequately staffed rarely have adequately trained staff. The only newspaper "division" known to give its staffers long times to develop stories about fairly arcane matters was *The Wall Street Journal* editorial page. Alas, in this case, its attention was directed elsewhere.

Financial journalists, in particular, are geared to getting their stories by interviewing "experts" rather than doing the investigation themselves. This is a matter of efficiency. Obviously, it's a lot quicker and easier to ask a stock analyst what he thinks about 3M than to undertake a careful study of the company and its competitors. It's a lot easier to go to an accountant at Touche to ask about Executive Life than to learn some little bit of accountancy and study numbers yourself.

In the case of Milken, asking the experts was a disaster. Most of them were participants in the game. The Milken accountants had no complaints. They were happily writing up financials and getting well paid. The lawyers had no complaints either, except the few engaged in legal actions against some Drexel-related maneuver, and even they did not see the full scope of the web until rather late in the day. Thus, when the journalists talked to experts, they got information in bits and pieces, most of it complimentary, rather than the full story.

Further, the idea of inserting some kind of smell test into the analysis of a particular financial story seemed to occur to almost no one covering the financial beat. Almost no one analyzing the Milken world seemed to have much knowledge of history or ethics. Milken was essentially promising investors something for nothing, or at least that he had defeated the entire theory and history of markets. But— and this was a huge but—in the financial press, no one paused to ask how this could be true.

The something-for-nothing part should have prompted some questions. So should Milken's association with financial daredevils like Steinberg and Riklis and Posner. But blood dries quickly, at least the blood of ordinary investors. If any journalists recalled the shenanigans of Milken's friends and early buddies and pondered how similar they were to what Milken was doing, no one wrote about it in the national press.

There was one other particularly odd part about Milken's position with the financial press: the absolute absence of an adversary feeling about the relationship between the newshounds and the fat cat. At least in the post-Watergate era, there has been a distinct adversarial feeling between politicians and the press, although its intensity has ebbed and flowed. In the world of professional athletics, there has sometimes been even more generic hostility. The rich and the famous of movies and music are dogged relentlessly by reporters and photographers in almost open warfare. But when the press attends upon the doings of professional financiers, it is diffident to a fault. The London press pays far less respect to the royal family than the American financial press pays to successful manipulators in finance. With Milken, that kind of toadying was raised to an unprecedented level. But even in general terms, the obeisance of the media at the height of the Milken era to American billionaires beggared the imagination.

Perhaps it had to do with the fact that journalists so rarely know anything about finance that it offers a halo of knowledge to the financiers. Perhaps it had to do with a certain awesome power radiating from men with money. Perhaps it had to do with the fact that, in the 1980s, the worship of money had become the national religion even in newsrooms, and men like Milken could take friendly journalists and make them truly rich. The example of Steve Anreder, a likeable reporter who wrote for *Barron's,* then went to work at Drexel and wound up vigorously and cheerfully defending Milken night and day, as well as becoming a multimillionaire partner in a number of Drexel/ Milken partnerships, must have been in some other minds.

For whatever reason, the protective walls of his own financial fortress and the lack of anyone willing or able to scale those walls allowed Milken to continue to sell his bonds and finance his takeovers and make his billions. When the walls finally came tumbling down, it was because, by 1987 and 1988, a small group of students of finance at Harvard Business School had actually dared to do some research, and not just accept the claims that the wizard was really a whiz.

CHAPTER FOURTEEN

STATISTICS

"Mathematics, rightly viewed, possesses not only truth, but supreme beauty . . ."

BERTRAND RUSSELL, 1902

IN THE MARKETPLACE, there is an intimate connection between power and money. Michael Milken was smart enough to understand that his path to unique power in finance was a highway paved with the faulty figures of captive Drexel statisticians, respectful journalists, complaisant accountants, and supine politicians and civil servants. He attracted an armada of academics, lawyers, publicists, friends in high places, and economic soothsayers who protected a myth about the value and default rate of junk bonds. But that myth, in turn, was in the service of a unique power: Milken's ability to fix junk bond prices at above their true value.

Contrary to the opinion of many students, there are some extremely useful things to be learned in Economics 101. The most useful is probably the concept that true wealth accrues to price fixing beyond any other business practice. Few get rich in this world by making a product and selling it for the economic definition of market price: that price which repays the costs of production and capital. The wheat farmer selling his fabled bushel of wheat at exactly the price that keeps him going rarely gets rich. The laborer, selling his labor in competition with other laborers who underbid each other until their wage just barely covers their cost of sustenance (defined differently in different times and places), also never gets rich.

But the physician who has a government-granted monopoly, plus a lengthy education requirement that inhibits competition, can charge fees far above his cost of staying alive. The famous corporate lawyer who knows that some unknown cannot undercut him because who would hire that guy anyway can charge fees vastly above his cost of replacement. In the game of capitalism, however, at least on a level playing field, it is the laws of supply and demand, and the competition among suppliers to provide whatever goods or services are in demand, that generally determine their price. And those who play by the rules of supply and demand rarely get rich.

The same is true for the seller of bonds. The sales volume of competitively-priced bonds is huge, but the markup is virtually nil. And to prevent that dreary prospect, Milken had to make sure that he could sell his bonds at a price greater than their real value allowing for defaults. If he could do that, mainly by suppressing the truth about default rates, he could also charge fees to underwrite original issues, get the equity warrants and stock that were part of his deals, trade the bonds at his discretion, and make the uniquely high profits he had come to love and expect as his due.

If there had been a real market in junk, Milken's boundless energy would have made him a major player, but not a King Kong. If the market had known the true rates of default for junk, his bonds would have had to carry a much higher interest rate than they did. That would have made the mathematics of their issuance extremely problematical for many issuers, because they would have been even less able to afford to service the debt. If the true rate of default had been known, those bonds already in the market would have been traded at prices far lower than the fictitious prices that Milken set. In turn, that would have required the owners of the junk—S&Ls, insurers, pension funds—to take huge reserves for realized and unrealized losses, which would have drastically lowered their net worth. If they did not, in due course, such buyers rapidly would have failed or would have been barred from buying any more Milken junk (which is, in fact, what eventually happened). And finally, if the true rates of default were known, even the most thoroughly captive buyer would have had difficulty buying Milken junk. The Drexel network would have dried up, the endless hyped-up demand for Drexel issues would have evaporated, and

Milken would have had to peddle his bonds out in the market like any other salesman.

Thus the big lie about rates of default was at the heart of Milken's scheme and, in turn, was the underpinning for the collection of what economists call "monopoly rent"—profits far in excess of what is needed to sustain the costs of production of the goods in question. That lie, so ably protected by the Milken circle, enabled Milken to artificially fix bond prices. It was his license to steal. But the lie was finally and conclusively revealed in March of 1988 by the self-effacing professor Paul Asquith of Harvard University's Graduate School of Management and his two fellows, David W. Mullins, Jr., and Eric D. Wolff, assisted by their researchers and fact-checkers, Ben Bisconti, Paul Bonner, and Bruce MacLennan.

Asquith could hardly have been a more unlikely iconoclast. He was known as a highly competent researcher and mathematician. A work of his about the rates at which bond prices rose or fell after mergers and acquisitions was by no means hostile to the investment fashions of the 1980s. His study, done along with a colleague, noted that—contrary to the position of many lawyers and economists— there was no clear evidence that takeovers of industrial investment-grade companies resulted in clear falls in price or investment-grade rating. The study was subject to discussion and to some modest criticism for the years that he chose to include, but was otherwise accepted as a creditable piece of the body of work on bonds, neither iconoclastic nor hidebound.

Operating with a grant from the George F. Baker Foundation (one of the first, if not the first grant to be given for the study of this field by someone not making money in the field), Asquith and his team started their examination of junk bonds in 1988 by acknowledging that the methodology that had previously been used to study junk default was badly flawed and in fact useless. They easily spotted the fallacy of deriving a default rate by comparing small amounts of junk from early Milken days with the total float of junk in years when that total had become enormous. Asquith and his colleagues instead studied junk by using an "aging" analysis. By this method, they followed the junk issued in any given year for the succeeding years to see what its fate was, thus simulating the experience of the real life buyer of junk.

163

The results, as summarized by Asquith in the introduction to his paper, contradicted the bulk of the Altman studies virtually point by point.

> Buying and holding all [junk] bonds issued in 1977 and 1978 produces cumulative default rates exceeding 34% by November 1, 1988. . . . Cumulative default rates rise markedly as the time since issue increases and are 0–8% three years after issue, increase to 18% to 26% seven years after issue (for all but the first of the issue years) and exceed 34% eleven years after issue.
>
> Exchange offers are also a significant factor in the high yield debt market. However, exchanges are often followed by default on the securities received in the exchange, and thus exchanges do not seem to be an important factor in reducing the reported default rate for high yield debt. Moreover, by November 1, 1988, a significant percentage, 23%–43%, of the high yield debt issued in 1977–1982 had been called.
>
> The first half of the sample period, 1977–1982, presents a summary picture of the high yield debt market from an aging perspective. By November 1, 1988, about one-third of the bonds issued in these years had been called and only a small percentage had reached maturity. On November 1, 1988, the residual issues outstanding without default represented, on average, only 30% of the original issues of 1977–1982. Finally, there is no clear evidence in this study that more recent issue years will produce results that differ markedly from early issue year results.

In its calculated, calm, measured way, this introduction to the Asquith study was as devastating to the established reign of Milkenism as "We hold these truths to be self-evident . . ." was to George III in 1776.*

---

* Professor Edward Altman also made one such "aging" study, but acknowledges that he made a flood of others reaching different conclusions. His pro-Milken studies were, of course, the ones that were the most widely promoted and advertised. The Asquith study found a somewhat lower reported rate of default for certain years for Drexel issued bonds as compared with other issuers' bonds. The Drexel rate soon soared, however, as the Milken empire cracked, to rates far above the Asquith study's data, themselves lethal.

Every part of the study attacked the pillars of Drexel/Milkenism. By pointing out that the default rate on junk was roughly three times what Drexel claimed (and what Altman had "substantiated" in his work), the Asquith team radically devalued junk of original issue. If bonds defaulted at at least 3.5 percent per annum on average over time, then they were worth much less than if they defaulted at about 1 percent (the Drexel line). First, they paid far less money over the course of their lifespan to their owners. The exact amount of shortfall would be determined by the time of default and what investment alternatives were available at that time. In short, junk was not a way to "get rich quick" as Drexel claimed. Just the opposite, at the prices Milken was commanding, especially for fiduciary institutions.

For example, if junk defaulted at a rate of 3.5 percent per year over roughly ten years, that meant an insurance company that held a large portfolio of junk bonds with an average life to maturity of ten years should prudently take a reserve equal to very roughly 35 percent of the value of the portfolio (reduced by real rates of recovery on default) and amortize that amount against earnings from the portfolio or account for it in some other way. Such an insurer, a First Executive or a First Capital Holdings, or a Zenith National, would then have to report sharply lower earnings from its portfolio (or take a charge against assets). And it would have to offer sharply lower implicit and explicit interest rates on its annuities, life insurance, "guaranteed" investment contracts, and every other kind of product.

That, in turn, would mean that a reputable insurer such as Prudential or Metropolitan Life would no longer have to "reach for yield" to keep up with First Executive or First Capital's insurance units. They would not think they had to buy Milken junk to compete with a now defunct Fred Carr. Thus would topple one of the pillars of the Milken temple of finance.

Furthermore, if there really were exchanges in the ranges indicated by Asquith, and if many of those exchanges were followed by defaults (or involved an exchange of a non-interest-paying security for an interest-paying security), the overall yield on Milken junk would be even lower, and additional reserves would have to be taken for the certainty of nonpayment of coupon by some of the exchanged issues in the portfolio. If the new securities were non-interest-bearing

165

and also had no ready market, prudent accounting would require still larger reserves or charges against earnings, or both.

For a Milken captive junk-bond-holding S&L, such as Columbia or CenTrust or Ben Franklin Savings, the consequences would be extremely serious. The S&L would have to take a reserve against earnings, or a charge against its capital for the likely rate of default, *plus* the likely rate of loss upon exchange. Since even the best S&Ls operate with an equity capital of only a few percent of assets and liabilities, such a significant charge on its bond portfolio could easily put it below legally required capital requirements and very possibly into negative capital territory. And again, this would mean that a huge slice of Milken's captive bond-buying universe would disappear.

If the Milken bonds (and all junk bonds) were accounted for at their real rate of default, pension funds that held such bonds would also have to make large allowances for default. They, too, would have to set aside reserves, take charges against earnings, or otherwise account for the inevitable losses they would suffer upon default of great hunks of their portfolios. Under federal laws governing standards of prudent conduct by pension fund trustees, especially ERISA, owning Milken junk might then simply be disallowed. And this, in turn, would knock out yet another prop of the Milken empire. Even the captive Drexel issuers who habitually stocked their pension larders with Milken bonds would be barred from buying any more. In addition, if true rates of Milken and junk default were known, and the likes of First Executive failed, there would be no possibility at all of any entity bundling junk bonds, having an affiliate put its stamp of approval on them, and then calling them investment-grade credits, thus making them permissible for pension funds.

Yet another Milken captive buying realm, his own issuers, would have to take big hits to their capital or earnings if they had to consider true rates of junk default. A Stone Container, a Reliance, an Enstar, or an MDC Holdings could not hold large amounts of junk in their portfolio of marketable securities at par. Even though accounting standards allowed junk holders and bondholders in general to carry bonds held to maturity at cost, there was a devastating catch: a realistic reserve for likely losses also had to be kept against bonds, even those planned to be held to maturity. Again, this was a potentially catastrophic prospect for Milken. His repertoire had always included overfunding junk issuers and making them take in his other junk. If they could no longer do so, yet another buying segment was gone.

The sad truth for Milken was that once the real rates of default were known, hardly anyone with any degree of supervision could continue to be a captive buyer of Drexel junk. And almost all Drexel buyers had to have some degree of supervision, because almost all were fiduciaries, spending other people's money. There simply were no large Drexel buyers paying out their own personal funds. The S&Ls were spending their depositors' money. The insurers were spending their policyholders' money. The pension funds were spending workers' and retirees' money. That meant there would always be at least nominal standards, however laxly enforced. As long as the wishful default data from Drexel, Altman, and others was believed, and reserves not compulsorily taken, supervision could be held at bay. But once the Asquith data was out, the handwriting was on the wall in flashing neon and the regulators could ignore it no longer.

To be sure, there were other enormous problems within the Milken empire. The insider trading scandals involving Ivan Boesky, Dennis Levine, Martin Siegel, and others had angered the public and regulators. Boesky, a "speculator" on mergers and acquisitions on a gigantic scale, Levine and Siegel, investment bankers, and various lawyers involved in insider trading looked like spokes originating from a Milken hub. And from these scandals emerged the clear fact that Milken had made Drexel the center of insider trading nationally. Breaching and trading on clients' confidences seemingly was a basic part of his enterprise and it had startled and dismayed many players even within the Milken tent.

Furthermore, the business problems of many junk issuers, including Continental Airlines, LTV Corporation, ICH, Integrated Resources, and Imperial S&L, had made some legislators wary of the so recently touted "miracle" of junk bonds. And the reaction by potential target companies against the many Milken junk-financed hostile takeovers of the 1980s had also aroused public concern. Outcries against the legacy of joblessness, abuse of the environment, and

167

mistreatment of employees and public investors left behind by the raids, successful or unsuccessful, on Disney, Pacific Lumber, TWA, Crown Zellerbach, Safeway, Burlington Industries, Phillips, Gulf, Unocal, Prime Computer, Damon Medical, MCA, Carter Hawley Hale, and many others had finally reached Congress as well as state legislatures.

Some large savings and loans, most notably Imperial Savings & Loan of San Diego, were already reeling, by 1988, largely due to their losses on junk bonds, a fact that had been recognized even before the Asquith study received widespread currency. The Federal Deposit Insurance Corporation, even in its hypnotized state under the Reagan regime, and its sister agency, the Federal Savings and Loan Insurance Corporation, were beginning to notice that despite the glib words of the "watchdog" General Accounting Office about how great junk bonds were for federally insured S&Ls, losses were piling up in junk portfolios at insured institutions. Major reform greatly inhibiting investment in junk by federally insured S&Ls was nearing legis- lative completion, in the form of an act known as FIRREA (the Financial Institutions Reform, Rehabilitation and Enforcement Act), which would basically curtail junk ownership by federally insured S&Ls.

Congressman John Dingell of Michigan had revealed, in meticulous studies by his staff, the manipulation of junk prices within Drexel by Milken. Dingell's staff investigators had found that Milken as a com- mon practice sold junk upon issue to himself and his friends (as well as his "charitable" foundations), then immediately resold it to captive third-person buyers such as S&Ls and insurers, at hefty increases in price. Dingell had also shown, in hearings in 1987 and 1988, that Milken routinely paid himself, his friends, and his foundations far more for his junk than was paid to captive third-party nonrelated sellers. Milken had appeared at the hearings, but had refused to tes- tify at all, seeking shelter in the Fifth Amendment.

By 1989, Milken's troubles were coming not as single spies, as they say, but in battalions. But it was the Asquith study that was not just a small tear, but the unraveling of the entire fabric of Milkenism. The insider trading could have been seen as the aberration of a few men, even if one was Milken. The wild favoritism and chiseling on trades

168

could also have been seen as something personal. The losses at the S&Ls might have been described as bad investment picks or salvaged by some kind of diversification guidelines (always a favorite Drexel dodge, as if any form of diversification except away from Milken would have worked). But when Asquith showed that junk was simply not a good investment at the prices Milken was charging, the bottom fell out. It was not just a few bad men or a bad year, it was a basically questionable product at the Milken price. But at a lower price, Milken would not have been able to make the scheme work to throw off such huge profits.

The Drexel forces fought back vigorously against the Asquith study. In fact, a long-time friend, Professor Michael Jensen of Harvard, was on the board of editors of the financial journal in which Asquith's study was to have first been published. He questioned it and kept it under review for so long that it was feared by some who had seen the piece that it might never appear. In the event, however, Jensen could not bottle it up forever, and might not even have wanted to.

Professor Edward Altman, eternal optimist about junk, produced reply studies attempting to obscure the facts and put the best light on the Drexel junk world and on junk generally. But even he was forced to admit in caveats that by some standards junk was far from the good investment he might have led investors to believe. (Interestingly enough, Altman was continuing to defend junk, using his same questionable methodology, in mid-1992. He had even teamed up with Merrill Lynch and a number of former Drexel-era junk bond "researchers" to create a Merrill-Altman junk index, still using questionable data.)

With Milken running into choppy water, the Milken empire put its media campaign into high gear. It stepped up production of its commercials about its successes. It mobilized its many friends to write endless, obscurantist letters whenever any criticism of Milken appeared anywhere in print. Led by Linda Robinson and Ken Lerer of the high-powered public relations firm of Robinson, Lake, Lerer & Montgomery, the Milken army counterattacked its critics with ad hominem smear campaigns, rather than responses on the merits of their criticisms.

The friends of Michael Milken placed newspaper advertisements, in fact created by the Milken publicity machine and Robinson. These ads, which read, in huge headlines, "Mike Milken, We Believe in You," appeared in national newspapers such as *The New York Times* and *The Wall Street Journal*. They briefly praised his works, citing many fraudulent claims that had already been debunked about job creation from junk, and then listed the names of men whom Milken had helped to enrich.

As underwriters, the Milken team also attempted to grind out more junk issues than ever to show that the Ponzi was still alive and well. The Milken machine was so powerful and effective that even after he left the firm permanently, in 1989, Drexel placed by far the largest underwriting in corporate history, junk or nonjunk, the collection of securities used in the KKR takeover of RJR/Nabisco. These bonds, although offered through the Milken apparatus, turned out to be perhaps the best, least junky bonds Drexel ever placed. Many now trade for a premium above offering price, which was rare indeed in the Milken world. It may be simply an irony that the bonds issued after Milken left performed so well, or it may be that in his absence, superior underwriting standards prevailed, or that buyers now bought with their eyes open.

Some of Drexel's most amazing underwritings indeed took place in the late 1988–1989 period, when the wolves of justice were at its door. One, according to a lawyer who recently worked for Drexel, consisted of about $100 million of bonds in a private placement subscribed to by the usual suspects, such as CenTrust, Columbia, First Executive, and Far West. This offering, under an innocuous name, placed its proceeds directly into the hands of the Milken junk department for its unfettered use. They did not go to build a factory or lease an airplane or even to pay off the coupons on another offering from an earlier day. The beneficiaries were simply described in the offering memo as "HYCANY," which, in the Milken world, meant "High Yield Department, California and New York." The proceeds went right to Milken and his pals. No middlemen, no need to waste any time with boring details about how much commission there would be. It was the entire amount raised by the issue.

Even after the Asquith studies, the power of Milken was still so great that in the academic community, especially at business schools, hardly a voice could be heard against him. But the rubber band was getting ready to snap back. The gravity of arithmetic, which is a basic form of truth, simply could not be suspended much longer.

CHAPTER FIFTEEN

BUYING BACK THE BROOKLYN BRIDGE

. . . where the sun beats,
And the dead tree gives no shelter, the cricket no relief,
And the dry stone no sound of water.

T. S. ELIOT, 1922

THE END OF THE Milken junk bond scam finally came about in late 1989 and early 1990 as several trends converged. First, Drexel had by 1989 pleaded guilty to six felony counts of federal securities law violations. By mid-1989, Milken and his brother, Lowell, had been indicted on ninety-eight felony counts of violations of federal securities laws, laws involving misuse of charitable organizations and tax evasion statutes, including extremely blatant misuse of Milken's supposed charities, and parking of stocks to help his very junior partner, Ivan Boesky, and himself avoid securities laws. Other violations involved helping his long-time friend David Solomon evade federal income tax laws.

Milken had gathered about his person a capable and frighteningly large legal team, but the burden of preparing for protracted litigation was taking a great toll on his ability to manipulate his Ponzi. Further, the effective date of FIRREA in August of 1989 had been a black day

172

for junk and for Milken in particular. On that day, the Milken S&Ls were no longer able to buy Drexel junk and had to start the clock running for a five-year process of liquidating their junk portfolios.

Milken left Drexel—although he kept an office down the hall from his trading floor, and he did still *own* the building—in December 1988. His presence was felt, of course, but he was rapidly losing his power to control events. By the fall of 1989, when the S&Ls wanted to unload junk, there was hardly anyone left to buy it. The data was clear that, at par, on average it was a losing buy. The Milken who had always promised to take buyers out of issues—at an acceptable price—was no longer able to do so. With the Resolution Trust Corporation (RTC), a new federal agency created to clean up the S&L debacle, and the Office of Thrift Supervision looking on, albeit belatedly, thrifts were certainly not buyers. Insurers were backing away, too. First Capital, never as fully engulfed by Milken as First Executive, became a less likely buyer. Zenith National, run by Milken's cousin, was rapidly disposing of junk rather than buying it. Persons close to Drexel said that Milken wished to spare his cousin the loss of his company and might have warned him to get out of junk long before he even hinted at his own corporate demise. It was, if made at all, a warning he did not share with many other junk buyers.

Integrated Resources, a Milken-influenced financial services company, and I.C.H., another dicey financial services company, both of which had been enormous buyers of Drexel junk, were in trouble and wanted only to get out while they could. But some noncaptive fiduciaries, perhaps not completely aware of the facts about Drexel junk, were still small buyers even into late 1989. A few state pension funds, a number of foreign governments, even the pension fund of the World Bank, were buyers of Drexel junk until just before the end of the firm. The power of propaganda and disinformation was still great. Many fiduciaries missed the obvious, but they did not show enough interest in Drexel junk to keep the market going.

In December of 1989, with the junk market reeling from FIRREA, the truth about junk rates of return, and the criminal case against Milken, Drexel stepped up its efforts to keep the junk market afloat. It began to liquidate its own huge capital in Treasury instruments and cash equivalents and to *buy back* from its network of junk bond holders. Drexel itself turned out to be the buyer of last resort for Milken junk issues that were unsalable elsewhere. It used up a large portion, perhaps more than half, of its available capital at the end of 1989 and early 1990 to make some of its buyers liquid.

Of all of the acts of Drexel Burnham Lambert, this was surely among the most quixotic. Drexel, the house that had been built upon the fraud of the value of Milken's junk, the house that had grown rich trading highly overvalued bonds for cash, was now making the ultimate bad trade in the con man's world: buying back the Brooklyn Bridge.

A Wall Street trader knowledgeable in the ways of Drexel said that there were several *conceivable* reasons for this disastrous maneuver. For one thing, it was possible that the top players at Drexel, in Milken's absence, were not wholly aware of the real value of the Drexel bonds. Many of the high players on Milken's trading floor were salesmen and glad-handers, not experts at valuing bonds. Above all, they were True Believers. That, explanation, however, would appear to be a little bit far-fetched, since many of these players knew well that buyers had to be bribed to buy Milken's bonds. Presumably they would at least suspect that if the bonds required bribes to be sold, there was something questionable about their value. It was much more possible that some of the higher officials at Drexel in New York did not fully realize how overvalued Milken's bonds were. Many of these men were basically relationship builders and publicity people, perhaps unable to keep track of what the true rates of default were or the proper means of computing them.

Second, it was possible that the buybacks were a sales tool, similar to the car salesman's promise to buy back the car himself at a certain price in a certain time if the buyer doesn't like it. Drexel might have been trying to resuscitate the junk market by the bravado of buying back the bonds and thus showing its confidence in them. Of course, at no time did Drexel buy back more than a tiny fraction of the bonds outstanding, but if it was that kind of sales trick, it was a highly dangerous one. It was somewhat like playing Russian roulette; eventually the gun will go off. To take in a large hunk of junk bonds to be used as capital for a securities firm that had to have available, bankable capital to live was self-defeating. If Drexel could not swiftly resell its junk and get creditworthy capital, it would simply stop functioning.

Third, and closely related as an explanation for Drexel making itself illiquid to buy junk, perhaps there were some at the firm who believed, and persuaded others to believe, that the price was right. There was and is a right price for junk, after all. Even Milken's junk was far from worthless. It may have been that it had declined sufficiently in price in the fall of 1989 so that, adjusted for its likely rate of default, it looked like a good buy. But that move, too, would have involved a certain bravado on the part of the firm, because it was difficult to know whether Drexel junk really was a good buy. That decision would have to be based on so many completely unknowable factors that any bet on it at all was risky in the absence of insider information about the prospects and conditions of Drexel issuers—and maybe even in its presence, unless Milken himself was the buyer.

Fourth, as an explanation of why Drexel used up a good chunk of its capital buying back its bonds, was the possibility that the firm was bailing out and paying back its pals for their help in years past. It was reported that in its final month Drexel bought back tens and maybe hundreds of millions of junk from Columbia Savings, CenTrust, and First Executive. It may well have been that this was no more than honor among thieves, or a simple exercise in backscratching or one hand washing the other. Certainly, inasmuch as the Drexel empire was built upon personal connections and friendships, it would not have been at all out of the ordinary for the powers that be at the firm to attempt to make their friends look as good as possible, just to keep them available for future use.

The backscratching element in this explanation made some sense because often the final buybacks of Drexel junk were apparently from partnerships in which individual Drexel players such as fund managers and Drexel issuers had jobs at risk. It would be very much part of the Drexel way of doing business to protect its friends on a personal level, no matter what might happen to their trustors.

In an eerie echo of that same maneuver, when First Executive was seized in the spring of 1991, even as the regulators' footfalls could be heard in the hallway, it liquidated some of its real estate partnerships with its remaining cash. Fred Carr himself was a beneficiary of some of these investments. He was, so to speak, cashed out during a liquidity crisis, following the Drexel pattern or practice at the moment of its demise.

But the most likely explanation for the suicidal behavior of Drexel in making the positions of holders of Drexel junk liquid came down to Milken's Law: The Constant ME Is Always Greater than the Variable U. According to an extremely well-placed analyst of Drexel/Milkenism, a large amount of the buyback of Drexel junk was from the partnerships owned partly or mostly by Milken himself. The conversion to cash of junk bonds was just possibly done to benefit Michael R. Milken, or so it was said.

In its death throes as well as in its birth and life, Drexel/Milkenism very possibly existed mainly to benefit Milken, so why not bail him out? By late 1989, he had left the firm, at least nominally. As far as he was concerned, it was simply an obsolete skin he had worn and then shed. The firm was his creation, and to be fair its wealth came from his work. Why, in that case, should he leave it with any more money than he absolutely had to? The persons who ran the "trading" department in Beverly Hills were still his troopers, not Fred Joseph's. Their loyalty, should he wish to ask for it, was unquestioned, at least as far as bond sales went.

In any event, by January of 1990, Drexel was a goner. By the beginning of February, it had stopped answering its telephones in Beverly Hills, at least to the uninitiated. In the middle of a night in late January, workers began to haul away files from first-floor storage rooms on Rodeo Drive, and into those rooms moved a high-end dress shop named Amen Wardy.

In New York, Drexel's lenders stopped rolling over its commercial paper as of the first week of February. Drexel was unable to borrow on a secured basis on the collateral of the junk it had bought back. No federal official was willing to step in to plead for a bailout. Joseph's friend John Shad was now the *former* head of the SEC and could do nothing.

Then in typical Drexel fashion, the firm paid out several hundred million dollars in bonuses and bond buybacks to its high-ranking employees—while it knew it would have to delay or cancel payment to various labor union pension funds that had advanced money to the firm. It was, in legal terms, a "fraudulent conveyance" in that the "conveying" or transferring of something had resulted in a fraud being perpetrated on an innocent party. It was deeply revealing indeed that Drexel approved these payments while two former chairmen of the SEC sat on its board of directors.

Having thus stripped itself of its last big hoard of cash, and clinging to the notion that it was a victim rather than the perpetrator of the biggest fraud in financial history, Drexel filed, on February 13, 1990, a plea for protection from its creditors under federal bankruptcy laws. To the end, Drexel knew how to use the law.

On the day it declared bankruptcy, a visitor to the main Drexel lair at the corner of Rodeo and Wilshire talked to a guard, still wearing the badge of Drexel's own security company. "I just can't believe it," he said. "Just a few days ago, Mike himself told me I should take my life savings and buy stock in First Executive. Now it's gone to shit like the rest of it, and I can't see Mike anywhere." In fact, it took almost another year for First Executive to go under, along with every other captive Drexel player in finance.

On that same day, in the cavernous room that had housed the mortgage trading operation of Drexel, there was only one piece of paper visible. It was a clipping from *The Wall Street Journal* about how the fall of Drexel and the collapse of junk might do lingering damage to many pension funds and retirees who had depended on Drexel junk. In the Milken junk-trading room itself, there were only light blue plastic sacks of shredded paper, dozens of litigation boxes of corrugated cardboard with law firm initials on them, and a sleek, humming shredder in the middle of the room where Milken's desk had been.

CHAPTER SIXTEEN

RUINS

All for ourselves, and nothing for anyone else seems, in every age, to have been the vile maxim of the masters of mankind.

ADAM SMITH, 1776

WAS THERE ANY TRUTH at all to Milken's claims about junk bonds? There are some plausible—but flawed—reasons to include them in a portfolio. For one, it is possible that the timing of the flows of coupons from Drexel junk would have had a major effect upon their value. If a bond defaulted fairly late in its life, after it had already paid most of its stream of high (or relatively high) coupons, it might have been a far better investment than if it paid for only a few coupon periods and then defaulted. It might even be superior to a risk-free Treasury bond.

This calculation would be affected by the current market rate of interest. If interest rates were high, then the present value of coupon payments far in the future would be much less than if market rates were low. The value of payments in the period close to issue would also be correspondingly higher than they would otherwise be. Thus, if a Milken bond paid a high coupon, then continued to pay that coupon for most of its life, and if interest rates were high, and if there was a sufficient spread between the Milken rate and the investment-grade rate, that Milken bond could have been a better buy than an

178

investment-grade bond. Again, this is because the discounted present value of the last few coupon payments would have been small in a time of high real interest rates. Also, the surplus coupon amount from the paying years could have been reinvested and it would have been earning interest as well even after the original bond default.

To determine whether this was true would be a highly complex investment calculation, requiring knowledge of the real interest rate at the time of issue and at the time of each coupon payment of every Drexel issue. It would also require knowing the exact spread between the Drexel bond and the investment-grade bond at every month during the Milken reign, and the cost of reinvestment, as well as the cost of purchase and of salvage upon default of the Drexel bonds, and reinvestment rates at those times. In short, it would be an extremely complicated calculation.

It is fairly certain that the powers that be within the Milken orbit will now do such calculations and that they will show that, indeed, Milken's bonds were the best buy available when he was still operating. Even now, there are statisticians grinding out data that claim that Milken's bonds were and are superior investments. Although these studies have been completely debunked as based upon incorrect, incomplete, explicitly fabricated data, they are still cited in major newspapers.

But the evidence that Milken bonds were, in fact, a disaster is real and all around us. To paraphrase what Justice Robert K. Jackson said when he donned the mantle of a Nuremburg War Crimes prosecutor, "If we were to say there were no crimes, we would have to say there were no dead."

Milken's bonds were not entirely worthless, by any means. He was not selling sea water and calling it champagne. The bonds had some value. If they had been kept in portfolios and proper account taken of their likely real rates of default by means of reserves or charges against earnings, they would have been a legitimate investment— although nowhere near as good an investment as Milken claimed. But taken at Milken/Drexel's claimed value, using the phony default rates claimed by Milken, without accounting or reserving for losses, they were a catastrophe. If the proper reserves for default had been put aside, it would have been lethal to the Milken empire at any point.

Still, a few other exculpatory points for Milken and his world must be made.

Milken might have been using his argument about the "democratization of capital" only as a selling tool, but the truth is that it was and is a good idea for underwriters to be available to sell the bonds of smaller, less-seasoned companies. A functioning, active market in below-investment-grade bonds is an extremely useful adjunct to American finance. But to have such a market, and have it mean something beyond what Milkenism has come to mean, that market would have to have several characteristics:

- Full disclosure about real, not fanciful rates of default, which would give investors an idea of real yield.
- A free market with known prices, and with several firms making the market, not a single "market-maker" who could simply make up any prices he felt like for different buyers of the same bond at the same time.
- Issuance of bonds with all of the income going to the buyers of the bonds, not with huge chunks of the yield pocketed by the issuer and agents for the issuer in secret deals.

With those features, a bond market for companies that do not rate investment grade from S&P and Moody's would be extremely helpful. If Milken alerted us to the need for such a market, he would have done some service. Such a market did exist on a large scale in the prewar period, and would be useful right now.

As a second exculpatory point, in certain financial environments, Milken junk can indeed shine. In 1991's waning months and the early months of 1992, nominal interest rates simply collapsed in the United States. By the spring of 1992, real rates on short-term money were often negative. Rates on medium-term government bonds were at historic lows. In that situation, those Milken bonds that had not defaulted and showed some likelihood of not defaulting in the immediate future were in high demand. By definition, if they had survived a few years of recession and had not been issues from the defunct junk insurance, S&L, or financial services sector, they were sounder than most original-issue Drexel junk.

To say that, however, is to say no more than that in a period of low interest rates, a high-yielding bond will do well. If it is still paying after a number of years, it has lost some of its speculative (or guaranteed to fail) quality, and it will rise in value just as other bonds issued in a higher-interest-rate environment will rise.

Some Milken bonds are definitely not junk. But how many are sound is hard to say since there are still many years to go until their maturity. So far it appears that roughly 30 percent have neither defaulted nor been called or defaulted in some concealed way. But this stunner, that only about 30 percent should have survived as high-paying instruments, must be weighed along with the fact that some Milken bonds now trade at high prices, close to par and in some very, very few cases above par.

To offer that as proof that Milken's bonds were in fact a good investment is, however, like attending a reunion of veterans of the Battle of the Somme, noticing that all present are still alive, and concluding that no one was hurt or killed in that worst of all bloodbaths. The Drexel survivors are just that—survivors. The combination of the living *and* the dead tells the tale.

The Drexel/Milkenites have claimed that the companies they funded provided America with most, or even all, of its employment growth through the 1980s. There is no evidence of this at all, and none has ever been produced in any convincing way. The Milkenites, and specifically George Gilder, have also claimed that the Milken junk bond efforts increased national productivity and enriched the lives of American workers. There is simply no evidence of this effect either. In fact, worker wages and productivity through the Milken era, basically the 1980s, did not rise in any unusual way. Worker pay per hour in 1988, adjusted for inflation and not counting fringe benefits, in many cases was actually lower than in 1978.

The claims that Milken junk in some way added measurably to the well-being of the American republic are at the very least unproved. The ruined lives from the Milken years are extremely real:

- The workers who lost their jobs because Milken raiders armed with Milken junk bought their employers, looted them, and then turned the employees out.

- The employees who lost their pensions because their companies' pension funds were invested by Milken cronies in Milken junk-backed "guaranteed" investment contracts, which turned out to be anything but guaranteed.
- The policyholders, annuitants, and survivors of Drexel captive insurers who are not ever going to get the benefits they contracted for, and who must lead poorer lives because their "insurers" existed mainly to ensure that Milken and his friends would become rich.
- The taxpayers of this generation and generations to follow who will have to pay their hard-earned money to make up the losses in the federal deposit insurance fund caused by the default of Milken bonds in the vaults of the Milken captive S&Ls, while Milken and his cronies grew unimaginably rich.
- The investors in junk bond funds who saw their investments fall dramatically in value as losses on principal of bonds in their portfolios exploded.
- Stockholders and bondholders of the hundreds of Drexel companies that melted into thin air as reality overtook their false promises.
- And, finally, the American people whose faith in the system has been demolished by the spectacle of Drexel/Milkenism both in its promises and its reality—and especially the reality of Milken riding roughshod over every ethical principle and every legal institution that was supposed to protect them and their savings.

On the scales of economics and justice, the weight of evidence against Milken and his work is overwhelming.

CHAPTER SEVENTEEN

PRECEPTORS

Something deeply hidden had to be behind it all.

ALBERT EINSTEIN, 1964

MICHAEL MILKEN PLEADED GUILTY to a number of what are generally called "white-collar" crimes—as opposed to "blue-collar" crimes or those Godfather-type underground activities known as "organized crime." But on examination, much of Milken's white-collar work bears a startling resemblance to the methods of organized crime in schematic if not case by case. Milken was no capo, but he certainly applied the general mindset of the gangster to finance. And by so doing, he created a vastly more powerful operation than anything that John Gotti could ever have imagined.

After all, what were the greenmail raids of Milken associates Goldsmith, Icahn, Steinberg, Pickens, Boesky, and others except the old protection racket writ very, very large? What were the threats to subvert the finances of target companies except a shakedown, with plenty of immoral complicity by target company management. What was the cleverly planned pillage of the federally insured S&Ls except the familiar criminal tactic of buying a business for pennies (in this case, the trivial equity required to buy a pool of federally insured assets) and then simply stealing its assets instead of operating it as a long-term entity? What was First Executive, which could not avoid failure eventually, except the looting of a financial company to enrich the men who had captured it? What was the demand by Milken for huge slices of equity in the deals he made, the movement of those pieces to him personally, and the fact that those demands were often made at the very last minute except the most fundamental strong-arm tactics? But at an even more basic level, the Milken operation had at its core a basic unethical principle: *The quickest and easiest way to make a lot of money is to borrow it and not pay it back.* Milken simply raised that principle to a form and scale that were unheard-of.

There is a passage in the movie *Goodfellas* in which a restaurant is bought by a Mafia chieftain whose restaurateur-partner hopes for great things. Instead, the Mafia guy (played by Paul Sorvino) buys liquor on the charge account of the restaurant, has it "stolen" and resells it, leaving his partner to go into bankruptcy because he can't pay his liquor bills.

If the Paul Sorvino character then claimed he was doing a good thing by looting his partner's restaurant because he was enlarging demand for stolen liquor and creating new jobs for all of the loaders and lifters who carried it off, that would be Drexel/Milkenism fairly precisely. Indeed, if one imagines that the looted restaurant is a whole series of S&Ls and the defrauded partner—whose name is on the bills—is the taxpayer, the parallel seems to be almost precise.

Even if the Milken players did not violate—or at least were not prosecuted for violating—any laws, their tactics bear a striking similarity to those of organized crime. If, at the end of the day, the Drexel player (or any other businessman) has enriched himself while draining the assets of a company to which he has a fiduciary obligation, that is at the very least highly organized misconduct.

Drexel and Milken and their many confederates cannot, of course, be compared for evil-doing with Al Capone or Legs Diamond or "Lepkele" Buchalter, but in their basic approach to the conduct of business, they certainly borrowed far more from the captains of crime than from the captains of industry and finance like Andrew Carnegie, Henry Clay Frick, and J. P. Morgan. That is, while J. P. Morgan and the steel barons of the nineteenth and early twentieth centuries enriched themselves wildly out of any scale of fairness to their stockholders or employees, at the end of the line they left the largest and best and most profitable steel-manufacturing facilities in the world.

Milken and his entourage could hardly make such a claim. At the end of their line, they had enriched only themselves, leaving vast sectors of American business and industry reeling.

The Milken group was really more similar to the species that investigative journalist Steven Pizzo called "the artists of the bust-out" than to the steel magnates. A "bust-out," according to Pizzo, is a hybrid animal, somewhere between a straight Mafia operation and a straight heads-up business like Mom and Pop's corner store. It is a business that is in a legitimate line, such as insurance, but that is taken over ("busted out" in Pizzo's phrase) and then used for the illegitimate purpose of enriching its owners and principals at the expense of its stockholders or creditors. Fred Carr's First Executive was, by that definition, a "bust-out," a small insurance company that Carr and Milken took over and then "busted out" to make themselves a large amount of money. So, each in its own individual way, were CenTrust, Imperial (of San Diego), Columbia, Ben Franklin Savings, and many others.

In fact, Drexel itself could be thought of as a "bust-out." It was a small but well-regarded firm doing its job much as other investment banks did theirs. When the Milken players took it over, all of that changed drastically. Drexel became an organization that was puffed up beyond normal scale by its sales of an essentially fraudulent security, the overpriced, incorrectly valued junk bond. It was bound to grow extremely rich by the sale and use of that item for takeovers, restructurings, insider trades, and greenmail. But it was also eventually bound to fail as real rates of default caught up with inadequate reserves for loss.

In the certainty of defaults, it could have put aside reserves for losses and lawsuits over the junk it sold. But if it had, it would have had to admit that its bonds were not what they were cracked up to be, and it would not have seemed to be an eighth wonder of the world. Instead, Drexel did what bust-outs do. It enriched its principals and left someone else holding the bag, in this case, pension funds, policyholders, S&L stockholders, junk bond fund holders and, most of all, taxpayers.

Even those Drexel companies that were not classic bust-outs and that left some food on the table for stockholders had much in common with that kind of operation. When Nelson Peltz and Peter May, complete unknowns in business, took over National Can and American Can with Drexel financing and made it into Triangle Packaging, they did not run it into the ground. In fact, for a variety of reasons, their packaging company made excellent returns, had a high-flying stock for many years, and was more than intact when it was sold in late 1988 to the French packaging giant, Pechiney.

Peltz and May were by no means to be equated with Fred Carr or Tom Spiegel. But along the way from buying the nation's largest can company with basically no money down and selling it for over a billion dollars, some things were done that would have meshed nicely with bust-out philosophy. At several decisive turns in the history of Triangle, Milken players were there with large positions in the stock directly or through partnerships just before it moved skyward. Coincidence, perhaps, but a number of Milken confederates were miraculously on the right side of trades involving Triangle that Milken would have had to know about.

Also along the way from nothing to plutocracy, in a series of cunning maneuvers that would have made Boris Spassky envious, Peltz and May, with basically no money down, and with loans from their own stockholders paying the freight, issued several kinds of stock in various companies they controlled, traded shares back and forth from one company to another, and then, again, without having to come up with any money, gained control of a huge block of Triangle that was then taken over by a holding company they also controlled—all with the advice, consent, and aid of Milken.

Peltz and May did not have to borrow money to buy the whole common stock capitalization of Triangle. They did not have to obligate themselves or put themselves at any risk at all. They merely issued supervoting, ten-votes-per-share preferred stock, and then made sure they got enough of it—with borrowed money from the very stockholders they were fleecing—to control Triangle. It was so smoothly done that it made the usual unethical management buyout look comically lame.

At the moment of truth, when Pechiney stepped up to buy Triangle, the French company obviously had to pay a vast premium to Peltz and May, who, since they had the supervoting preferred in the holding company, were the control block. The other holders of control stock—mostly Milken insiders—also got paid off. The ordinary stockholders, who had been bought out of their stock with (what turned out to be) a small amount of cash and security, could only look on and gasp.

Then, in a truly amazing turn of events, it was discovered that some Pechiney officials and others who had paid such a lordly price for Triangle had been allowed to buy Triangle's stock for themselves before the announcement of the buyout and thus to make millions. A number of these people have since been indicted or convicted in France.

To be sure, no government agency has alleged that Peltz and May or their associates possibly arranged the whole transaction with Pechiney by recommending the stock to the officials in question. But the circumstantial evidence is dismaying. Into the Drexel world, where no one did anything except for money, along came the French in 1987 and 1988 to make Drexel players rich beyond avarice. Peltz and May got about $900 million out of a virtually nil initial investment. And the French buyers were lavishly enriched by insider trading in the same deal. It might well have been coincidence, like the lucky stock buys of Drexel players earlier in the Triangle saga. Or it could have been a bust-out that any hood would understand and envy.

In the final analysis, then, the true similarity between Milkenism and organized crime can be found in the mindset of Michael Milken and his colleagues and the use of the underworld tactics of the con and the shakedown, the swindle and the heist, in the world of finance on a national and international scale.

During the Kefauver Hearings into organized crime in the late 1950s, a common topic of conversation was roughly this: Considering how cagey and tough all of these hoods taking the Fifth before Kefauver were, how much more money that type would have been able to make if instead of street-corner gambling and loan-sharking they worked in "legitimate" business?

Now we know.

EPILOGUE

What is past is prologue.

SHAKESPEARE, *The Tempest*

IN THE LONG COURSE of learning and writing about Michael Milken, I have come to have some appreciation of the power of the Milken engine. Even though he is in Pleasanton Federal Correctional Facility his apparatus is by no means idle. To plead his case and protest his innocence, with a fortune of billions still left, he can and does hire publicists and lawyers the way other people buy Lifesavers. In August of 1992, Milken's lawyers persuaded the same federal judge who sentenced him to ten years for his six admitted felonies to lessen his sentence to 24 months, despite his minimal cooperation with prosecutors and his consistent refusal to divulge his assets in detail. Both had been supposed conditions for a reduction of sentence. Milken will be a free man in early 1993 at the latest—ample testimony to the power of money. And as I have learned to my bitter cost, Milken apologists have often diverted almost any careful questioning of his career by heaving grimy personal smears at the questioner, leaving the facts and the analysis out to rust.

In the late 1970s, when I was working as a consultant to a successful TV production company, I noticed something interesting. Down the hall from the headquarters of the company in Century City was a door. I often saw business-suited men walking through the door, but it had no sign on it. One day, however, a sign appeared, which said DREXEL BURNHAM LAMBERT HIGH-YIELD SECURITIES, or something very similar.

Because I have always had an interest in finance, I was curious. I had studied economics at Columbia with Lowell Harriss, and while at Yale Law School I had taken courses in corporate finance with the legendary Henry Wallich, later a well-regarded governor of the Federal Reserve System. I had also attended seminars and lectures of Milton Friedman and James Tobin. But most important of all for my interest in what lay behind that door, my parents were both economists. I had grown up hearing about free markets and equilibrations in returns on capital all of my youth, the way other children might hear about bad times in wheat or women's ready-to-wear.

One day I walked through that door and said, truthfully, that I often wrote articles for *The Wall Street Journal,* plus I had some small (very small) savings of my own to invest, and I wondered what kind of high-yield securities might be for sale. As I was talking to a receptionist or some other greeter, a fit young man walked by. He had heard me mention *The Wall Street Journal,* he said, and he would like to tell me what he was doing. His name was Milken.

The securities he was selling, he said, were the bonds of low-rated offerers, which paid more than the issuers of investment-rated bonds. But, he assured me, these bonds had been carefully investigated by him and his colleagues and their rates of default would not be much greater than those of investment-grade bonds. Therefore, their overall yield would greatly exceed that of the bonds of, say, General Motors.

I asked him why, if the bonds really had so little risk of default, they paid a much higher coupon than investment-grade bonds. Why would the issuers have to do that? In reply, Milken explained to me with a little irritation that the issuers were not to be compared with General Motors. They were—of course—far less creditworthy than General Motors, and that was why they paid a higher coupon by far.

I knew something about bonds and I told Milken that what he was selling seemed to be like the bundles of bonds of distressed or bankrupt issuers that were sometimes advertised and that Henry Wallich sometimes used to talk about. I asked him if I had it right. No, he said, because his issuers were not distressed and not bankrupt. In fact, he said, his issuers had mandatory sinking fund provisions to retire the bonds in question and generous reserves set aside to cover the coupons.

Then I asked Milken why, if the bonds in fact had sinking fund provisions and reserves for coupons, they had to be issued with the high interest rates he described. Was this not a contradiction in terms? Even very large and rich companies, after all, often did not have sinking funds of any size, and frequently did not have mandatory provisions for reserves for coupons. To me, although I did not say so, high yield implied high risk.

At this point, Milken simply looked disgusted and without another word, walked away. Someone else handed me some materials and I left. As far as I know, I have never seen Michael Milken again, although I am told I have been with him or at least in the same room with him in restaurants.

Time passed. In the mid-1980s, I, as a very small stockholder, was badly mistreated by a company called Narragansett Capital Corporation in a transaction involving a management leveraged buyout of the company. I took time to study the field and began to write about that management buyout as well as others at Metromedia and elsewhere. Little by little, my time came to be occupied primarily with study, writing and lecturing about finance, and with the ethical and economic issues in the world of finance generally. Most of my writing about finance appeared in *Barron's*.

I focused mainly on management's abuse of clear duties to stockholders, especially in terms of theft of corporate assets through the leveraged buyout. Occasionally, however, I was drawn to look at what seemed to me to be economically pointless deals in the mergers and acquisitions arena. Some of these deals seemed to me to be driven more or less solely by the fees to be gained by the investment bankers and their associates, rather than by any expectation of long-term profit or strength for the company. Some of them seemed like just plain greenmail. The names of Drexel Burnham Lambert and Michael Milken turned up in a fair number of these deals, especially in management buyouts or proposals at Metromedia and Viacom, which I wrote about extremely critically, and in mergers and acquisitions at Disney, MCA, Goodyear, and TWA. Drexel and Milken seemed to be the suppliers of huge sums of capital and I questioned

190

whether their junk bonds, as they were now being called, could have the wonder-working properties that Milken claimed for them.

Still, I was not truly beguiled by Drexel until the late spring of 1988. At that time, I was renting an office in a small building in the cheaper portion of Beverly Hills, south of Wilshire. Only two blocks away, also south of Wilshire, were the grand, sprawling offices of Drexel Burnham Lambert. I had as an assistant a young woman who had a beau in the corporate finance department at Drexel. She wanted me to meet him. So one day, we three and one other friend went to lunch at a restaurant called Yanks.

The young man did not know I wrote for *Barron's* about financial misconduct. He apparently thought I was a doctor of medicine, a mistake people often make. He regaled us for over an hour with tales of his and his firm's coups. Some involved selling bonds for a company that could not possibly pay the interest on them. Others involved generating fraudulent income predictions for a client firm in the entertainment business. Yet another involved a phony raid on a medical lab company, which was really nothing but a device to move the stock, with Drexel taking a huge slice of the upside in the stock movement.

The next day, I got a call from my assistant. She had told the young man that I was not a physician, and that, in fact, I wrote about financial misconduct for *Barron's* and planned to write a story about Drexel based on what he had said at lunch the day before. She reported that her beau had become hysterical and said he would kill me "with his raw hands" (sic) if I ever wrote about him. He also pleaded via my assistant that he had not meant to talk in front of a writer and that his whole life and career would be over if he was ever revealed as the source of a story about what he had said about Drexel.

This message was followed by another, also from the young man, via a mutual friend. She reported that he said he knew my office address and had promised to come over and kill me "with his raw hands" if I wrote about what he had told me. He would get into such bad trouble at Drexel, she told me, that he said it would only be right to kill me over it.

These threats, on top of the already startling information about the workings and attitudes at Drexel, made me begin to think that per-

191

haps it was not just another extremely aggressive investment bank, not just a West Coast competitor of Salomon or Morgan Stanley. Perhaps this was an organization that intentionally did exactly what laws were enacted to prevent, and on an ongoing basis. Perhaps, as a routine practice, it was making really big money in exactly those areas the laws were supposed to protect most rigorously. Further, perhaps this organization had a code of conduct (or had at least recruited one man with a code of conduct) that involved threats of death as a way of protecting the franchise.

I discussed this with my editor at *Barron's*. He pointed out the youth of the threatening young man and suggested that I not go public with the story but discuss it with the Drexel lawyers to see what their reaction would be. He also said, fine editor that he is, that one such incident did not mean much to the serious investors *Barron's* serves, and that this should be a beginning of scrutiny, no more.

Within the next few days, I talked to at least two lawyers from Cahill Gordon, Drexel's firm. When I told them of the incident, they were extremely apologetic and asked me to tell them the name of the man in question. I said I thought that perhaps just a note to the head of his department that death threats were not a good idea when dealing with financial writers would do the trick. The lawyers thanked me profusely for not writing about the incident and then one said that I really should go over and talk to Milken, that he knew me and liked my work. We had a lot in common, said the lawyer, and would get along great. Just drop him a line and it would be all set up. I did not pursue the suggestion at that time.

In the fall of 1988, while I was working on a finance case as an expert witness, I met and became friends with a young securities lawyer named Daniel J. Mogin. In a hallway at the federal court building in downtown Los Angeles, we discussed at some length the world of Drexel. I said that I could not understand certain Drexel deals, which seemed to me destined to fail. What was the point of issuing bonds for such and such a company, I said, when the likelihood that they'll default is so great? In a truly insightful reply, Dan Mogin said something like, "Maybe the point isn't whether the deals work out in the long run, but just whether or not Drexel can continue grinding out the bonds and get their big fees, and forget tomorrow."

This insight, that Drexel might be operating as an irresponsible polluter of the financial environment, collecting its fees and letting third persons pick up the tab for the pollution, was a fascinating way of looking at the firm. As an analogy, Drexel could be compared to a sawmill that dumped chemicals used in wood treatment into the river. By so doing, the mill saved money on pollution control equipment and made unusual profits. The profits were larger than the likely fines for pollution, and so pollution became a way of doing business. This was Drexel, dumping its junk into the rivers of finance, or so it seemed.

In November of 1988, on my birthday, I wrote letters to a number of investment banks offering my services as a lecturer on ethics in finance. In return, I asked to talk to young investment bankers about their ethical standards. I was extremely eager to see how many of them had an attitude similar to my erstwhile lunch partner's. I had been lecturing about ethics, gratis, at UCLA's Anderson School of Management, and in the process had learned a great deal about what was on the students' minds. I hoped to do the same with young investment bankers. I would speak about why my experience and work had led me to believe that certain business deals were not ethical, and they would give me insights into the state of mind of the young financial type. That would be my recompense. My letter to Milken and Drexel, like my letter to Morgan Stanley, noted that I would like to talk to them, examine their deals before they went public, and explain my questions about them. I said that I would, of course, continue to write about them. I never received a reply—at least not directly.

I continued to write more pieces about the world of finance, sometimes mentioning Drexel and sometimes not. Then in the spring of 1989, Paul Asquith published a justly famous study about true default rates on bonds. This work showed far higher default rates on bonds of the junk grade, both from Drexel and from others, than had been touted by Drexel. And to me, it was the hinge on which everything swung. I wrote a series of pieces about Drexel's problems, including one that asked if Drexel generally was running what might be called a Ponzi scheme.

Milken's response was to release to the media a negative press kit about me. It had a bad photo, a series of lies about other parts of my life, and then the completely erroneous claim that I had once applied to Drexel for a job. It was hard for me to see the relevance of the job application even if true, except as a pretext to allege a "sour grapes" approach to my work. To be sure, I had let myself in for the attack, since my letter to Milken had been ambiguous. Had I known it would be seized by the Milken public relations juggernaut, I would have drafted it more carefully. In any event, my letter hardly seemed important. No matter what my motivation, I had written extremely detailed analyses of bond defaults, reserves, and trading practices. These, not my personality, needed to be addressed. Alas, they never were.

Several papers ran excerpts from the press kit, as did *Esquire* magazine, even though I had long before written to and orally told Steve Anreder, chief publicist and a multimillionaire Drexel player, that I would never take one penny from Michael Milken's Drexel for anything. Those letters from the Drexel files somehow never saw the light of day.

In July of 1992, an authorized version of Michael Milken's life came out in the form of a book by Jesse Kornbluth called *Highly Confident* —*The Crime and Punishment of Michael Milken*. This astonishing book, arranged by Ken Lerer, the tireless, resourceful publicist for Milken, and written with Milken's cooperation, made a few almost comical points about Milken that had been part of his standard authorized public persona. He really did not care about money; he only wanted to help the little guy; he was led astray by his own kindness and gullibility. It never once mentioned any data about the key element in Milken's world—true rates of default on junk bonds.

Highly Confident did, however, take the attempt to discredit me a quantum leap further. In a blistering five-page attack, it painted a picture of me as a loose cannon indeed. First, the book tried to make it seem as if I was not sufficiently well educated even to comment upon Milken's world. Never mind that I was a lawyer and economist and offered as an expert witness in many legal proceedings about junk bonds. Never mind that my theory of the case, set forth in testimony and in articles in *Barron's,* had become the standard approach in almost all civil litigation about Drexel. To Jesse Kornbluth,

Vanity Fair show-business writer, and Ken Lerer, p.r. man, I was not sufficiently knowledgeable or well-credentialed.

Next, Kornbluth and his book brought up an incident in my life that had occurred in 1983. In that year, when I was renting a vacation house in the seaside town of Aptos, California, I had been told of prowlers. As a measure for protecting my wife and me, I had bought a gun at a gun shop and planned to bring it to that house. On the day I was to fly up to the San Jose Airport (the most convenient to Aptos), I had several meetings before departure and frankly forgot that I had even packed the gun in my suitcase. At the airport, I was in a mad rush and carried the suitcase through the metal detector, again, forgetting that I had the gun. The metal detector rang, and I was arrested for carrying an unloaded gun. The charges were later dropped and I had no criminal record from my unintended mistake. The Burbank police rightly concluded that I was not a potential hijacker.

Somehow, possibly through an editor we had both worked with, Kornbluth got that story, which I had told to almost no one, and put it in his book. He noted the arrest, but not that the charges were dropped or that I had no criminal record. What it had to do with my analysis of Drexel bonds default notes was hard to say.

Kornbluth then brought up a defunct lawsuit between the comedienne Joan Rivers and me over an article I wrote following the death of her husband. He again neglected to tell the story's real ending: that the case had been settled with my assuring the world that I had no reason whatsoever to believe that Ms. Rivers's grief was anything but sincere, or that she was anything but a devoted wife, and with Ms. Rivers stating that she wished to emphasize that she did not mean to question my integrity as a journalist. Kornbluth also brought up a wicked and wholly imaginary story about Joan Rivers and my wife and lesbianism, a story that for real sliminess can hardly find an equal in my experience (except, perhaps, for a long passage in *Highly Confident* in which Kornbluth detailed homosexual activity allegedly performed by Ivan Boesky in prison—only to say a few paragraphs later that it was all probably not true).

Kornbluth then made an attempt to portray me as an addict, writing my long, detailed pieces about Milken under the influence of a drug. One might imagine a sort of economist/William Blake hybrid, pounding away at the typewriter keys, thumbing through default printouts, all on dope, if one took Kornbluth seriously. That accusation, again, was a fiction, without even the slightest connection with fact. I have never written under the influence of drugs, nor can I even conceive of anyone writing detailed analyses of complex subjects under the influence of drugs.

The book by Kornbluth also brought up the shopworn and wholly fantastic story that I had only started to criticize Milken because I had applied to him for a job and been turned down. It was clear and on the record before Kornbluth wrote his book that, in fact, I had not sought a job with Milken and had said I would never take money from him. It was also clear that even if I had acted out of spite (which I certainly had not), that did not dispose of the factual arguments I had made in my articles about Milken. These merited some reply on their own terms, which the Milken forces never gave to them.

The Kornbluth book put me in mind of two other bizarre Milken-related incidents possibly having to do with attempts to impair my credibility. In one of them, in 1988, a relative of Milken who had gone into the film business contacted me and asked me to do some writing for him. I declined. Then, in 1991, a famous former casino operator and long-time friend of Milken and his circle, long retired, approached me with an amazing plan: He would put half a million dollars into an account for me, we would choose stocks together, and at the end of one year, I could have all of the money in the account. The man said it would just be a way for him to have fun talking to me about stocks through the days and months of his retirement. Again, I declined.

In both cases, I could well imagine how my credibility as a student of the world of Milken would have been affected by my taking money from either a Milken relative or a Milken pal who once owned casinos in Havana. But all of these efforts—the negative press kit, the Kornbluth book, the offers of money from persons connected with the Milken world, and, most of all, the death threat—struck me as part of a pattern. The pattern had little to do with legitimate business and, again, had much in common with the mindset of the thug. It was well worth bearing in mind although only a personal feeling.

Milken was indicted on about one hundred felony counts and

pleaded guilty to six trivial ones. He is in federal confinement and will probably get out in early 1993 if not sooner. He is allowed to work on his investments, give interviews, talk on the phone, and see his wife while in jail. When he gets out, he will still be one of the richest men in America. Although no sane person wants to go to jail, Milken's punishment for costing the American taxpayers billions of dollars is comically trivial.

All charges were dismissed against Lowell Milken, the clever, devoted brother, with a staggering fortune of his own. Richard Sandler, the lawyer who set up many of the Milken partnerships, has not even been charged. Of all the multimillionaire insiders at Drexel, only one, the extremely loyal and well-liked Bruce Newberg, even went to jail, and that briefly indeed. Like all Drexel players, he will still be a multimillionaire when he gets out after serving only a few months.

Fred Carr has not been indicted, and as far as is known, is not even under grand jury scrutiny, despite his role as "the one indispensable player" of the Milken empire besides Milken himself. The savings and loan impresarios have faced more severe punishment. Charles Keating, Jr., his name now synonymous with sanctimonious hypocritical theft, is likely to spend the balance of his life behind bars for his misconduct in the management of securities issues and other fraud involving Lincoln Savings and its parent, American Continental Corporation.

Tom Spiegel, who took over Columbia Savings & Loan from his father and ran it into insolvency while amassing a fortune for himself, has just been indicted on about fifty felony counts of fraud and illegality in various forms. David Paul, chairman of CenTrust of Miami, is fighting dozens of federal charges in Florida. Perry Mendel and Richard Grassgreen are either in jail for very brief sentences or in halfway houses preparing their return into civilized society.

Not one person at any of the large law firms involved in Drexel deals has been charged with any crime related to that work. No accountant who used his firm's prestige to paper over the glaring untruths in the Milken empire has ever spent a day in jail because of it. Yet clearly without the imprimatur and approval of the mighty law firms and accounting firms of the Drexel empire, the whole scam could not have worked. If at any time at all a partner at Skadden or

Touche Ross, for example, had stood up and said, "Wait a minute. These deals just don't make sense. There's some basic error of fact here in these bond defaults and the reserves taken against them," the whole structure would have trembled. If a powerhouse like Touche had refused to handle the dealings of a firm that it knew or should have known was making fraudulent boasts for its bonds, Drexel might well have died on the spot.

Again, no one said such things. Instead, the accountants got vast fees and the lawyers got even more, and the game of musical chairs rolled on until at last there was no seat for the taxpayers, small investors, pensioners, and beneficiaries caught in the Drexel web, and that was the end of the dance.

The Milken name may be in disgrace in criminal courts, but in Los Angeles it is still magic. Money from the Milken family foundations, clearly traceable to large-scale misconduct by Michael Milken, is sought by worthy causes all over Southern California, from orphanages to operas. UCLA still seeks donations and promises to name a building after Milken. In the San Fernando Valley there is a huge community center named after Bernard Milken, built with gifts from Michael and Lowell and their foundations. Up and down the most prestigious beaches in Malibu are the multi-million-dollar mansions of the Milken players. At the polo field in Carpinteria, near Santa Barbara, there are the horses of a Milken player.

A major Milken player, Leon Black, has taken over the residue of First Executive in California. Others are busily making deals for this or that piece of Drexel wreckage. Teams of Drexel players wheel and deal in the millions and billions at firms such as Canyon Partners in Beverly Hills, across the street from the old Drexel headquarters.

The giants of American finance, especially Merrill Lynch, are endlessly struggling to make a name in junk bonds. Merrill, as noted, has even created a questionable junk bond index to make it seem as if junk bonds are a far better investment than they are. In this venture, their partner is none other than Drexel's favorite professor, Edward Altman of New York University, as noted above.

Salomon, First Boston, and Morgan Stanley all bid eagerly to take up the mantle as leaders in the field of junk, without even a nod to indicate that junk from Drexel carries a certain taint that must be fully disclosed. In short, the power players of junk are still powerful. More important in the land of the dollar, they are still rich, some richer than any Rockefeller. The government has taken away money from Milken, but enough has been left to allow him to be rich and his descendants to be rich for generations if they choose to be. The works of the Milken crew are still protected, still praised by powerful organs of the media. In time, if the Milken billions continue to be spent to burnish his image, he may emerge as the innocent victim of cunning and evil men or, perhaps, a financial genius who loved making money not wisely but too well.

To the next generation of financial wizards, with their own some-thing-for-nothing, promises-for-cash scams, the lesson of a swindle big enough to buy your own historical salvation in a world where everything is for sale is this:

Milken got away with it.

ACKNOWLEDGMENTS

This book would have been impossible to write without the aid, insight, hard work, energy, and devotion of Susan Gayle Reifer, my comrade in arms, collaborator, ace researcher, and scholar of financial misconduct in her own right. She has been working with me on my inquiries for *Barron's* into financial misconduct since my first long piece on Metromedia (a Drexel client) almost six years ago, and I could not have made progress in this field without her. She is a treasure. Her long tomes about the key Milken players were the building blocks of the story I have told here, and impressive by themselves. She has been with me every step of the way.

Bill Lerach, the world's premier trial lawyer, and Daniel J. Mogin, the smartest lawyer under forty I have every met, were invaluable help in all of my efforts to investigate Milken and Drexel. For Dan Mogin's wife, Laura, perpetual apologies for my many, many late night calls consulting his wisdom and experience on a myriad of Milken-world questions. For Kathy L., Bill Lerach's world-class secretary, thanks also for patient understanding of my persistent calls to test this or that hypothesis.

Thanks to a very smart Hollywood agent and top drawer investor, George Diskant, for an insight about Drexel a few years ago which started me thinking about how and why the scam worked. George has learned much from Warren Buffett about suckers and money, and he's shared a little of it with me. Steve Greene has been teaching me over the years about how telephone boiler rooms work. His insights about how Drexel under Milken was organized were also invaluable to me.

My thanks to Elizabeth Dow Hoyt for an unexpectedly useful entree into the Drexel world.

John Barber's help as a sounding board about Drexel practice was extremely meaningful, as was his partner's, Warren Schlicting. Larry Lissitzyn's ideas and experience about law and finance were also invaluable.

My brilliant father, Herbert Stein, was always willing to go to the well of his thoughts and to his keyboard to work out various hypotheses about Drexel/Milkenism. He insisted that I write about Milken in terms of economic theory, especially price-fixing, and this really explained everything. Even when his own offices were invaded by Milken and his handlers, my father stood on the principle of truth and service to the ordinary investor. This was heartening to me beyond measure. Herbert Gold told me years ago that a son who, when choosing between his father and truth, chose truth was a fool. My father has always made it easy to choose both. My mother, Mildred Stein, with her careful reading of the manuscript many times, often found errors in typing or usage that needed correcting. My sister, Rachel, had a basic insight into Wall Street practice by noting that it had as much to do with misshapen personalities as with laws. That also opened many doors.

The people at *Barron's* could not have been better or more supportive over the years that I followed this tale in their pages. Alan Abelson is not only a great editor, writer, and wit, but simply fearless. He is as unafraid of the big boys as he is eager to serve the honest investor. He is a titan in the world of little people. My own editor and soul mate over the years, Jim Meagher, not only humbled me with his fast comebacks and his range of humor, but also taught me a thing or two about explaining by example of wit. He was as fearless as Abelson, and as careful and remorseless as a surgeon in considering my work. Thank you, Meagher. At *Barron's,* Shirley Lazo also deserves lavish praise, and so does Margo Whitehead.

Still within Dow-Jones, I doff my hat to my former editor at *The Wall Street Journal,* Bob Bartley. Although he is—I think—on the wrong side of this issue, he taught me much about organizing my thoughts, as well as about what counts in human behavior. I applied his standards and came to very different conclusions from his, but I must still thank him for the yardstick.

My economics teacher of almost three decades ago now, Lowell

Harriss of Columbia, was exactly what a teacher should be. Much of what he said lingers and is valuable day by day. My brilliant teacher of finance at Yale, the late Henry Wallich, and his very much alive colleague, James Tobin, taught me about how things that look too good to be true usually are, and that's a lesson indeed. More or less in passing, Edward Dennison of Brookings explained some things about management that have been important to me. Murray Weidenbaum of Washington University has likewise been instructive about management behavior in general and in specific. Michael Thomas sees, understands, and inspires with his glimpses into the Drexel world week by week. Thanks, Michael.

I am grateful as well for the insights and example of Peter Flanigan of Dillon Read, who showed me something about what an investment banker should be. Roy Ash, cofounder of Litton Industries and an authentic genius, shared many experiences on finance and the history of conglomerates. Thank you both.

The men and women of High Yield Associates and Securities Data, Inc., in New York provided extremely important data about default rates on bonds, which is really the crux of the Milken story. I also learned some useful things about the default rates on bonds from the publishers of the *Defaulted Bonds Newsletter*.

John Meroney, Mary Beth Smith, and Jayne O'Donnell helped in specific research tasks.

There are some very important books on the subject of Drexel and Milken which should be considered the most basic documents on the subject. They are *The Predators' Ball,* a genuine work of genius, by Connie Bruck, and *Den of Thieves,* likewise a superb resource, by James Stewart. Students of the Milken world should know them well. *Eagle on the Street,* by Vise and Coll, is a truly insightful examination of just how badly the SEC failed in its responsibilities to the investors of America. It's a valuable document of history and law.

Stephen Pizzo, a fearless and gutsy writer on the general subject of the infiltration of business by crime, has also been a resource of major value to me.

I also thank many writers at the *Los Angeles Times, The New York Times, The Wall Street Journal,* the *Daily News* (which used to be called the *Valley News,* and which knows the Milken family well),

Vanity Fair (especially Marie Brenner), *M, Forbes, Fortune, Barron's, The Montgomery Advertiser,* a fine small city paper, and its twin, *The Alabama Journal, The Las Vegas Sun* and *The Washington Post.* Mary Beaudoin at the *Minneapolis Star-Tribune* found extremely helpful articles about Meshulam Riklis and I thank her as well.

I had many sources who expected confidentiality and they will get it. In general, I also sought comments from the people I criticize in this book. In particular, I have sought to talk to Michael Milken a number of times, and have not been granted an interview. I am going to assume that everyone I mention in this book in a critical way absolutely, categorically, and sincerely denies any wrongdoing.

As for Milken himself, his life and career are indescribably rich texts of the workings of the material world. His understanding of how to make things happen, how to make the world go his way, how to wheel and deal and control was stupendous. No one I talked to who had worked face-to-face with Milken thought he was particularly impressive, but if one considers what he accomplished, even for ill, he must be some sort of genius, a real magician in his understanding of the human spirit, almost a force of nature. I learn from him every day.

I owe a unique debt to my editor at Simon & Schuster, Fred Hills, who was not only insightful, dedicated, and tireless, but had that rarest of qualities, a sense of humor about the modern world. Our editor's editor, Burton Beals, a startlingly deft physician of text, made his gift felt on every page. Our lawyer, Eric Rayman, was a fine attorney and also a good editor and sounding board in difficult moments, and I thank him. Daphne Bien, Fred Hills's assistant, was also a valuable asset.

Thanks to my beautiful once and future wife, Alexandra, who put up with much more discussion of junk than anyone should have to. She became a target of the Milken smear machine simply by being near me. Unearned suffering is redemptive, said Martin Luther King, Jr., and she has had her share. She learned about courage from her father, Dale Denman, Jr., a genuine combat war hero—Silver Star in World War II and Vietnam. It was my feeling at seeing the likes of him ripped off by the likes of Milken that inspired this book.

203

APPENDIX

The Casualty List

The following lists give some idea of the scope of the damage wrought by Drexel Burnham Lambert's "high yield" bond department under the leadership of Michael Milken.

The first list details the thirty largest bankruptcies of the past decade. It's worth noting that of those bankruptcies that were not caused by litigation, more than half, fifteen out of twenty-seven, were Drexel-related.

The second one lists the names of fifty-five federally insured S&Ls that were Drexel issuers and/or controlled or influenced by Drexel and that were seized by the federal government, thus incurring huge costs to federal taxpayers that may yet increase.

There are well over one hundred additional casualties—bankruptcies, defaults, and exchanges—of smaller but still significant companies for which Drexel issued junk bonds.

Largest Bankruptcies 1/1/80–9/1/91

(All amounts in millions)
(Rankings from Securities Data Company/New Generation Investments)

	Date of Bankruptcy	Company	Pre-Bankruptcy Total Assets	
1	04/12/87	Texaco, Inc.	35,892.00	+
2	09/09/88	Financial Corporation of America	33,864.00	
3	01/07/91	Bank of New England Corporation	29,773.00	
4	03/31/89	MCorp	20,228.00	
5	05/13/91	First Executive Corporation	15,193.43	*
6	02/08/90	Gibraltar Financial Corporation	15,011.00	*
7	02/28/90	Imperial Corporation of America	12,263.00	*
8	05/30/91	First Capital Holdings	9,675.16	*
9	09/26/83	Baldwin-United	9,383.00	
10	07/14/89	Southmark Corporation	9,161.00	*
11	02/13/90	Integrated Resources, Inc.	7,876.00	*
12	12/03/90	Continental Airlines Holdings	7,656.00	*
13	09/24/89	Lomas Financial Corporation	6,645.00	
14	07/17/86	LTV Corporation	6,307.00	
15	01/04/91	Enstar Group, Inc.	5,594.00	*
16	04/13/89	American Continental Corporation	6,645.00	*
17	09/17/90	Santa Barbara S&L Assn.	4,666.00	*
18	08/03/89	Texas American Bancshares	4,383.00	
19	03/09/89	Eastern Air Lines, Inc.	4,037.00	*
20	06/12/89	Lone Star Technologies	3,894.00	
21	02/13/90	Drexel Burnham Lambert Group	3,698.30	*
22	01/15/90	Allied Stores Corporation	3,502.00	
23	12/27/89	Hillsborough Holdings Corporation	3,462.00	*
24	10/24/90	Southland Corporation	3,439.00	
25	03/16/89	First Columbia Financial	2,786.00	*
26	06/30/89	Rothschild Holdings, Inc.	2,778.00	
27	01/28/88	Public Service Company of NH	2,639.00	+
28	01/08/91	Pan Am Corporation	2,440.83	
29	08/26/82	Manville Corporation	2,298.00	+
30	04/25/90	Ames Department Stores	2,130.00	*

* indicates Drexel issuer and/or Drexel-controlled or -influenced.

+ indicates non-operating bankruptcy, for example, Manville to shield assets pending asbestos litigation, Texaco pending Pennzoil litigation.

Failed Federally Insured Savings and Loans

(The date listed indicates the date of first conservatorship or receivership after failure.)

ABQ Bank, A Federal Savings Bank
  Albuquerque, New Mexico
  2/8/90

Altus Bank, A FSB
  Mobile, Alabama
  5/17/91

Ambassador Federal Savings & Loan
  Tamarac, Florida
  8/24/90

American Pioneer Federal Savings Bank
  Daytona Beach, Florida
  5/25/90

Atlantic Financial Savings, F.A.
  Bala Cynwyd, Pennsylvania
  1/11/90

Baltimore Federal Financial Federal Savings Association
  Baltimore, Maryland
  2/7/89

Benjamin Franklin Federal Savings Association
  Houston, Texas
  3/8/89

The Benjamin Franklin Federal Savings & Loan
  Portland, Oregon
  2/20/90

Bright Banc Savings Association
  Dallas, Texas
  2/10/89

Central Savings and Loan Association
  San Diego, California
  4/10/87

CenTrust Federal Savings Bank
  Miami, Florida
  2/1/90

Certified Federal Savings Association
  Georgetown, Texas
  1/11/90
Charter Savings Bank, FSB
  Newport Beach, California
  6/15/90
City Savings Bank, FSB
  Bedminster, New Jersey
  12/7/89
Columbia Savings
  Englewood, Colorado
  12/30/88
Commonwealth Federal Savings and Loan Association
  Ft. Lauderdale, Florida
  7/19/89
Community FS&LA
  St. Louis, Missouri
  12/14/90
Coral S&LA, F.A.
  Coral Springs, Florida
  1/25/91
Coreast Federal Savings Bank
  Richmond, Virginia
  2/1/91
Ensign Federal Savings Bank
  New York, New York
  8/31/90
Far West Federal Bank, S.B.
  Portland, Oregon
  5/23/91
FarWest Savings and Loan Association, F.A.
  Los Angeles, California
  1/11/91
First Columbia Savings & Loan
  Beverly Hills, California
  1991
First Texas Savings
  12/27/88

Franklin Savings Association
  Ottawa, Kansas
  2/15/90
Germania Bank, FSB
  Alton, Illinois
  6/22/90
Gibraltar Savings, F.A.
  Beverly Hills/Simi Valley, California
  3/30/89
Gibraltar Savings Association
  Houston, Texas
  12/28/88
Great American Bank, A Federal Savings Bank
  San Diego, California
  8/9/91
Guaranty Federal Savings and Loan Association
  Dallas, Texas
  9/30/88
Home Federal Savings Bank, F.A.
  Waukegan, Illinois
  12/14/90
Home Owners Savings Bank, FSB
  Burlington/Boston, Massachusetts
  4/27/90
Imperial Federal Savings Association
  San Diego, California
  2/22/90
Lincoln Savings and Loan Association, F.A.
  Los Angeles, California
  4/14/89
MeraBank, A Federal Savings Bank
  Phoenix, Arizona
  1/31/90
Mississippi Savings Bank, FSB
  Batesville, Mississippi
  5/8/90
MountainWest Savings and Loan Association
  Ogden, Utah
  2/16/89

Nowlin Federal Savings Association
  Fort Worth/North Richland Hills, Texas
  2/22/90
People's Heritage Federal Savings and Loan Association
  Salina, Kansas
  8/10/89
Pima Federal Savings and Loan Association
  Tucson, Arizona
  3/1/90
Santa Barbara Federal Savings and Loan Association
  Santa Barbara, California
  4/27/90
San Jacinto Savings Association, F.A.
  Bellaire, Texas
  11/30/90
Security Savings and Loan Association
  Scottsdale, Arizona
  2/16/89
Sooner Federal Savings Association
  Tulsa, Oklahoma
  11/15/89
Southwest Federal Savings Association
  Dallas, Texas
  5/18/90
Statesman Federal Savings Bank
  Waterloo, Iowa
  7/26/90
Sun State Savings and Loan Association, FSA
  Phoenix, Arizona
  6/14/89
Sunbelt Savings Association of Texas
  Dallas, Texas
  8/19/88
Texas Western Federal Savings Association
  Houston, Texas
  11/15/89
United Federal Savings Bank, FSB
  Windon, Minnesota
  5/10/90

United FSA of Iowa
  Des Moines, Iowa
  3/22/91
United Savings Association of Texas
  Houston, Texas
  12/30/88
Western Empire Federal Savings and Loan
  Yorba Linda, California
  2/15/90
Westwood Savings and Loan Association
  Los Angeles, California
  3/27/86
Williamsburg Federal Savings and Loan Association
  Salt Lake City, Utah
  1/25/90

INDEX

Ackerman, Peter, 19
Adams, Abigail, 28
Alliance for Capital Access, 24, 134
Allied Supermarkets, 107
Altman, Edward, 129–36, 164, 165, 169, 198
A. M. Best, 150
Ambrit, 107
Amen Wardy, 13, 176
American Can, 186
American Colortype, 44
American Continental Corporation, 17, 42, 51, 81, 197
American Express, 24, 93
American Family Products, 106
American Financial Corporation, 50, 78
American Savings & Loan, 108, 112, 117
Anderson School of Management, 193
Anreder, Steve, 139, 160, 194
Arthur Andersen, 138
Asquith, Paul, 163–65, 168, 169, 170, 193
Atlantic Capital, 114
Atlantic Financial, 121
Avco, 123
Aylward, David, 24

Bache, 87
Bally's, 107
Banner, 107
Bantam Books, 50
Barron's, 148, 160, 190, 191, 192, 194
Beatrice, 120, 125, 126
Ben Franklin Savings, 18, 102, 121, 166, 185

Berkshire Hathaway, 118
Best & Co., 45
Beverly Hills Hotel, 155
Birmingham High School, 20, 46
Bisconti, Ben, 163
Black, Eli, 51
Black, Leon, 19, 51, 198
Blinder, Meyer, 153–54
Blume, Marshall, 135, 136
Boesky, Ivan, 24, 27, 30, 72, 102, 103, 104, 119, 123, 167, 183, 195
Bonner, Paul, 163
Brant, Sebastian, 15
Bruck, Connie, 142
Buchalter, Louis "Lepkele," 96, 184
Buckingham Distributors, 45
Buffett, Warren, 118
Bulova Watch, 91
Burlington Industries, 168
Burnham & Co., 66
Burns, Arthur F., 31
Bushman, Jackie, 117

Cahill Gordon & Reindel, 12, 138, 192
California, University of, at Berkeley, 20, 30–31, 33, 34, 35
Cannon Group, 107
Cannon Holdings, 91
Canyon Partners, 198
Capital Foundation, The, 141
Capone, Al, 45, 184
Care Investors, 116, 117
Carnegie, Andrew, 184
Carr, Fred, 46, 72, 85–96, 107, 165, 175–76, 185, 186, 197
Carroll, Lewis, 127
Carter, Jimmy, 24, 100

Carter Hawley Hale, 168
Cartier, 47
Cellu-Craft, 44
CenterBanc, 112, 117
Central States Teamster's Pension
    Fund, 71–72
CenTrust Federal Savings, 15, 102,
    108, 121, 166, 170, 175, 185, 197
Chase Manhattan, 21, 60
Chemical Bank, 130
Chrysler Financial, 83
Chrysler Motors, 83
Chubb Insurance, 51
Cincinnati Enquirer, 50, 51
Circle K, 51
CityFed, 15
Clarendon, 93
Clay, Henry, 152
CNA Financial, 64
Coast, 121
Coastal Corporation, 107, 113
Colt, 107
Columbia Savings & Loan, 11, 15,
    102, 103–7, 113, 121, 148, 149,
    166, 170, 175, 185, 197
Columbia University, 189
Combined Communications, 51
Comdisco, 70
Commercial Credit Corporation, 63
Compact Video, 107
Consumer Price Index, 38
Container Corporation of America,
    106
Continental Airlines, 167
Continental Connector, 46–47
Control Data, 63
Coopervision, 107
Cornfeld, Bernard, 46
Corporate Bond Quality and
    Investor Experience (Hickman),
    20, 31–33
Council of Economic Advisers, 23
Cox, Charles, 154
Crown Zellerbach, 168

Dahl, James, 19, 102, 103, 147, 149
Dalitz, Moe, 72
D'Amato, Al, 23–24
Damon Medical, 68
Dart, Justin, 24

Deloitte, Touche, 34
DeNiro, Robert, 27
Deukmejian, George, 155
Dingell, John, 76, 121, 168
Director, Aaron, 100
Drexel Firestone, 66
Drexel Harriman Ripley, 42, 48, 66
Duff & Phelps, 143–51
DWG, 54, 55

Eagle on the Street (Vise and Coll),
    154
E. F. Hutton, 154
Eichenwald, Kurt, 139
Einstein, Albert, 183
Eizenstat, Stuart, 24
Eliot, T. S., 172
Eller, Carl, 51
Embry, Talton "Tally," 22
Emerson Radio, 70
Enstar, 18, 110–18, 166
Enterprise Fund, 46, 87–88
Equitable Life Assurance, 130
Equitable Life Insurance, 72, 93
Esquire, 194
E-II Holdings, 11, 18
Executive Life Insurance, 16–17,
    159

Farnham Partners, 105
Far West, 121, 170
Federal Deposit Insurance
    Corporation, 168
Federal Home Loan Bank Board,
    98–99, 100, 156
Federal Reserve Board, 31
Federal Reserve System, 189
Federal Savings and Loan Insurance
    Corporation, 98, 103, 135, 168
Fidelity Funds, 108
Fiduciary Trust Company, 22
Firestone Tire and Rubber, 66
First Boston, 198
First Capital Holdings, 17, 93, 121,
    150, 165, 173
First Executive Corporation, 11, 16–
    17, 72, 86, 88, 89, 90–94, 95, 101,
    113, 121, 150, 151, 155, 165, 166,
    170, 173, 175, 177, 183–84, 185,
    198

First Investors Fund for Income
  (FIFI), 22, 70, 71, 108, 121
First Stratford, 94
Fitch, 144
Forbes, 24–25, 26–27, 60
Fortune, 52
Frary, Richard, 108
Freeman, Brad, 144
Freeman, Spogli, 144, 145, 146, 147,
  149
Freeman Spogli Equity Partners II,
  146, 147, 148
Frick, Henry Clay, 184
Friedman, Bill, 78, 81–82
Friedman, Milton, 31, 100, 189
Friedman, Rose Director, 31
FSLIC, 135
Fusco, Joseph, 45

GAO, 135, 157
Garn, Jake, 100
Geffen, David, 82
General Host, 107
General Motors, 104, 121, 189
Genger, Ari, 115
George F. Baker Foundation, 163
Georg Jensen, 47
Gibraltar, 18, 102
Gilder, George, 24, 26, 181
Gillespi, Roxani, 155
Gillette, 113
Gillett Holdings, 124
Glen Alden, 44
Goethe, Johann Wolfgang von, 66
Golden Nugget, 22, 107
Goldsmith, Sir James, 123, 183
Goodyear Tire and Rubber, 123, 190
Gotti, John, 183
Goulet, Victor, 107–8
Government Employees Life
  Insurance Company, 51
Grand Hotel, 63
Grassgreen, Richard, 81, 83, 111–12,
  113, 114–18, 125, 197
Great American Insurance, 50
Green Tree Acceptance, 123
Grosset & Dunlap, 50
Grundfest, Joseph, 23
Guarantee, 121
Gulf, 168

Haberler, Gottfried, 100
Haifa Chemical, 116, 117
Harriss, Lowell, 189
Harvard Business School, 36, 140, 160
Harvard Law School, 63
Harvard University Graduate School
  of Management, 163
Heller Packing, 44
Hewitt, John, 152
H. H. Robertson, 91
Hickman, Walter Braddock, 20, 31–
  33, 35, 36, 41, 128, 132
Highly Confident (Kornbluth), 27,
  194–96
"High Yield Newsletter, The," 73,
  74, 75
Hoffa, Jimmy, 71
Horowitz, Harry, 137
Hughes, Howard, 57
Hume, David, 161
Hunter, 50
Hurwitz, Charles, 114

Iacocca, Lee, 83
IBM, 57
Icahn, Carl, 18, 23, 123, 183
ICH Corporation, 18, 167, 173
Imperial Corporation of America,
  18, 102, 107–8, 147, 149, 185
Imperial Savings & Loan, 167, 168
Ingersoll, 107
Inland Credit, 45
Integrated Resources, 17–18, 78,
  104, 167, 173
Internal Revenue Service, 57, 118
International Bank for
  Reconstruction and Development,
  see World Bank
Investors Diversified Services, 46
Investors Overseas Services, 46

Jackson, Robert K., 179
Jade Corporation, 91
Jensen, Michael, 23, 169
Johnson, Roy, 93
Joseph, Fred, 77, 154, 176

Kauffmann Alsberg, 117
Keating, Charles H., Jr., 51, 52, 81,
  83, 102, 108, 155, 197

Keim, Donald, 135, 136
Kennedy, John F., 137, 153
Kennedy, Joseph P., 153
Kenton, 47
Keynes, John Maynard, 43
Keystone B 4, 70
Kinder-Care Learning Centers, 18,
    81, 108, 111; see also Enstar
Kleiner, Bell, 87
Kohlberg Kravis Roberts (KKR),
    105, 113, 125, 170
Kornbluth, Jesse, 194–96
Kroger, 51

La Costa Resort, 72
Lake, James, 24
Lakeland Packing, 44
Lanes Stores, 45
Lansky, Meyer, 45, 67
Latham & Watkins, 138
Laurel in the Pines, 63
Leasco, 58, 59, 60
Lehman Brothers, 69
Lerer, Ken, 24, 169–70, 194, 195
Lerner Stores, 44
Levine, Dennis, 20, 167
Liberty Service Corporation, 106,
    148
Limited, The, 11
Lincoln Savings & Loan, 15, 17, 81,
    102, 108, 121, 197
Lindner, Carl, 21, 50–55, 56, 61, 62,
    67, 68, 69, 81, 93, 126, 138
Lindner, Robert, 50
Linsey, Joseph, 45
Lipton, Martin, 157
Loan Insurance Corporation, 98
Lodestar, 117
Loew's Corporation, 52, 63, 64
Lord Abbett Bond Debenture Fund,
    70
LorSan Partners II, 121
Los Angeles Times, 139
LTV Corporation, 69, 167
Lutheran Brotherhood Life, 93

McCarthy, Crisanti & Maffei, 144
McCrory Corporation, 18, 42, 44,
    91
McGraw-Hill, 147

MacLennan, Bruce, 163
Magnetek, 107
"Managing the Corporate Financial
    Structure" (Milken), 40–41
Mark Cross, 47
Massachusetts Mutual, 70, 72–73
Max 10, 113
May, Peter, 88, 186–87
MCA, 168, 190
MDC Holding, see Mizel
    Development Corporation
Megra Partners, 114, 115
Mendel, Perry, 81, 111–12, 113,
    114–18, 125, 197
Mendelson, Morris, 35
Mercury, 18
Merrill Lynch, 101, 121, 144, 145,
    169, 198
Metromedia, 190
Metropolitan Life, 165
MGM, 63
Michigan General, 70
Milken, Bernard, 22, 28–29, 198
Milken, Ferne Zax, 22, 28, 29, 30
Milken, Lori Hackel, 30, 34, 35
Milken, Lowell, 22, 29, 172, 197,
    198
Mission Insurance Group, 52–53
Mizel, Larry, 77, 78, 81
Mizel Development Corporation
    (MDC), 17, 77, 80, 166
Mogin, Daniel J., 92, 192
Monarch Capital, 51
Monarch Life, 93
Moody's, 143, 144, 150
Moore, Geoffrey, 31
Morgan, J. P., 184
Morgan Stanley, 129–30, 144, 192,
    193, 198
Mullins, David W., Jr., 163
Mutual Benefit Life, 72–73, 93, 121,
    150

Narragansett Capital Corporation,
    190
National Association of Insurance
    Commissioners, 154–55
National Can, 186
National Forge, 91
National Propane, 54, 55

National Vulcanized Fabric, 54
Nelson, E. Benjamin, 155
Newberg, Bruce, 197
New Haven Railroad, 132
New Street Securities, 15
New York, State University of, at Stonybrook, 134
New York Stock Exchange, 153
New York Times, 139, 170
New York University, 62, 129, 169, 198
Nissan, 83
Nixon, Richard, 100
Nortek, 78
Northwestern, 93

Occidental Petroleum, 107
Office of Thrift Supervision, 173
O'Sullivan Rubber, 60
Otter Creek, 104, 153

Pacific Lumber, 91, 114, 168
P&C Foods, 149
Pantry Pride, 78, 107
Parks, Rosa, 110
Paul, David, 102, 108, 197
Pechiney, 186, 187
Peltz, Nelson, 20, 88, 186–87
Penn Central Corporation, 21, 51
Pennsylvania Engineering Corporation, 54
Pension Benefit Guaranty Corporation, 91
Peralta Hospital, 91
Perelman, Ronald, 23, 113, 114
Phillips, Gene, 78, 81–82
Phillips Petroleum, 23, 123, 168
Pickens, Boone, 23, 113, 183
Pioneer Insurance, 117
Pioneer-Western, 93, 112
Piper, Jaffray & Wood, 44
Pizzo, Steven, 185
Playtex Holdings, 106
Pleasanton Federal Correctional Facility, 188
P. Lorillard, 42, 45, 52, 63, 64
Polychrome, 70

Pope, Alexander, 157
Posner, Victor, 21, 54–56, 61, 64, 67, 68, 69, 70, 83, 126, 138, 159
Pound, Ezra, 143
Predators' Ball, The (Bruck), 142
Prime Computer, 168
Provident, 50
Prudential, 93, 165
Prudential-Bache, 121
Pulte Home, 61

Rapid-American, 11, 42, 44, 51, 52
Rapid Electro-type, 44
Reagan, Ronald, 24, 90, 100, 128, 153–54, 155
Regency Equities, 155
Reliance Corporation, 52, 58–59, 60, 61, 93, 166
Resolution Trust Corporation (RTC), 16, 173
Revlon, 18, 91, 113
Riklis, Marcia, 115
Riklis, Meshulam "Rik," 21, 43–50, 51, 53, 55, 56, 62, 64, 67, 68, 69, 70, 83, 95, 115, 116, 126, 138, 159
Riordan, Freeman, Spogli, 144
Riordan, Richard, 144
Rivers, Joan, 195
RJR/Nabisco, 170
Robinson, Lake, Lerer & Montgomery, 139, 169–70
Robinson, Linda, 24, 169–70
Rockefeller, David, 60
Rockefeller, Nelson, 60
Rudd, Mark, 37

Safeway Stores, 106, 113, 168
St. Germain, Ferdinand, 100
Salomon, 192, 198
Sandler, Richard, 137, 197
San Jacinto Savings, 15, 108, 121
Santa Barbara Savings, 121
Savings and Loan League, 98, 99, 100
Schenley Distributors, 45–46, 63
Securities and Exchange Commission (SEC), 23, 46, 51, 52, 53, 55, 61, 77, 87, 138, 144, 152, 153, 154, 156, 177

Securities Data, Inc., 120
Security Management Corporation, 54
Security Pacific, 143–44, 147
Selected Utilities, 145
Shad, John, 23, 77, 154, 176
Shenker, Morris, 46–47
Shoe City, 113, 116
Siegel, Martin, 167
Silverado Savings, 78
Simon & Schuster, 51
Simply Six, 113
Skadden, Arps, 138, 197
S. Klein, 45
Smith, Adam, 7, 153, 178
Smith's Transfer, 70
Solomon, David, 22, 70, 71, 172
Sorvino, Paul, 184
Sosnoff, Martin, 104
Southeastern Public Service, 54, 55
Southmark, 17, 78, 81–82, 107, 108
Spassky, Boris, 186
Spiegel, Abe, 102, 103
Spiegel, Tom, 20, 102, 103–7, 108, 113, 125, 148, 186, 197
Spogli, Richard, 144
Sportsman's Lodge, 35
Spurge, Lorraine, 137
Standard & Poor's, 143, 144, 150
Standard Gravure, 91
Steel, Sharon, 54, 55, 56
Stein, Herbert, 7
Steinberg, Saul, 20, 21, 52, 56–62, 64, 67, 68, 69, 89, 93, 102, 108, 123, 138, 159, 183
Stevens, Wallace, 110
Stewart, James, 142
Stigler, George, 100
Stone Container, 166
Storer Broadcasting, 105, 113, 114, 120, 124, 125, 126
Strachan Shipping, 91
Sylvan Learning Centers, 112, 117

Tannetics, 70
Texas Air, 18, 107
Texas International, 70

Texstyrene, 107
Thomas, Michael, 153
3M, 159
Tisch, Al, 62
Tisch, Laurence, 21, 52, 62–65, 67, 69
Tisch, Robert, 62
Tisch, Sayde, 62, 63, 64
Tobin, James, 189
Tops Markets, 149
Touche Ross, 34, 138, 159, 198
Toyota, 83
Transmark, 93
Trans Pacific Resources (TPR), 115–116
Traymore, 63
Triangle Packaging, 78, 88, 126, 186, 187
Tsai, Gerry, 88
TWA, 18, 168, 190

United Brands, 51
United Fruit, 51
Unocal, 113, 114, 168

Vanderbilt, Cornelius, 97
Vanity Fair, 195
Vesco, Robert, 46
Viacom, 190

Wallace, George C., 110
Wallich, Henry, 189
Wall Street Journal, 12, 21, 24, 25, 139, 140, 142, 158, 170, 177, 189
Walsh, Leo, 72, 93
Walt Disney, 23, 123, 168, 190
Walter, James, 35, 37, 40, 42
Walter Kidde, 91
Wanniski, Jude, 24
Warner Communications, 51
Webcraft, 149
Weingarten, Robert, 93, 121
Western Reserve Insurance, 117
Wharton School of Business, 20, 34, 35–40, 57, 62–63, 135
Wickes, 107
Wilson Brothers, 54, 55
Wirth, Timothy, 24
Wolff, Eric D., 163

Wometco, 126
World Bank, 71, 73, 173
Wygod, Martin, 72
Wynn, Steve, 22

Xerox, 121

Yago, Glenn, 134
Yale Law School, 189

Zadora, Pia, 47
Zax, Stanley, 93
Zenith National, 93, 121, 165, 173

About the Author

Benjamin J. Stein is a lawyer, economist, and writer whose coverage of Milken and Drexel in *Barron's* and elsewhere first revealed the scope of the junk bond disaster across the nation. The author of *Financial Passages* and *Money Power* and winner of awards for his financial writing, he lives in Los Angeles, California.